ignite

Unlock your brain's true potential and change your life

ignite

Unlock your brain's true potential and change your life

Neeltje van Horen

First published in the UK in 2025 by Bedford Square Publishers Ltd,
London, UK

bedfordsquarepublishers.co.uk
@bedsqpublishers

info@bedfordsquarepublishers.co.uk

© Neeltje van Horen, 2025

The right of Neeltje van Horen to be identified as the author of this work has been asserted in accordance with the Copyright, Designs and Patents Act 1988. All rights reserved. No part of this book may be reproduced, stored in or introduced into a retrieval system, or transmitted, in any form or by any means (electronic, mechanical, photocopying, recording or otherwise) without the written permission of the publishers.

Any person who does any unauthorised act in relation to this publication may be liable to criminal prosecution and civil claims for damages.

A CIP catalogue record for this book is available from the British Library.

The manufacturer's authorised representative in the EU for product safety is Easy Access System Europe, Mustamäe tee 50, 10621 Tallinn, Estonia
gpsr.requests@easproject.com

ISBN
978-1-83501-075-4 (Hardback)
978-1-83501-076-1 (Trade paperback)
978-1-83501-077-8 (eBook)

2 4 6 8 10 9 7 5 3 1

Printed in Great Britain by CPI Group (UK) Ltd, Croydon CR0 4YY

*To oma, mama and Femke
whose warmth, wisdom and strength inspire me every day*

Contents

Preface	ix
Introduction	xi

Part 1: Elevate Yourself: Achieving Clarity and Control

1. The Art of Prioritising What Matters	3
2. From Distracted to Disciplined	25
3. Igniting Your Inner Drive	51

Part 2: Elevate Your Brain: Strategies for Cognitive Enhancement

4. Memory Magic	81
5. Learning How to Learn	113
6. When Creativity Strikes	145
7. The Brain Gym	171

Part 3: Elevate Your Mindset: Freeing Yourself from Limiting Beliefs

8. Inner Truths	199
9. Letting Go	227
10. Dance to the Music	267

Epilogue	297
Acknowledgements	299
Endnotes	303
Index	333

Preface

Looking at the big, white machine in front of me, I feel a mix of anticipation and curiosity. I have spent so much time researching and thinking about the human brain, yet I've never seen my own. Sure, I've seen images of other people's brains, but this feels different. This is personal. This brain of mine – the one that has evolved and transformed so much over the past few years – is about to be revealed to me in vivid detail.

The room is slightly chilly, and the hum of the machinery fills the background as I lie down on the narrow table. Paul, the technician, hands me earplugs and a stress ball, then carefully secures my head. 'Try not to move,' he says, which, of course, makes me hyper-aware of every little itch and twitch. Slowly, I'm guided into the snug tube of the MRI scanner. The rhythmic clicking begins, almost like a mechanical heartbeat. Oddly enough, I feel a sense of serenity, knowing that each pulse is capturing another aspect of my brain.

After it's done, we gather around the computer. Then there it is – in vivid detail – the organ that has shaped every moment of my life. I'm struck by its symmetry, its intricate folds and curves. I recognise my prefrontal cortex, my hippocampus and my amygdala – the brain regions I've learned so much about yet never truly connected to myself.

As I pore over the scans, I marvel at how this isn't just an organ; it's a living record of every thought, every choice and every leap of faith I've taken. Within these folds and curves, decisions were weighed, memories created and lessons learned. It dawns on me how much of what defines me is housed within these patterns of grey and white.

As I stand there, a deep sense of connection washes over me. This isn't merely a collection of neural pathways; it's the physical embodiment of my experiences, my struggles and my triumphs. This is my brain – an inseparable part of me. Standing here I can't help but wonder – where would I be now, if I hadn't managed to unlock its true potential?

Introduction

The phone sits in my hands, a silent witness to my indecision. I want to accept my friend's invitation, but the weight of my workload pulls me back. My inbox is overflowing with unanswered emails, my day is crammed with meetings and I've just realised I only have twenty-four hours left to prepare my presentation for a conference in Frankfurt. The fear of falling short, of not delivering the flawless presentation I demand of myself, hangs over me like a storm cloud.

Yet, a small voice inside me urges me to say yes to my friend's offer. In this new city where I hardly know anyone, I yearn for connection, the laughter and warmth that friendship brings. The loneliness is like a heavy blanket, but the thought of putting my responsibilities on hold sends a jolt of apprehension through me. What if stepping away leaves me even more behind?

I wrestle with the decision, but finally, I take a deep breath and type out a simple, 'Yes, I would love to' and hit send. Immediately, unease settles in, my stomach tightens as if caught in a vice. My hands tremble slightly, revealing the tension between the relief of prioritising connection and the anxiety of putting it before work.

Glancing at the clock, I realise I need to get serious about my to-do list. The fact that I only have seven hours left until I meet my friend sharpens my focus in an unexpected way. No more fiddling around. I turn off my phone, close my email and zero in on the most important task: my presentation.

I quickly reschedule a few meetings and politely excuse myself from others, buying myself precious time. With those distractions out of the way, I dive into outlining my presentation. The ideas start flowing easily now that I've committed my full attention to the task. The initial pang of guilt for prioritising friendship over work is replaced by a strong sense of purpose. My fingers fly across the keyboard as I structure each slide with precision. My focus deepens, allowing me to execute with an efficiency I didn't know I had. It's as if deciding to meet my friend unlocked a hidden reservoir of energy, fuelling my determination to get everything done.

As I put the final touches on the presentation, a wave of accomplishment sweeps over me. Glancing at the clock, I realise I've managed to navigate a packed day with unexpected finesse and can now enjoy the evening. As I pack up my bag, I look forward to a guilt-free night with my friend.

The next morning, I wake up feeling unexpectedly refreshed. There's a lightness in my step as I remember the previous evening – a reminder of the joy I've been missing, the warmth of connection that work had slowly drained from my life. The satisfaction I feel from spending time with my friend forces me to confront the hidden costs of dedicating so much of myself to work. How many other moments have I sacrificed over the past few years? Is this really how I want to keep living – always prioritising work over life?

The questions linger like a quiet storm, fuelling a rebellion against the status quo. I start diving into books and articles on time management and personal productivity, eager to find a better way to balance my life. I begin experimenting, trying out tools like the Pomodoro Technique and carving out focus hours, searching for a rhythm that feels natural, sustainable.

As I test new strategies, I slowly learn to set clearer boundaries and become better at saying no. With each small victory, I feel a shift – tasks that once overwhelmed me are now tackled with more focus and intention. Slowly but surely, I start to reclaim my time, rediscovering a sense of freedom I hadn't realised I'd lost. It feels like I've unlocked a new level of control, not just over my work but over life itself.

However, beneath my newfound success, the familiar voice of self-doubt lingers, nagging at the edges of my consciousness. As I celebrate more victories, the hold of my imposter syndrome tightens, whispering that my achievements are merely a fluke – that I am not truly capable or deserving of them. Even being appointed as professor of economics fails to quell my feelings of inadequacy. My internal struggle casts a shadow over even my proudest moments, clouding them with a persistent haze of self-doubt.

Desperate for relief from the stress and anxiety that have become my constant companions, I decide to diverge from my meticulously curated professional path and embark on a five-month sabbatical – a period fully dedicated to life's simple pleasures. No hectoring voice, no pressure, no stress or anxiety that have infested my personal and professional life. With an enormous sense of relief, I shut down my computer and leave the office on 26 February 2020, ready to reclaim my life.

But the universe has different plans. Just three weeks into my sabbatical, the world has changed beyond recognition. As the pandemic tightens its grip, I find myself confined to my apartment, allowed out only once a day for exercise. The sabbatical, which was supposed to be a time of joy, exploration and nourishment quickly loses its purpose. The futility of persisting with this hollowed-out version of a sabbatical becomes glaringly obvious. With a heavy heart, I decide to end it prematurely and plunge back into work.

It only takes four days for the voice of self-doubt to creep back into my thoughts, more insidious than ever. Each time I sit down to work, it whispers that my ideas are shallow, that my contributions to economics are insignificant and that I'm simply not smart enough for this role. The constant barrage of doubts is suffocating. It gnaws at me, chipping away at my motivation and resolve.

One afternoon, as I gaze out of my window at the eerily quiet city below, I realise that I'm standing at a crossroads. Two distinct paths stretch out before me. The first is one of surrender – an escape route where I leave behind the career I've spent years building, trading it for something easier, something that demands less of me. The second path is far more daunting; a path of confrontation where I must face my fears and anxieties head-on, challenging the very doubts that have plagued me for so long. The choice is clear, but the journey ahead is anything but.

Unsure of where to begin, I reflect on the progress I've already made in self-management. These improvements have boosted my productivity, freeing up time for activities that energise me. I wonder if there's more I can do – other strategies that can enhance my work efficiency and help alleviate the stress and self-doubt I feel. My search leads me to a course taught by Jim Kwik, a renowned brain and memory coach, titled *Superbrain*. Intrigued by the promise of unlocking new cognitive abilities, I decide to enrol, eager to discover what more my brain might be capable of.

With a mix of curiosity and scepticism, I sit down behind my computer for the first class. The silence of my quiet room is quickly filled by Jim's confident voice, instantly capturing my attention. 'There is no such thing as a good or bad memory,' Jim begins, his tone both reassuring and persuasive. 'Only a trained or untrained one.' His words linger in my mind. Could it really be true? Can I actually train my brain to excel at memorisation? The idea feels both intriguing and hopeful, stirring a sense of possibility within me.

As the days unfold and I immerse myself deeper into the course, I begin to uncover something remarkable about my brain. I realise I've significantly underestimated its potential, focusing too much on its weaknesses rather than leveraging its strengths. In economic terms, I've been operating my brain with surprising inefficiency.

As the thirty-day course comes to an end, I realise my journey is far from finished. Having mastered memory feats that once felt way out of reach – easily recalling lists, facts and sequences – I find myself grappling with deeper questions. Why are these techniques so effective? If my memory techniques were flawed, what else might I be missing? Are my learning strategies inefficient too? And what about my creativity? Is there a way to enhance that as well?

Determined to explore these questions, I dive into the world of cognitive performance. It's not long before I meet Philip Bond, a professor of creativity and innovation, and a Guinness World Record holder for memorising the first ten thousand digits of pi and correctly identifying random sequences within them (a feat known as the Mount Everest of memory challenges). Meeting Philip opens the door to a world where the limits of my brain are both tested and redefined.

Under Philip's guidance, I embark on an exploration of cognitive training that stretches beyond memory, delving into problem solving and creativity as well. His techniques and exercises push me to new heights, revealing that significant improvements in cognitive abilities are possible within just a few months. The process is demanding, requiring considerable time and effort. Yet, even as progress sometimes feels slow, each small victory fuels my determination.

As I delve deeper into the mysteries of the brain, I uncover more methods to sharpen my memory, learn more effectively and spark my creativity. Some of these techniques are familiar, but many are entirely new. The irony isn't lost on me: despite years of study and learning, no one has ever told me how to optimally use my brain.

As my cognitive skills steadily improve, the sharp edges of my self-doubt begin to soften. I start to feel more confident as I see the tangible results of my efforts. The overwhelming self-doubt of the past now seems more manageable, but the shadow of my imposter syndrome remains. It's a delicate balancing act – juggling the newfound confidence in my cognitive abilities with the persistent fear of inadequacy.

This internal struggle becomes starkly evident after delivering a keynote speech at an international conference. While I'm met with enthusiastic feedback from fellow academics, my mind fixates on minor stumbles and a few inadequate responses to questions. The small flaws loom large, casting a shadow over the entire experience and making me question my credibility as a researcher. In that moment, it's clear: I must confront the final hurdle – silencing the inner critic that continues to undermine my accomplishments.

At the suggestion of a friend, I sign up for another online course: *Personal Mastery*, taught by Srikumar Rao, a renowned author and life coach. The course promises to challenge my perspectives, and as the weeks go by, I find myself drawn into its thought-provoking lessons. Then, during one particular session, Rao says something that stops me in my tracks. His voice – calming yet authoritative – pauses for effect before delivering the statement that changes everything: 'You can't change behaviours without changing beliefs.'

The impact is striking, as if his words are cutting through a dense fog that has clouded my understanding. In that moment, the breakthrough I've been seeking crystallises. I realise that true transformation requires more than just tactical adjustments; it demands uncovering and reshaping the beliefs that quietly steer my life. This insight marks the beginning of a deeper, more introspective phase – one that forces me to confront and reimagine how I view myself and the world.

Thus begins the final, most challenging phase of my journey: confronting and transforming my limiting beliefs. Again, I dive into a sea of resources, this time gaining insights into how beliefs are formed and the challenges involved in altering them. Gradually, I come to realise that my self-defeating thoughts are not immutable truths but merely outdated beliefs I internalised long ago. Consciously, I work to replace them with more empowering ones. Over time, I learn to shift my focus to the present moment, embrace the journey and accept failure as part of growth.

The transformation unfolds gradually, yet its effects are profound. As I reshape my beliefs, I begin to notice a marked shift in my inner world. The self-criticism that once dominated my thoughts starts to take a back seat, making way for a growing appreciation of my worth and capabilities. What used to feel like a burden – my work – now brings me joy, and finding balance between my professional and personal life becomes more natural.

As my inner critic recedes, a newfound self-assurance takes its place. With the confidence I've cultivated, I start to embrace my potential, trust in my abilities and meet challenges with resilience. Freed from the constraints of my old self-doubt, I now move forward with a clear vision of who I am. My journey has transformed me from merely existing to truly thriving. At last, I am free to be fully and authentically me.

*

Having witnessed the great benefits of harnessing my brain's capabilities, I wondered whether my peers had given it some thought as well. It seemed logical; after all, the advantages are manyfold – improved productivity, less stress, a better work-life balance – so I assumed they would have given the topic at least some attention. To my surprise, most had not.

Some colleagues mentioned reading books on focus, deep thinking or time management, while others had stumbled upon effective strategies through trial and error. A few said they refrained from trying to excel at everything, accepting that trade-offs are inevitable. Yet, when I introduced the idea of actively working to enhance brain function, most responded with mild surprise. They admitted they had never really considered it.

What fascinated me most is that they're all economists. Economists study how individuals and societies make the best possible choices given the resources at their disposal. Central to this is so-called *constrained optimisation*: the process of maximising utility – our overall satisfaction or happiness – within the limitations we face, such as time, money or other resources.

Through this lens, we analyse decision-making processes, and the trade-offs people make to reach their goals.

Every decision we make involves weighing pros and cons to find the best possible outcome within our constraints. This is something we do every day, often without thinking about it. Imagine you're deciding between two options for your evening meal: cooking a healthy dinner at home or ordering takeout from your favourite restaurant. Cooking allows you to control the ingredients, ensuring a nutritious meal that aligns with your health goals, plus it's typically cheaper. However, it requires time and effort after a long day. Ordering takeout, on the other hand, is convenient and saves time, but the meal may be less healthy and more expensive.

The right choice hinges on your circumstances and priorities. If you have the time and energy to cook and are focused on improving your diet, preparing dinner yourself might be the better option. However, if you're exhausted and short on time, and your budget isn't too tight, opting for takeout might be more appealing for that night.

To make the right decision, you need all the relevant information. This includes knowing how much time and money you have, your remaining energy levels, what ingredients are available at home and how important maintaining a healthy diet is to you at that moment. You also need to consider how ordering takeout might impact your long-term health and saving goals. Without this information, you might impulsively choose takeout, only to regret it later when you feel sluggish or guilty about straying from your health plan – or when you realise you don't have enough money left for those concert tickets you've been eying.

Decisions about dinner are usually straightforward, yet this example underscores a deeper truth: optimising outcomes requires informed decision making. This principle applies not only to our daily tasks and major life choices but also to how we utilise our most valuable resource – our brain. Just as selecting the right meal relies on a clear understanding of each option's pros and cons, maximising our brain's potential requires access to the right knowledge.

Our brain is incredibly powerful, but it needs proper care and effective strategies to function at its best. During my journey, I discovered that finding that knowledge is surprisingly difficult. Countless books have been written on the brain, yet the sheer volume of information can be overwhelming, making it hard to identify strategies tailored to our specific needs. Furthermore, harnessing our brain's full power necessitates a holistic approach that addresses various aspects of how we think, feel and perform. Unfortunately, many books focus on one topic – be it memory enhancement, time management or mindset – leaving us to piece together a comprehensive strategy on our own.

That's why I set out to create the resource I wish I had – a comprehensive guide that integrates the fragmented pieces into a cohesive whole. In the pages that follow, I've distilled everything I've learned into a book that covers time management, motivation, cognitive performance, mindset and happiness. My goal is to share the practical tools and techniques that not only helped me optimise my brain's cognitive capabilities but also enabled me to reduce stress, overcome self-doubt and step into my true power. As you read, you'll gain insights from my extensive exploration of neuroscience, psychology and economics. Many strategies I share are grounded in scientific research, while others stem from personal experiences and practices that have proven effective in my life.

This book explores both the 'why' and the 'how' of various aspects of cognitive enhancement, helping you to make better decisions about your brain. Think of it as a buffet of ideas. There are many options to choose from and you can pick the ones that fit your preferences, constraints and lifestyle best. You'll find that making trade-offs is unavoidable, but by giving up certain things, you'll gain a sharper, more productive, more creative and more empowering brain. Successful people know that deciding what not to do is just as important as deciding what to do.

The book is divided into three sections, each reflecting a key stage of my personal journey. The first part focuses on clarifying your goals and staying on track by learning to prioritise and manage your time more effectively. You'll find techniques to sustain concentration, minimise distractions and boost both motivation and self-discipline.

Part two offers a variety of tools and techniques that can significantly improve your cognitive abilities. I provide practical strategies for memory enhancement and effective learning. You'll discover that creativity isn't merely a stroke of luck, but a process you can actively control. I'll also discuss the vital roles of mental and physical exercise, restorative sleep and mindfulness practices in optimising your brain's performance.

The final part delves into the transformative power of mindset and beliefs. You'll discover how your brain forms and reinforces beliefs, often ones that hold you back. I'll share practical strategies to begin reshaping these beliefs, paving the way for personal growth and empowerment. In the final chapter, I'll share effective ways to bring more positivity in your daily life.

As you reach the end of this book, you'll find yourself armed with a newfound understanding of your brain and how to harness its power. Some parts may resonate strongly with you, while others may not. Take what's helpful; let go of the rest. This book is simply an invitation to embark on your own journey of discovery. You might want to revisit it every now and then, as different insights may resonate as your life evolves.

Unlocking your brain's full potential isn't about making monumental, drastic changes overnight. It's about making small, thoughtful adjustments that, over time, can lead to big improvements in your life. I've experienced firsthand how challenging it can be when your brain is working against you. And how powerful it can be if it's tuned to help you instead. Let's dive in and unlock our brain's true potential together.

PART 1

Elevate Yourself: Achieving Clarity and Control

In a world brimming with distractions and endless demands, using our time and energy effectively can seem like a distant dream. As a result, we often find ourselves drifting through days of relentless multi-tasking, our focus splintered and our goals elusive. It's easy to feel overwhelmed by the constant barrage of notifications and obligations, often pulling us in multiple directions. Yet within each of us lies the power to reclaim our time and energy; to make deliberate choices that align with our deepest goals; to transform the chaos into a more organised and purposeful life.

Everything we do requires time, a finite and precious resource. Each day, we make numerous decisions, but we often neglect to consider the trade-offs involved. We focus on the benefits without considering the costs. And all too often, we fail to consider if our decisions help us reach our desired goals. By becoming more mindful of how we allocate our time and evaluating the true impact of our choices, we can steer our lives in the direction that aligns better with whom we aspire to be.

Similarly, our mental energy is limited, but we often stretch it thin across multiple tasks. When we allow ourselves to get bogged down by endless distractions and low-priority tasks, we deplete our mental reserves, leaving little room for the activities that truly matter. Our brain thrives when it can concentrate on a task and then has time to rest and wander. By learning to pay attention to the things that truly matter, we can use our mental energy much more effectively.

Motivation plays a crucial role in this process. It's the spark that ignites our desire to learn and grow, and the fuel that helps us sustain the effort. Motivation isn't merely a trait we possess; it's an active practice that we engage in that requires clear, achievable goals, self-discipline and an environment that supports our ambitions. This enables us to keep our enthusiasm high and our efforts consistent as we work towards our goals.

In this first part we set out to master these skills. We'll explore practical tools to manage time in line with our priorities (Chapter 1), strengthen our 'focus muscle' (Chapter 2) and maintain a high level of motivation for the things we set out to do (Chapter 3). These tools should help you unlock a new level of clarity and control over your personal and professional life.

1

The Art of Prioritising What Matters

It's just after 6 p.m. and I finally lean back in my office chair, staring blankly at the computer screen. My desk is cluttered with research papers, half-empty coffee mugs and scribbled notes – the remnants of a long and demanding day. Outside, darkness has settled in, and I am almost alone in the office, bathing in the harsh sterile glow of the fluorescent lights.

As usual, my day has been a whirlwind – various meetings, a deluge of emails and urgent tasks that demanded my immediate attention. Now, in the quiet of the evening, I am trying to focus on my research. Yet, the more I try to delve into it, the more I feel like I am treading water. For months, my productivity has been waning and the constant pressure is starting to take its toll.

I've had a demanding career for years and I am accustomed to long hours, but tonight feels different. I'm not just tired; I am frustrated by my inability to make any real progress. The constant interruptions and shifting priorities have drained my energy and focus, impacting not only my work but my personal life as well.

As the office grows quieter and the day fades, a realisation begins to take shape. Despite my best efforts to stay on top of everything, I am spinning my wheels. The days' incessant urgencies keep pulling me away from what really matters, and my effectiveness is suffering as a result. I am caught in a cycle of reacting to demands rather than moving forward with purpose.

I pause for a moment, close my laptop and allow the stillness to settle. It's becoming clear that my current approach isn't working. There is an obvious gap between my efforts and the results I'm seeing. I need to break free from this reactive mode and find a way to take back control. It's time for a new approach – one that involves making intentional choices that lead to real progress.

The Power of No

Most of us would rather not face the harsh truth of how many hours a week we actually spend scrolling mindlessly on Facebook, Instagram, TikTok or X. When it comes to social media, we often apply what Cal Newport, author of *Deep Work*, calls the 'any-benefit approach': we justify using it if we can find it provides any kind of benefit, such as entertainment.[1] We don't ask ourselves whether we lacked entertainment before we joined the platform, or whether we would be better entertained doing something else.

Often without realising, we apply this 'any-benefit approach' to many other decisions in our lives as well. How often have you agreed to take on an additional project at work, knowing perfectly well that it would mean working late nights? How often have you accepted an invitation to a social event even though you really needed a night by yourself on the couch? We tend to focus on the benefits of saying yes to something, without factoring in the full cost of doing so.

Of course, in some cases we don't have much of a choice. But when a choice is available to us, why do we struggle so much to utter that two-letter word 'no'? One explanation lies in so-called *hyperbolic discounting*: our tendency to exaggerate the present moment in our decision-making. Even if a future reward holds more value than an immediate one, we often opt for the short-term gain. For instance, when a friend invites us to a last-minute social gathering, we may say yes, lured by the excitement of the moment. We do this despite knowing that declining would allow us to rest and recharge, and feel more energized tomorrow.

Another reason is that we fail to consider the trade-off involved. Saying yes to one thing inevitably means saying no to doing anything else in that timeframe. Economists call this an *opportunity cost*. The opportunity cost of something is whatever you had to give up to do it. It's an important concept to understand.

Requests such as delivering a presentation abroad, reviewing a colleague's report or attending a friend's party can seem perfectly reasonable. However, to make sound decisions, it's essential to examine them through the lens of opportunity cost. This way, the true implications of each choice become much clearer.

Should I agree to present, knowing it means being away from home for two days and nights? Should I commit to reviewing a colleague's report, which would delay my own work? Should I attend my friend's event at the expense of time I could dedicate to self-care? Economic journalist Tim Harford suggests a useful reframing of these choices: rather than simply focusing on what you're agreeing to by saying yes, consider what you are passing up – the opportunity cost.[2]

Another reason we struggle to say no is the pressure to meet expectations – whether personal, professional or societal. The fear of letting others down or being perceived as less committed or engaged can make us feel obligated to say yes. At work, the expectation to be a team player can lead us to accept additional responsibilities, even when they push our limits. Socially, the desire to fit in and not miss out can prompt us to agree to plans we'd rather skip. On a personal level, the desire to meet our own high standards can trap us in a cycle of doing things we don't have time or energy for. Such expectations, whether genuine or perceived, can cloud our judgment and make it difficult to prioritise our true needs and values, ultimately preventing us from setting the boundaries we need.

It turns out that learning to say no is especially important for women. In their book *The No Club*, professors Linda Babcock, Brenda Peyser, Lise Vesterlund and Lauri Weingart provide ample evidence that women are disproportionately expected to perform what they call 'non-promotable tasks', like planning the office party, screening interns, attending to a time-consuming client or simply helping others with their work. These are all important tasks in an organisation but won't help the person doing them advance their career. This leaves many women overcommitted but underutilised, contributing to loss of confidence, erosion of time with family, increased stress levels and stagnating careers.

So, the next time you're faced with a request, take a moment to pause and reflect. Consider what you will have to decline if you agree to this new task. Think about any prior commitments you've made. This reflection is particularly important for tasks that have future deadlines, as the demands on your time and energy can change significantly as those deadlines approach. Most importantly, ask yourself whether saying yes aligns with your overall goals.

It can be difficult to say no to an opportunity when the exact costs of doing so are unclear. For instance, refusing an extra work task frees up time now, but could limit chances of future professional development. To make informed decisions, you need to weigh such potential abstract losses against concrete benefits and have a firm grasp of your long-term goals. If a task brings you closer to a goal, take it. Otherwise, it's best to decline.

Saying no can be tough. But it helps to keep in mind that declining one opportunity opens the door for another. Instead of taking on another client, you can use the time to take your partner on a romantic getaway and strengthen your relationship.

Goal-setting 101

Learning to say no to unimportant things is a key step towards making room for things that do matter – our goals. Goals are important as they act as a compass in our life. They're like stepping stones, leading us to our ultimate destination, be it a promotion, finding a life partner or creating unforgettable family moments.

Effective goal setting begins with a heartfelt conversation with ourselves, reflecting on our values, passions and aspirations. Unfortunately, we often overlook this self-reflection amidst constant distractions, societal pressure to always be busy or the fear of confronting uncomfortable emotions and uncertainties. However, taking the time to pause and reflect allows us to stay focused on what we would like to achieve.

Yet, merely setting goals isn't enough; it's the clarity and strategy behind them that truly makes the difference. This is where SMART goals come in. SMART is an acronym that stands for Specific, Measurable, Achievable, Relevant and Time-bound – criteria that provide a structured approach to ensure we're not only dreaming big but also take the necessary steps to achieve our desired outcomes:

- **Specific**: A goal should clearly define what you want to achieve, creating a focused target to aim for.
- **Measurable**: Quantify your goal or provide a way to measure progress, so you know when it has been achieved.
- **Achievable**: A goal should be realistic, challenging you while still being attainable. Breaking down large goals into smaller milestones, makes them more achievable.
- **Relevant**: It should be meaningful and align with your values and long-term objectives.
- **Time-bound**: There should be a deadline or timeframe, which provides a sense of urgency and helps to prioritise.

S M A R T

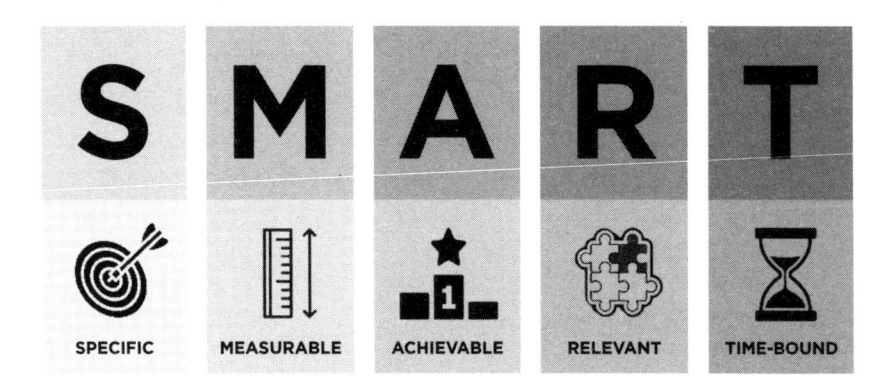

SPECIFIC | MEASURABLE | ACHIEVABLE | RELEVANT | TIME-BOUND

The SMART framework was first introduced by George Doran in 1981 and remains widely adopted.[3] And for good reason – there's plenty of scientific evidence that it works. Well-defined goals have been shown to enhance performance across a wide variety of tasks and settings by sharpening focus, boosting effort, increasing persistence and encouraging the development of effective strategies and plans.[4]

The brilliance of setting SMART goals lies in their power to bring clarity and focus. They transform vague aspirations into actionable plans. It's the difference between setting a nebulous goal, such as 'I want to get fit', and a clear, specific target: 'I'm going to complete a 5k run in under thirty minutes by July.' As we'll explore in Chapter 3, this shift makes a world of difference for motivation and accountability. SMART goals encourage commitment, allow for progress tracking and offer tangible milestones to celebrate along the way. Each milestone we hit fuels a sense of accomplishment, reinforcing our drive to continue moving forward.

So, the next time you set out to achieve something, try making your goal SMART. By doing this, you create a mental blueprint that gives you purpose, direction and a yardstick against which to measure your progress. This simple shift makes you far more likely to succeed. While we'll dive deeper into goal setting in Chapter 3, why not start now? Set a SMART goal for finishing this book – you'll be surprised how much more rewarding the journey becomes when you've set a clear destination.

Setting medium- and long-term goals is important, as they give us direction, but how do we manage the daily grind when tasks keep piling up? How do we stop feeling overwhelmed by everything on our plate?

The Priority Compass

Imagine you have a bank account that deposits £1,440 each morning. The account doesn't allow you to carry over any remaining balance to the next day. Every evening, whatever money you failed to use during the day disappears. What would you do? You'd draw out every dollar each day!

We all have such a bank. Its name is *Time*. Every morning, it credits us with 1,440 minutes. Every night, it writes off as lost whatever time we have failed to use wisely. It carries over no balance from day-to-day. It allows no overdraft. We can't borrow against ourselves, nor can we borrow someone else's time. If we fail to use the day's deposits, it's our loss, and we can't appeal to get it back.

The time we have is the time we have. It's ours to decide how we spend it, just as we decide how to spend our money. Often, it's not the case that we don't have enough time to do the things we want to do. It's that we don't prioritise those things.

After reading this analogy one morning, I couldn't shake it off. As I moved through my day, I started noticing the small decisions that filled my time – responding to emails that weren't urgent, getting caught in another meeting that didn't need to happen. The minutes were spent, but not on what I really cared about.

As the day continued, I became more aware of how easily time slipped through my fingers – scrolling through updates, chatting with colleagues and handling tasks that seemed important in the moment. Before I knew it, the day had ended, leaving me to wonder where all those hours had gone. The list of things I'd wanted to do remained untouched. It wasn't a matter of not having time; I just let it slip away without conscious thought.

Planning every minute of the day to avoid 'wasting time' feels exhausting and unrealistic – I've never been able to stick to that kind of rigid schedule. But I've learned that simply stepping back to observe how I spend my time, especially at work, makes a noticeable difference. I began to see where my efforts aligned with my goals and where they didn't. The more attention I paid, the clearer it became that much of my time went to tasks that seemed urgent but weren't truly important. By focusing on what really mattered, I gradually started gaining control over my day, one small decision at a time.

I had to begin with a clearer understanding of my goals. What was I trying to accomplish? What were my key responsibilities? So, I sat down and took stock of everything on my plate. As a researcher, my primary responsibility is to publish research papers, which involves a whole host of tasks: conducting experiments, analysing data, reviewing literature, writing and editing, and presenting at conferences. But there's also a mountain of additional responsibilities that I hadn't really accounted for – department meetings, coordinating with co-authors, answering a flood of emails, reviewing papers for journals, updating my online presence, mentoring and more.

Once I laid everything out, it became clear just how many small, overlooked tasks were eating away at my time. That's when I knew I had to start prioritising, and the Eisenhower Matrix, popularised by Stephen Covey in *The 7 Habits of Highly Effective People*, came into play. It's been a game-changer for me, helping me sort through what's really important versus what just feels urgent.

The Eisenhower Matrix is a simple yet powerful tool for prioritising tasks by urgency and importance. It divides tasks into four quadrants, helping us to determine what requires immediate attention and what can be handled later – or not at all. Let's break down how the four quadrants work, using examples from my typical day as a researcher.

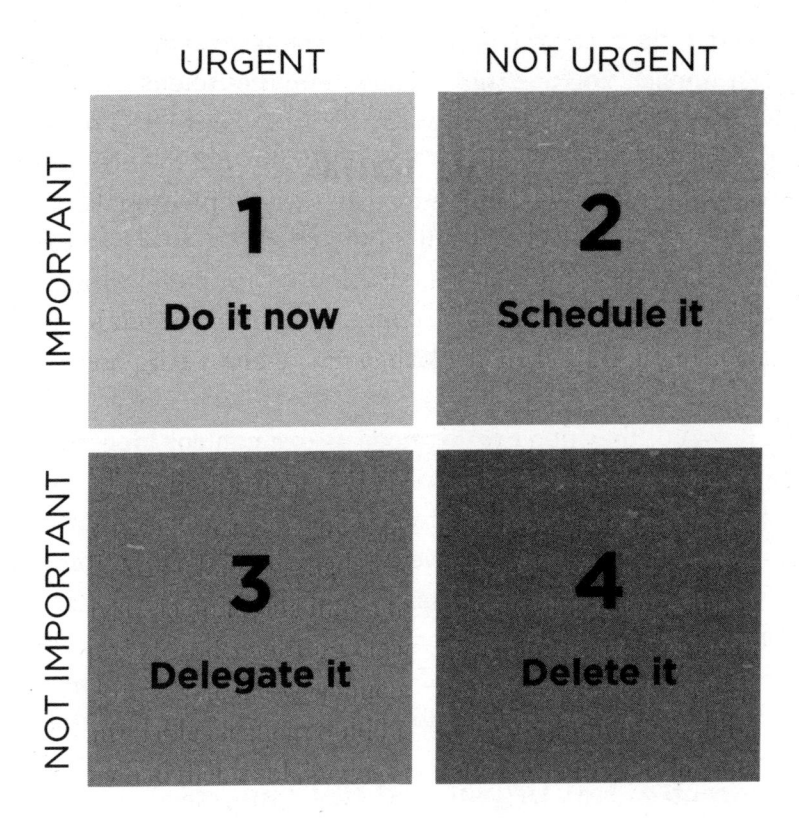

	URGENT	NOT URGENT
IMPORTANT	**1** Do it now	**2** Schedule it
NOT IMPORTANT	**3** Delegate it	**4** Delete it

Quadrant 1: Urgent and Important
This quadrant is for tasks that demand immediate action and are crucial to achieving our goals. These are the fires we need to put out – urgent deadlines, crises or critical problems that, if left unattended, could have serious consequences. In my case, this could be a rapidly approaching deadline to submit a research paper or an unexpected issue with an experiment that needs immediate troubleshooting. These tasks require immediate focus and can't be pushed off.

Quadrant 2: Not Urgent but Important
This is the sweet spot for long-term success. These tasks are important to our goals but not time-sensitive. They often get overlooked because they don't press for our attention, but

investing time in them consistently is what ultimately makes the biggest impact. For me, this includes activities like planning out new research projects, writing sections of a paper in advance or mentoring junior researchers. These tasks may not have an immediate deadline, but focusing on them ensures progress towards larger goals. The challenge is that they often get delayed because Quadrant 1 and 3 tasks feel more pressing in the moment.

Quadrant 3: Urgent but Not Important

These tasks are urgent in the sense that they demand our attention now, but they don't really move us towards our bigger goals. They often come from external pressures – like responding to routine emails, attending non-essential meetings or dealing with last-minute requests that someone else has deemed urgent. In my work, this might be replying to department-wide email chains or attending meetings that don't really require my input. These can eat up valuable time, and the key here is to minimise or delegate them whenever possible.

Quadrant 4: Not Urgent and Not Important

This is where tasks that neither advance our goals nor require urgent attention belong – essentially, time-wasters. These might include mindlessly scrolling through social media, getting distracted by unproductive conversations or handling minor tasks that could be done at any time. For me, that might look like getting sidetracked by non-work-related content or spending too long on website updates. These activities may feel like breaks, but they can also lead to wasted hours if we're not mindful of how much time they consume.

By taking stock of my tasks and sorting them into the four Quadrants, I found it much easier to pinpoint and concentrate on my Quadrant 2 activities. This approach has enabled me to make meaningful progress in what truly matters in my work, rather than merely reacting to whatever seems urgent. I encourage you to try applying this framework to your own tasks; it can

THE ART OF PRIORITISING WHAT MATTERS

help gain clarity on where your time and energy are currently allocated – and more importantly, where they should be directed for maximum impact. You might be surprised at the insights you uncover

However, identifying those important tasks is just the beginning. To prioritise effectively, we need more than just an understanding of the Eisenhower Matrix. We need systems and habits in place that help us consistently stay on track. This is where Rick Pastoor's book *Grip* offers some valuable insights. Pastoor focuses on practical strategies for taking control of our day-to-day work in a way that aligns with our larger goals.

One of the core ideas from *Grip* is the importance of structuring our week in a way that puts us in control of both our time and attention. He recommends breaking tasks into smaller, manageable pieces and blocking out focused work time in our calendars. This approach fits perfectly with the Eisenhower Matrix, particularly when it comes to Quadrant 2 tasks. These tasks need to be deliberately scheduled because their lack of urgency makes them easy to neglect. Without setting aside dedicated time, urgent tasks – including those driven by others' demands – will inevitably take over. Planning ahead allows us to make steady progress instead of waiting for a crisis to force us into action. In the next chapter, we'll explore the best times to schedule these Quadrant 2 activities.

Another insight from *Grip* is the importance of reviewing our commitments regularly. Pastoor suggests taking time at the start of each week to evaluate your tasks and projects, ensuring they align with your priorities. This practice helps avoid getting caught up in Quadrant 3 distractions – urgent but not important tasks. Additionally, he recommends reflecting at the end of the week to assess what we've accomplished. This helps determine whether your time was spent on meaningful work. By regularly reviewing and reflecting, we can fine-tune our priorities and make sure we become better at assessing how much time various tasks entail.

A particularly practical tip from *Grip* is to reduce our priority jobs for the week to only two or three, instead of the five, ten or thirty we might have on our list. This approach is crucial because it helps combat the *planning fallacy* – our tendency to underestimate the time needed to complete tasks, even when we have prior experience with similar tasks.[5] We just tend to be far too optimistic about how long it takes to finish a task. My personal guideline is to make an estimate of how much time I need to complete something and then multiply it by 5. Allocating time and scheduling your top 3 priority tasks, should also make it easier to say no.

The four quadrants and scheduling tips are valuable for managing all aspects of life, but it can be overwhelming to categorise every activity and determine priorities. I found it helpful to start by focusing on my job. Once I had a better handle on that, I gradually expanded to include my personal life as well. While distinguishing between urgent and non-urgent tasks is fairly easy, determining what tasks are important can be more challenging, since it's a sliding scale, rather than a binary choice. Fortunately, economics offers some handy tools.

Maximising Impact

In the late nineteenth century, Italian economist and sociologist Vilfredo Pareto noticed a curious pattern in the distribution of wealth: a small portion of the population seemed to control a disproportionately large share of the wealth. Intrigued, he gathered data on land ownership in Italy and discovered that 80 per cent of the land was owned by just 20 per cent of the population. Fascinated by this discovery, Pareto expanded his research to other countries, historical periods and outcomes. To his surprise, he found that this unequal distribution was not a mere anomaly but a consistent pattern.[6]

Pareto's observation that 80 per cent of the results come from 20 per cent of the causes is now known as the Pareto Principle or the 80/20 Rule. Although the exact shares may vary, this

THE ART OF PRIORITISING WHAT MATTERS 15

unequal distribution can be observed in many areas. For instance, in business, it's commonly observed that about 80 per cent of a company's revenue comes from just 20 per cent of its customers. Similarly, in shops, a small number of products usually account for the majority of sales. And a small portion of the workforce tends to generate the bulk of productivity.[7]

The Pareto Principle is relevant for time management as well: a few key tasks or activities usually drive the majority of our results. By focusing on our most impactful tasks – those that contribute most to our goals – we can greatly enhance our productivity and effectiveness. Recognising and prioritising these high-impact activities allows us to work more efficiently and achieve greater progress.

The question then becomes: how do we identify the critical few? A great starting point is to revisit the Quadrant 2 tasks you've just identified. Reflect on which of these tasks consistently yield the best results in your work. Start by asking yourself questions such as: which tasks align most closely with my current long-term goals? Which activities will likely have the greatest impact on my future success?

Another effective approach is to analyse your past performance. Take some time to review your completed projects or tasks from the last few weeks, months or even years. Which ones contributed most to your success or advancement? By identifying patterns in your past achievements, you can better focus on similar tasks that promise high returns in the future.

The next step is to concentrate your time and energy on your vital few. They should be part of your top 3 priorities. Aim to reduce the other 80 per cent of your responsibilities – those tasks that are less important, less urgent or less enjoyable – through elimination, delegation or automation. Note that this means that some tasks that you initially identified as Quadrant 2 tasks might actually fall into Quadrant 4 (I refer to them as Quadrant 2.5 tasks as they are important, just not as critical as my vital few).

This process requires you to set clear boundaries and learn to say no to less vital commitments – which can be challenging. However, having identified your vital few tasks should make this easier, as the opportunity cost of saying yes to non-essential tasks becomes clearer. By focusing on your vital few, you not only prevent yourself from spreading too thin but also alleviate the stress that comes with trying to juggle everything. This approach ensures that you maximise the return on the time and energy you invest in your work. You just can't do everything you wish you could; the key therefore is to focus on what will truly drive you forward.

Personally, I also found the 80/20 rule a powerful tool to combat my perfectionism. When I prepare a presentation (or anything for that matter), my natural inclination is to dive deep into every detail – tweaking each slide, refining the wording and adjusting the design to get everything just right. I can spend hours on what objectively are minor details, trying to make the presentation flawless. However, this meticulous approach often leads me to spend excessive time on my presentations at the expense of more important tasks.

Realising the need for a more efficient approach, I turned to the 80/20 rule for guidance. I now focus my energy on the parts of the presentation that are most critical – an impactful introduction and strong visuals that convey my message. By focusing on the core elements that truly matter, I am better able to concentrate my efforts without getting bogged down by small fixes (though I'll admit, my inner perfectionist still sneaks in for a final polish).

What about breaking commitments? Walking away from something, even when it no longer holds value, is often surprisingly difficult. Take this example: imagine you've enrolled in a series of cooking classes, only to realise that the teacher isn't great and you're not learning much. Despite this, having paid for ten classes and attended four, you might feel compelled to continue as quitting now would seem like wasting the time, money and effort you've already invested. But you shouldn't.

This is a classic example of the *sunk cost fallacy*. The time, money and effort you've already spent can't be recovered, so they shouldn't influence your decision to carry on. Yet, these factors often feel relevant because they represent an investment we're hoping will eventually pay off. Letting go is hard because it feels like admitting those past investments were for nothing.

Think about it this way: you've bought a movie ticket, and halfway through you find the movie boring. The sunk cost fallacy would have you believe you should stay to 'get your money's worth'. But really, that ticket price is gone whether you stay or leave. The smart move is to decide based on what's best for you now – maybe leaving and doing something more enjoyable instead.

It's easy to fall into the trap of persisting with something simply because you've already invested so much into it. However, recognising when to cut losses and redirect your resources is a valuable skill that can save a lot of time and trouble later. Time is a scarce resource, so try not to waste it on things that just aren't important enough – like I did, spending far too much time trying to save 25 cents on an avocado.

Easy Wins

The Dutch are generally considered to be masters of frugality. Indeed, we love sales and discounts, and we have expressions like, 'When it's free, it's even better', 'He who saves has something' and 'Look after your pennies'. We even optimised 'going Dutch' through a popular mobile app called Tikkie, which makes it super easy to ensure that each person pays his or her share of the bill.

Of course, as with all such stereotypes, we should take this one with a grain of salt. But being frugal is part of my DNA. From my early childhood, I was taught to save for a rainy day and to spend my money wisely. We would only buy vegetables that were on sale and my dad would go to different supermarkets to find the cheapest products – not so much out of necessity, but just not to waste any money.

Without thinking twice, I followed in my dad's footsteps as an adult. Until quite recently, if I needed an avocado and found the price too high in one store, I would refuse to buy it, go to another supermarket, and buy one that was 25 cents cheaper. It was only when I started thinking about the opportunity cost – how much time I was spending going to another store to buy a slightly cheaper avocado – that I realised I was wasting my time. Surely ten minutes out of my busy day were worth much more than 25 cents. Nowadays, when I am at a shop in need of an avocado and find it too expensive, I just buy it, make a mental note not to buy avocados at that store again, and feel happy that I just saved myself ten precious minutes.

It's easy to overlook how much time we lose to seemingly innocent habits. Whether it's making an extra trip to a different supermarket for a small discount, scrolling endlessly through social media, scrambling to plan meals at the last minute or dithering over what to wear, these seemingly minor habits can add up to significant time wastage over days and weeks. Additionally, every decision we make consumes mental energy, as our brains work to evaluate various options and scenarios. While complex decisions can be particularly draining, even the smaller, daily choices can accumulate and become quite tiring.

This is why highly successful individuals often design their lives to minimise unnecessary decisions. Take, for example, figures like Barack Obama, Steve Jobs or Mark Zuckerberg. You might notice that they often wear similar outfits. This isn't just a fashion choice; it's a deliberate strategy to reduce *decision fatigue*. As Barack Obama mentioned in an interview with *Vanity Fair*: 'You'll see I wear only the same grey or blue suit. I'm trying to pare down my decisions. I don't want to make decisions about what I am eating or wearing because I have too many other decisions to make.'[8]

By automating repetitive decisions, we can streamline our daily routines, saving both time and mental energy. When we establish consistent habits, our brains create neural pathways that help us perform these tasks instinctively, freeing us from constant deliberation. This process helps to mitigate decision fatigue – a condition where too many choices lead to poorer decision-making, lower satisfaction with the choices made and even procrastination. Reducing the number of conscious decisions each day allows us to focus more on the things that matter.

Moreover, turning desired behaviours into automated habits makes it easier to resist temptations and stay disciplined. For example, if running on Monday nights is part of your routine, you're more likely to follow through even after a long day. Conversely, without a set habit, the temptation to relax on the couch with a snack will become much harder to resist.

In Chapter 7, we'll delve deeper into how we can effectively establish and maintain habits. For now, consider auditing your daily decisions to identify opportunities for automation or other ways to save time. Perhaps you can streamline your morning routine by planning outfits in advance, simplify grocery shopping with a standard online list, or set up automatic bill payments or recurring reminders for routine work tasks. Whatever; as long as it makes your life easier.

Remember to revisit and reassess your routines periodically. Just like the London commuters who discovered more efficient routes during the 2014 tube strike, you might find better ways to manage your tasks.[9] By occasionally questioning your routines, you might uncover smarter, more efficient methods.

Time is a precious resource. By taking a moment to reflect on how you're using it and exploring ways to automate and streamline your tasks, you can save valuable minutes each day. Over time, these savings add up significantly – fifteen minutes saved daily translates to roughly ninety hours a year. That means more than two full working weeks!

However, even with the time-management skills we've just discussed, there will inevitably be moments when you feel overwhelmed by the constant demands on your time. Getting everything crossed off your to-do lists is an impossible ideal. New tasks are always popping up, and we tend to underestimate the time needed to complete the ones we've already set. That's why maintaining balance isn't about constantly being productive but recognising when to pause. Sometimes, the best way to regain control is to allow ourselves the space to relax and enjoy life without purpose.

'Alles Mag Dag'

As a kid, there was a day I eagerly awaited every year. We called it *'Alles Mag Dag'* or 'Anything Goes Day'. It was this magical twenty-four hours where the only rule was that there were no rules (well, within safety perimeters of course). I was the master of my time and total freedom reigned. The list of possibilities was endless – munching on as many candies as I could, bingeing on TV until my eyes burned and defying bedtime hours.

As I grew older, though, these exhilarating days of freedom inexplicably vanished. I had somehow convinced myself that as an adult, I could already do as I pleased, right? Recently, though, it dawned on me that those 'Anything Goes Days' that I cavalierly dismissed are, in reality, of great importance as they offer a mental break from the constant pressure 'to be productive'.

So, I decided to dust off the concept of the *Alles Mag Dag* and weave it back into my life. Occasionally, I give myself a day where life follows my whims and not the other way around. Lounging in my bed till 11 a.m. reading a newspaper, spending the entire day in my bathrobe, savouring a bag of crisps sans guilt, soaking up the sun and enjoying my coffee without feeling the need to respond to all the WhatsApp messages, not cooking but indulging in takeout, diving into a book just for the sheer thrill of it – anything my heart desires at that moment.

I emerge from such a day fully revitalised, feeling as though I've been on a brief yet satisfying vacation (minus the hassles of travel and figuring out new cultures and customs). The benefits are twofold. Firstly, I grant myself the licence to unapologetically indulge in a day of leisure without the nagging burden of guilt

THE ART OF PRIORITISING WHAT MATTERS 21

that I should be 'doing something productive'. Secondly, because I'm not chasing future outcomes, I'm engrossed in the present, savouring every bit of it.

As it turns out, I'm not the only one who has (re)discovered the value of stepping away from the daily to-do lists and giving myself permission to be idle. Oliver Burkeman, the author of *Four Thousand Weeks*, shares these sentiments. He believes that our futile pursuit of time control leads to feelings of guilt and discontent. He advises accepting our time limitations and deliberately incorporating purposeless time into our schedules, which he defines as periods where we have no specific tasks or goals, permitting us to do as we wish, without any pressure or expectation of productivity, much like the *Alles Mag Dag*.

Olga Mecking takes it one step further in her book *Niksen: Embracing the Dutch Art of Doing Nothing*. 'Niksen' translates as 'doing nothing'. It's apparently a Dutch concept but nobody really knows why. *Niksen* isn't about being lazy or unproductive. Instead, it's about deliberately setting aside time to simply be, without any specific purpose or goal in mind. It's about allowing ourselves to exist in the present moment, without feeling the need to achieve anything.

The practice of *Niksen* can take many forms. It might involve sitting quietly and observing the world, taking a leisurely stroll with no destination in mind or even just lying down and staring up at the sky. The key is to let go of the need to be constantly occupied and to embrace the stillness and calm that comes with doing nothing.

Both concepts emphasise the value of downtime and non-productivity but apply it in different ways. *Niksen* promotes mental idleness, letting your mind drift freely, while the *Alles Mag Dag* grants the freedom to do anything without a set goal. The choice of which to embrace is yours, but incorporating such moments of purposeless time into your routine offers benefits far beyond relaxation.

Stepping away from constant productivity allows creativity to flourish. Activities without pressure – whether it's a stroll through the park, a nap or doodling – give our mind space to wander and spark innovative ideas. Additionally, periods of daydreaming can enhance problem-solving and boost mental agility. Downtime isn't just a break; it's essential for supporting our cognitive processes.

Last, but certainly not least, unstructured time is a potent antidote to burnout and stress. Our fast-paced lives often leave us overwhelmed, sacrificing rest for a never-ending to-do list. Prioritising agenda-free moments allows us to recharge, fostering a sense of well-being that spills over into every facet of our lives. The beauty of idleness lies not in the activity it avoids, but in the life it invites.

> ### *The Key Takeaways*
>
> Learning to schedule your priorities instead of prioritising what's on your schedule is the first step towards unlocking your brain's true potential. This small shift in perspective can already greatly improve your mental functioning. By aligning your 1,440 daily minutes with your goals and desires, you'll feel less overwhelmed as you juggle life's many demands.
>
> - Embracing the power of saying no is like clearing clutter from a crowded room – it creates space for what truly matters. By strategically declining requests that don't align with your core goals you free up time and energy for your top priorities. Adopt an opportunity cost mindset to evaluate choices, considering not just the benefits but also what you're sacrificing.
>
> - Setting SMART goals ensures your objectives are clear and actionable. By making them Specific, Measurable, Achievable, Relevant and Time-bound, you create a

THE ART OF PRIORITISING WHAT MATTERS

clear plan that improves focus and motivation. This approach makes it easier to track progress and increases your chances of achieving meaningful results.

- Quadrant 2 activities are key to long-term success and well-being, yet their lack of immediacy often causes us to neglect them. By intentionally carving out time for these important but non-urgent tasks, you create a buffer against future crises and pave a smoother path towards your long-term goals

- The 80/20 rule teaches that a small portion of your efforts often yields the majority of your results. Embracing this principle means focusing on high-impact activities and accepting that it's unnecessary to do everything equally well. Keep in mind that sunk costs – resources already spent – shouldn't dictate your decision to continue with a commitment.

- Seemingly harmless habits and daily decisions – like choosing outfits, meal planning or scrolling through social media – can take up a lot of time and energy. By looking for ways to save time and automate routine choices, you can reclaim valuable time and energy for more important things. Saving fifteen minutes daily translates into roughly two full working weeks a year.

- Integrating periods of unstructured idleness, like an *Alles Mag Dag* or practising *Niksen* can be a potent antidote to your never-ending to-do lists. These intentional breaks provide a mental reset, reducing stress and allowing creativity to flourish. By stepping back, you create space for rest, so you can return to your tasks with renewed energy and focus.

2

From Distracted to Disciplined

It's Monday morning, the start of a new week. Even though you slept the recommended 7.5 hours, your head is still groggy and you struggle to fully wake up. You decide to make yourself a cup of coffee, hoping to embrace the caffeinated bliss that follows. As you sip your first cup, the energising effect kicks in and you immediately feel more alert and focused.

You start your job and feel productive and invigorated. When you take a break, you decide to take another coffee hoping to increase your productivity further. Your energy levels rise, but not as dramatically as with the first cup. When you take your third and fourth cup, you notice even less of an impact. You've reached the point where the additional cup of coffee only provides a minimal increase in energy, if any at all.

What you are witnessing is the law of diminishing marginal returns. This is an economic principle which states that as you increase the amount of input or effort you put into something, the additional benefits or output you receive will gradually decrease and may even reach a point where they become negative. In simpler terms, at a certain point, putting in more effort or adding more resources doesn't lead to proportional increases in productivity.

We can apply the law of diminishing marginal returns to our brain as well. Our brain has limited capacity for things like paying attention, working memory and processing information. When we overload it with too much information or try to do too many things at once, we put a strain on these mental resources. As a result, our ability to stay focused, be creative and solve problems declines. The quality of our work drops and our overall performance takes a hit.

There comes a point when spending that extra hour poring over spreadsheets or cramming that additional chapter into a late-night study session, like having that third or fourth cup of coffee, doesn't help us achieve much more. In fact, it might even make our overall output worse. Our brain, much like our body, has its limits. It's not designed to be 'on' all the time, for multitasking or for churning through an endless barrage of information. Instead, it thrives when allowed to concentrate on one task at a time, to delve deep and immerse fully, and then take a break and relax. When we learn to channel our mental energy effectively, we can get a lot more done. Let's have a look at how that works.

The Brain at Work

With every step away from the office, the fatigue I've been ignoring finally settles in. I've spent the day racing against a looming conference deadline, pouring all my energy into completing my research paper. The moment I hit 'send', relief washed over me, but now, as the cool evening air hits my face, the weight of the day sinks in. My body is moving, but my brain feels like it has reached its limit.

When I walk through the door, my running shoes sit untouched by the entrance, mocking the morning's ambition. My stomach rumbles, but the idea of cooking feels too ambitious for tonight. Defeated by the day's mental marathon, I collapse onto the couch and opt for my favourite takeout. It's all the activity my drained self can muster tonight.

Why can we feel so tired after a mental workout? For a long time, it was thought to be linked to the blood glucose levels in the brain. But brain experts have known for quite some time that the brain doesn't consume more blood glucose when working on difficult tasks. It turns out that the brain just continuously slurps up huge amounts of energy for an organ of its size, whether we're tackling complex maths or watching funny cat movies. Short periods of intense mental effort require a little more brain power than usual, but not much more.[1]

Still, we do *feel* tired after a period of mentally challenging work. Why is that? One possible answer is that researchers have not pushed their study subjects long enough. In most experiments on the brain's use of energy, participants perform a single task of moderate difficulty, rather than exerting prolonged and sustained effort. It's possible that lack of energy does play some role in mental exhaustion, but it's likely a minor one.

Instead, research suggests that sustained concentration triggers changes in the brain that promote avoidance of that state. One of these changes may be tied to motivation. Mental fatigue, according to this research, isn't a physical limitation but an emotional one – a signal that we've lost the drive to keep going and it's time to do something else. It's not just the amount of time we've been focusing that matters; our attitude plays a crucial role too. When we're motivated, either by external rewards or personal satisfaction, we can push through longer and maintain our performance.[2]

Another change might involve the buildup of certain substances in the brain. Cognitive neuroscientists have discovered that after sustained mental effort a specific neurotransmitter, glutamate, accumulates in the region of the brain underpinning control (the prefrontal cortex).[3] This neurotransmitter plays a role in memory, learning, mood regulation and even our sleep-wake cycle. It could be that mentally demanding tasks trigger this accumulation, which presents behaviourally as fatigue. This then acts as a signal to pause so the brain can recover its balance.

Whether the fatigue we experience after a mental workout is an emotion or results from an accumulation of glutamate – or both – the impact is the same. Sustained concentration creates changes in the brain that encourage us to do something else. Our brain finds it hard to stay focused on one thing and demands change. The fatigue we feel forces us to redirect our attention somewhere else.

When we are mentally fatigued, our performance levels decline. It becomes much harder to sustain attention, and our working memory weakens. The law of diminishing marginal returns has kicked in and our best strategy is to switch to a different task. Pushing through will require a lot of willpower and brings only limited results. Even if you haven't finished all you've set out to do, it's more efficient to take a step back, let your brain rest for a while and come back to it later.

It's natural to experience mental fatigue. When we challenge our brain, feeling tired afterward means we've put our mental energy to good use. The key is to aim for fatigue that comes from focused attention on the things we want to accomplish. That way, we get the best out of our brain. On the other hand, if we spend our time constantly juggling tasks, we end up exhausted without accomplishing much. Here is why this scattered approach falls short.

The Myth of Multitasking

Most of us are habitual multitaskers. We check emails over our morning brew, plan our day while brushing our teeth and catch up on news during our commute. At work, we're often bouncing between tasks, juggling calls and emails, attending meetings while reviewing reports and even grabbing lunch while responding to messages. At home, we may cook dinner while helping our children with homework or watch TV while folding laundry.

All this multitasking, however, isn't as productive as we might think. Multitasking, particularly in the workplace, tends to reduce productivity, increase errors and elevate stress levels.[4] This is because our brain isn't designed to focus on multiple tasks simultaneously. When we think we're multitasking, we're merely quickly switching our attention from one thing to the next. We're forcing our brain to constantly switch gears, resulting in what psychologists call *task switch costs*.[5]

Each time you switch tasks, your brain needs time to reorganise itself. Furthermore, part of your attention remains stuck on the original task. This so-called *attention residue* is especially thick if you left the first task unfinished and you were working on it at low intensity. We incur switch costs when shifting between any tasks, but they are higher when we switch between complex tasks.[6] According to psychologist David Meyer, task-switching can cost us up to 40 per cent of productive time.[7]

If you have a hard time believing me, try this little test. On the first line below write the word 'multitasking' letter for letter. Then, on the second line, under each letter write the numbers 1–12. Time yourself.

_____

_____

Now, again write the word 'multitasking' on the first line below and the numbers 1–12 under each letter on the second line, but this time you oscillate between the letters and numbers (M and then 1, U and then 2, etc). Time yourself again. Do you see the difference?

_____

_____

Task switching not only consumes time but also compromises the quality of our work, making us more prone to mistakes. Students who multitask during lectures, for instance, often have lower GPAs.[8] Multitasking also affects our ability to retain information, since it disrupts our focus and makes us susceptible to distractions.[9] Furthermore, when we learn new information while multitasking, it's stored in the wrong part of the brain. Studying without distractions places information in the hippocampus, a brain region where facts and ideas are stored. When we study while watching TV, it goes to the striatum, a region meant for storing procedures and skills, making retrieval harder.[10] All these factors make multitasking less beneficial than it appears.

But why do we find it hard to stop multitasking? Most of us are not fully aware of the cost of multitasking, or we genuinely believe that we're good at it. For a select few, roughly 2 per cent of the population, this is indeed the case. But the rest of us are deceiving ourselves. In fact, those who believe they are good at multitasking are often the ones most negatively impacted by it.[11]

Another reason is that many of us are addicted to the rewards it gives. Our brain has what neuroscientists call a *novelty bias*: it's built to ignore the old and focus on the new. When an email or a notification pops up, our prefrontal cortex – the part of the brain that helps us focus – gets distracted. The novelty triggers a dopamine release in our brain, encouraging us to explore further. Novelty is so powerful because, for evolutionary reasons, we pay attention to what's new to determine whether it's a threat.

As neuroscientist Daniel Levitin explains: 'In multitasking we unknowingly enter an addiction loop as the brain's novelty centres become rewarded for processing shiny new stimuli.'[12] Every time we allow ourselves to get distracted by the arrival of a new email or message, we reinforce our automatic desire to react to new stimuli.

Breaking our multitasking habit can be challenging. Our brains, caught in an addictive cycle of multitasking, rationalise our need to be constantly reachable and respond to each email immediately. However, it's worthwhile to question this narrative. While certain jobs and circumstances require immediate responsiveness, often these expectations are not as rigid as they seem.

In our busy lives, some degree of multitasking is of course

unavoidable and often the consequence of the sheer volume of what's expected of us. Work deadlines, family obligations and personal commitments all pile up. You might be working hard to meet a deadline when an urgent message from a colleague demands your attention. Or you could be helping your kids with homework, while trying to order shopping for the week. Life doesn't always allow us the luxury of focusing on one thing at a time. In these moments, multitasking isn't so much a decision, but a response to the many demands we face daily.

At times, multitasking can also be effective and make mundane tasks more enjoyable. For instance, I find it much easier to do my morning workout routine while watching the news. Nevertheless, it's important to recognise that multitasking is often not the most efficient approach. Concentrating on one task at a time usually yields superior, higher-quality results. In a world full of distractions, what steps can we take to help our brain stay focused on one thing at a time?

Don't Distract Me

The village of my childhood is a simple, rural town, where cows graze in the fields and windmills turn lazily in the sky. The houses and gardens are well maintained, the locals easy-going and life moves at a leisurely pace. Interestingly enough, this seemingly ordinary village has produced a surprisingly high number of economics professors. One in particular stands out: Guido Imbens, the recipient of the 2021 Nobel Prize in Economics.

I had the pleasure of meeting Guido in a café overlooking the canals of Amsterdam. He greeted me with a warm, genuine smile, immediately putting me at ease. As the rain poured outside in typical Dutch fashion, we reminisced about our childhood village and the memories we shared. Eventually, I asked him the question that I had been dying to ask: what was the secret to his extraordinary productivity? His answer was surprisingly simple yet deeply insightful.

He attributed his success, at least in part, to the lessons learned from an unexpected teacher – the game of chess. As a young boy, Guido had been an avid chess player, a game that requires strategic thinking, patience and intense concentration for hours on end. It had taught him the invaluable skill of focus at an early age. He learned to shut out distractions, hone in on the task at hand and channel his cognitive resources effectively. These skills would later prove instrumental in his groundbreaking research in economics.

Even if you're not heading towards winning the Nobel Prize, the value of being able to concentrate without distraction is undeniable. We tend to feel drained and unfulfilled when we spend our days doing trivial, attention-grabbing tasks. The opposite happens when we're working hard to achieve our goals. Finishing tasks and being able to 'tick off a box' gives us a mental boost and a sense of accomplishment. And only when focusing intensely can we reach the state of flow, which is when we lose track of time and our efforts become effortless. It not only feels great but also allows us to perform at peak level.

Unfortunately, focusing deeply is easier said than done – the world around us is full of distractions. And, as we just learned, it's extremely hard for us to resist them. The modern-day office environment isn't making it any easier. With open spaces, hot-desking and constant messaging, our work environment doesn't exactly cultivate focused work. In a society that often praises busyness and multitasking, the ability to concentrate has become a rare skill.

The price we pay is pretty steep. And it often goes unnoticed. The difference in value we gain from an hour of scattered, unfocused work compared to an hour of concentrated effort is big. When we focus on the task at hand, things are done quickly and efficiently. When our attention is scattered, tasks take much longer to complete, if we complete them at all.

So, how do we reclaim our ability to focus? Fortunately, there's an old trick, named after a tomato-shaped kitchen timer, that still stands the test of time: the Pomodoro Technique. Developed in the 1980s by Francesco Cirillo, this timeless productivity method is stunningly simple, but highly effective.[13] It works as follows:

1. Pick a task

2. Set a timer (traditionally for 25 minutes)

3. Work uninterruptedly on your task until the time is up

4. Take a 3–5-minute break

5. After four Pomodoros, take a 15–30-minute break

This technique works wonders as it minimises the impact of both internal and external interruptions on focus. The timer also instils a sense of urgency and a desire to get things done within the Pomodoro window. Finally, there is a rewarding feeling when you successfully finish a Pomodoro and get to check it off.

I've been using the Pomodoro Technique for a couple of years now and it's been a great productivity booster. Those 25-minute blocks allow me to focus on what I set out to do, chipping away at tasks with undistracted attention. And after each session, I stand up, stretch and grab something to drink, returning refreshed and ready for another round.

Now, you might be wondering, 'What if 25 minutes is not my ideal work rhythm?' That's the beauty of the Pomodoro Technique; it's flexible and can be tailored to your unique working style and ability to focus. You don't have to do four Pomodoros; you can start with one. Or, instead of 25 minutes, you can set the timer for 15 or 45 minutes. It doesn't matter as long as the core of the technique stays in place: each block of time is dedicated to a pre-chosen task. The short breaks help to maintain productivity levels but be careful not to get sidetracked with activities that could potentially disrupt your focus.

The task you pick to do during your Pomodoro can be broad or specific. It might be 'edit a section of a report' or 'prepare for my annual performance review'. It can involve a single task or set of similar tasks, like 'responding to emails in my inbox'. By batching similar tasks, you reduce the need for your brain to change gears. This makes it easier to maintain focus and conserves mental energy.

Creating an environment that minimises interruptions is key to the effectiveness of the Pomodoro Technique. This might mean turning off your phone, silencing your inbox or moving to a workspace that isolates you from interruptions. Remember, distraction-free doesn't have to mean quiet. Some people work incredibly well in a busy coffee shop.

Like most new ventures, success with the Pomodoro Technique, and being able to focus in general, requires starting small. Imagine yourself preparing for a marathon. Would you start by running the full distance, or would you begin with short runs and gradually increase your stamina? The same principle applies here. Start with shorter focused sessions and gradually increase your concentration span, allowing your 'focus muscle' to strengthen over time.

I've been honing my ability to focus for years now. Initially, resisting the urge to check my phone or inbox took a lot of willpower. Now, on good days, I can maintain deep focus for 4–5 hours with only a few short breaks. Those days are without fail highly productive. Although I'm exhausted afterwards, it doesn't matter because I've achieved a lot. I use the hours after these focus sessions to respond to emails or tackle administrative tasks that require less concentration. Some days, my focus isn't as sharp, and that's okay too; we can't be productive all the time, but the successful days more than make up for it.

And the thing is, being able to focus unlocks the state of flow, where we are fully immersed in the task at hand and able to effortlessly perform at our best.

State of Flow

During the final year of my PhD programme, I worked as a consultant for the World Bank in Washington, DC. Juggling the two roles, I needed to work on the weekends to finish my thesis. Lacking a suitable home office, I dragged myself to my World Bank office every Saturday morning. I'd always stop at Starbucks first and treat myself to an iced caramel macchiato. By the time I opened my computer, the caffeine and gallons of sugar had kicked in and I was fully focused. Determined to spend as little time as possible in the office so I could hang out with my friends, I refused to let myself get distracted by anything.

Those Saturday hours, without fail, were highly productive ones. I was immersed in the task at hand and unbothered by my environment. I often found solutions to problems that had been impossible to solve earlier in the week. I felt like I could access and process new information almost effortlessly. Decisions, thoughts and actions followed each other smoothly. Even though I was working during the weekend, I enjoyed what I was doing, as I was able to get an enormous amount done in a small amount of time. When I was finished for the day and ready to catch up with my friends, I would feel tired but utterly satisfied.

Unbeknownst to me at the time, what I experienced during those hours in my World Bank office was the state of flow. This state, named by Mihaly Csikszentmihalyi in 1975, is the optimal state of consciousness for peak performance.[14] It's where you will feel and perform your best. In fact, in this state you'll likely produce work that is above and beyond what you normally think is your best.

The terms 'focused work' and 'flow' are often used interchangeably, but they are not the same. Focused work is the practice of blocking off time to focus on a cognitively demanding task. Flow is an altered state of consciousness. Focused work relates mostly to the workplace, while you can also experience flow in sports, meditation and art.

You can do focused work without reaching flow. Quite a few tasks, such as effectively managing emails and correspondence or grading exams, require deep focus but not necessarily flow. But to reach your highest quality work and optimum productivity, you want to do focused work in a flow state.

To enter the state of flow we need to tap into specific brainwaves. Brainwaves are electrical impulses in the brain. They are created by neurons communicating with each other, producing rhythmic or repetitive patterns of neural activity.

Our brainwaves change according to what we're doing and how we're feeling. At different times of the day, different wave patterns dominate. When you wake up in the morning, your brain moves from the slow delta waves of deep sleep into low-frequency theta waves that characterise the twilight state between wake and sleep. Theta waves only exist when dreaming, during deep meditation or in flow. They are associated with intense creativity.

Fast beta waves dominate our normal waking consciousness, when we're alert, attentive and engaged in problem-solving and decision-making. When we are in a more relaxed state, alpha waves take over. In terms of frequency, these waves lie between beta and theta waves. They're associated with a restive, meditative state in which we are more focused on the present moment and can more easily absorb new information. This state is considered the bridge between the conscious and subconscious.

The flow zone sits around the border of alpha and theta. In this zone, memory, learning, visualisation and concentration are further heightened. The conscious and subconscious meet, and awareness and creativity expand. Gamma waves can also occur; they are the highest possible frequency and enable higher-level processing and cognitive functioning.

Researchers have been studying flow for nearly fifty years, but they have only recently begun to decipher what is going on in the brain during a flow state. While more research is needed, neuroscientists have identified a few things that seem to be happening. The portion of the prefrontal cortex responsible for self-criticism and the amygdala, the brain's fear centre, becomes less active. We worry less about failure, and our prefrontal cortex is free to focus all its attention on the project at hand.[15] The cognitive control and reward networks in the brain start communicating with one another more effectively.[16] Finally, our brain releases more dopamine, a neurotransmitter which drives motivation and focus, and this heightened focus can diminish our awareness of sensations like hunger and tiredness.[17]

Reaching flow relies on finding the right balance between our skill level and the complexity of the task at hand. When these two align, we can enter a state of effortless engagement, where time seems to vanish, and we are fully immersed in what we're doing. If a task is too easy, boredom sets in; if it's too challenging, we can feel overwhelmed. We need to aim for that sweet spot, just a step outside our comfort zone to keep the challenge exciting.

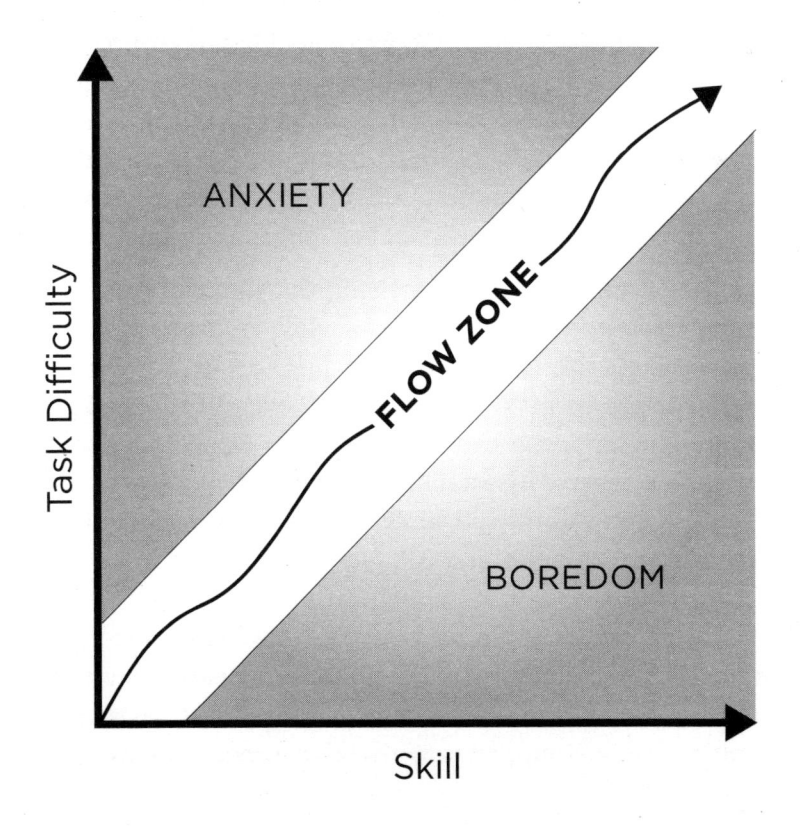

People enter into a flow state in many different ways, and by trial and error you can find out what works best for you. You're unlikely to reach a flow state every time you set out to do focused work, but here are a few practices you can implement in your work routine to help you achieve flow more often:

- **Set clear goals**: Knowing exactly what you need to accomplish makes it easier to get into flow. Intrinsic motivation – when you want to do something because it's satisfying, not because you will get a reward – further boosts your chances of entering a flow state.
- **Focus on the process, not the end goal**: Having a goal is important as it gives you direction. But achieving flow requires enjoying the journey. Allow yourself to simply live in the present moment without worrying too much about the result.
- **Avoid distractions and multitasking**: Achieving flow typically requires 15–20 minutes of focused attention. Once you're in this state, your brain instinctively filters out most distractions. However, if your concentration is interrupted, it can take another 15 to 20 minutes to regain that flow. This makes the Pomodoro Techniques less effective for reaching flow unless you opt for longer intervals.
- **Create a mental cue**: By pairing the sound of a bell with the presentation of food, Ivan Pavlov conditioned his dogs to associate the two. Eventually, just the sound of the bell was enough to make them salivate, even in the absence of food. Similarly, you can condition your brain to respond to specific triggers. By establishing a mental cue to signal you want to enter flow, your brain will eventually recognise this trigger and respond accordingly.

By treating myself to an iced caramel macchiato before each Saturday work session, I unknowingly established a powerful mental cue that set me on the path to flow. And that wasn't all. Without realising, I tapped into my golden hours as well.

Optimising Focus Time

As I enter the gallery, hushed voices and soft lighting surround me. My gaze sweeps the room until it settles on a striking piece – Frans Lanting's *Elephants at Twilight*. I'm instantly captivated by the sense of tranquillity it radiates. Set against a backdrop of muted oranges and pinks, a herd of African elephants is silhouetted in the warm, fading light of the setting sun. Their massive bodies casting long shadows on the water.

By capturing the elephants during this fleeting moment just before dusk, Lanting's created a scene of immense beauty. The soft, diffused light that characterises these 'golden hours' adds an almost otherworldly glow, transforming the image into something truly extraordinary.

Much like photographers, who await the perfect moment before sunset or after sunrise to capture the most breathtaking, well-lit images, we too have our golden hours. These are the hours when our focus and productivity peak. It's when we tend to produce our best work, solve complex problems and generate innovative ideas. Harnessing our 'golden hours' can greatly improve our efficiency and productivity.

To tap into these invaluable hours, we need to understand our body's unique rhythm or chronotype. Our chronotype is our natural inclination to feel most alert or require sleep at certain times of the day. It's closely linked to our circadian rhythm – our internal 24-hour biological clock that regulates key functions like our sleep-wake cycle and hormone release. While the circadian rhythm sets the overall timing for sleep and wakefulness, our chronotype acts as a personalised setting on this biological clock.

Our circadian rhythm primarily responds to sunlight exposure, while our chronotype is predominantly determined by genetics, though age and environment can also influence it.[18] Working harmoniously with our chronotype enables us to tap into the potential of our golden hours.

There are three generally recognised chronotypes: Morning, Evening and Intermediate:

1. **Morning chronotype (Larks)**: People with a morning chronotype, also known as 'larks', typically feel most alert during the early part of the day and prefer to go to bed early and rise early. They often have their most productive periods in the morning.

2. **Evening chronotype (Owls)**: People with an evening chronotype, sometimes referred to as 'owls', tend to stay awake late into the night and prefer to wake up later in the day. They often find that their productivity peaks in the afternoon or evening.

3. **Intermediate chronotype**: People with an intermediate chronotype fall somewhere between morning larks and night owls. They have some flexibility in their sleep and wake times and can adjust their schedules more easily than the other two types.

To discover your own chronotype, you can take the Morningness-Eveningness Questionnaire (MEQ) or the Munich Chronotype Questionnaire (MCTQ). This will give you a better understanding of your natural sleep-wake patterns and your dips and peaks in alertness. While exact percentages can vary depending on the study and criteria used, approximately 40–50 per cent of adults identify as larks, 30–40 per cent as owls and the remaining as intermediate.[19]

As our ability to focus fluctuates throughout the day, not all hours in a workday are equal. Even when your schedule is not entirely in your control, it's important to be mindful of this fact. For early birds, try to schedule your most demanding tasks in the morning when your concentration is at its peak. Night owls, on the other hand, better save such tasks for late afternoon and evenings. Using your precious peak hours for trivial tasks comes at a high cost. You not only hinder progress on your vital tasks but also miss the chance to tap into your most productive self.

Fortunately, we often possess greater control than we may realise when it comes to aligning our work with our natural energy levels. Consider taking a proactive approach and block a couple of hours each week when you're most alert (say every Monday and Friday from 10–12). This simple step transforms your intentions into concrete actions and prepares your brain for the work you need to accomplish. Protect these hours to the best of your ability. With this commitment, you minimise the likelihood of getting sidetracked and prevent less important tasks from encroaching on your peak hours. Even dedicating a few of your golden hours to concentrated work each week can have a substantial impact, especially when you dedicate them to Quadrant 2 activities – those tasks that are important but not urgent.

Once I realised I'm a lark, I shifted my workday to start earlier, dedicating my most alert hours to my Quadrant 2 tasks, such as working on my research projects. It took some adjustment, but by sticking to this schedule and communicating the importance of keeping my mornings meeting-free, I gradually regained control over my day and restored my productivity. This approach has been a game-changer. It gives me a sense of accomplishment early in the day and ensures that important tasks aren't lost in the daily rush. Your schedule and preferences might differ, but it's worth exploring how you can best leverage your own golden hours.

And then there are those times when things veer off course unexpectedly. Perhaps you indulged in an extra drink during a night out with a friend, which felt like a great idea at the time. But now, you're grappling with a foggy mind from lack of sleep. In moments like these, it's helpful to adjust your expectations and recognise that concentrating on a challenging task may not be feasible. Investing an hour in a demanding project often yields minimal returns and can lead to frustration. Instead, it's more productive to acknowledge the situation and redirect your attention to tasks that demand less mental strain, such as catching up on administrative duties. By taking this approach, you'll end your day with a sense of achievement as you successfully crossed multiple items off your to-do list.

Clearing Your Mind

So far, we've explored how to direct our brain towards what matters most, but it's just as important to train it to ignore distractions that aren't urgent. No doubt you have had an unrelated thought pop up when you were focused on a task: 'Oh no, I forgot to buy a birthday card for Mom; really should not forget to do it later.' This is your brain's *mind-wandering* mode kicking in.

For focused work, we engage the central executive part of our brain, or the so-called *stay-on-task* mode. In this state we are intensely focused on a demanding task. This mode is responsible for limiting what enters our consciousness. It prevents us from being distracted when engaged in a task so we can focus on what we're doing uninterrupted.

The mind-wandering mode is our brain's other mode of attention. It's our resting brain state when our mind is not actively focused on a specific task. Our thoughts wander or drift away from what we're currently doing, often leading to spontaneous and unstructured thinking unrelated to the present moment. It's particularly powerful and, unless we act, it usually wins against the central executive. Because of its tendency to dominate our attention, its discoverer, neuroscientist Marcus Raichle, named it the *default mode*.[20]

The problem is that once such thoughts pop up, they'll keep swirling in our head until we deal with them somehow. This can be explained by the *Zeigarnik effect*: people tend to remember unfinished or interrupted tasks better than completed tasks. Bluma Zeigarnik, a Lithuanian Soviet psychologist, discovered this psychological phenomenon in the 1920s.[21]

Legend has it that Zeigarnik was dining at a Viennese restaurant when she noticed that wait staff could easily recall ongoing orders but struggled with recalling ones that were already served. Intrigued, she conducted an experiment. Participants were given various tasks, like solving puzzles and stringing beads. Some tasks were interrupted before completion. Afterwards, Zeigarnik asked the participants which activities they could remember doing.

Interestingly, Zeigarnik found that participants were twice as likely to remember the interrupted tasks compared to the completed ones. This suggests that our brain perceives unfinished tasks as more important and relevant. In other words, if you have the thought, 'I need to buy toilet paper', but haven't taken any action, your brain will hold onto that until you do something about it. Once you've taken action, the thought will fade away.

To enhance your ability to focus and prevent this from happening, there is a simple solution. When a thought distracts you while focusing on a task, quickly jot it down on a piece of paper. By doing so, you give your brain permission to close the loop. This helps relax the neural circuits, allowing you to shift your focus back to the task at hand. So always keep pen and paper close by when you want to start a period of intense focus.

An effective long-term strategy to reduce the occurrence of random thoughts is to create a trusted system that transfers tasks to an external brain. This involves writing down everything you need to do so that you can free up space in your mind. People at the top of their profession, particularly those known for their creativity and effectiveness, often rely on an external brain as much as they can.

To make such a system work, you'll need to commit to two basic practices:

- Transfer *all* your tasks to your external platform
- Review them regularly, ideally on a daily basis

If you skip either of these steps, your brain will revert to nagging you about every unfinished task, leaving you right back where you started. The system doesn't need to be complicated and once established it becomes relatively easy to manage, as long as you adhere to these two practices.

A simple approach to creating an external brain is jotting down all your tasks on index cards, or some digital equivalent. Alternatively, efficiency expert David Allen developed a powerful method called 'Getting Things Done', which involves transferring all relevant information, tasks and projects from your brain onto an external platform and breaking them into actionable work items with specific time limits. This allows you to address each task as needed, rather than relying on memory.

A particularly effective part of the GTD method is its 2-Minute Rule: if a task can be done in two minutes or less, do it right away, even if it's not urgent. It doesn't have to be precisely two minutes; it can be three or five. If you need to read a short text to make a decision, just read it. Have to send an email or make a quick call? Do it. This rule helps clear your mind of distractions and improves overall efficiency. If a task can't be completed in two minutes, David Allen recommends sorting it into one of these actionable categories: Do it, Delegate it, Defer it or Drop it.

To effectively combine the 2-Minute Rule with your deep focus sessions, consider scheduling both into your day. Before or after each deep focus block, allocate a few minutes to tackle quick tasks that fall within the 2-Minute Rule. This approach not only helps you clear small distractions but also maintains your momentum throughout the day. For instance, once you finish a deep focus session, take a brief break to send emails or make quick calls. It's crucial to stick strictly to those 2-minute tasks to avoid getting sidetracked by more time-consuming activities. This strategy keeps you productive while preserving the quality of your focused work, enabling you to manage both urgent and important tasks effectively.

Sometimes, 'just doing' a task on our to-do list isn't that simple. It's common for us to avoid making decisions when we're uncertain of the outcome, leading to procrastination. In those cases, it can help to think about what the next actionable step should be and put that on your to-do list. For example, if you're unsure about accepting an invitation to speak at an event, don't let it linger. Take the initiative to email the organisers and ask for more information. By getting the answers you need, you'll eliminate a lot of uncertainty, making it easier to make a decision.

We now know how to improve our focus and make better use of our time, but what about the relentless busyness that often fills our days? It's time to challenge the belief that being busy is synonymous with being productive.

A Note on Busyness

Meet David. From the moment he opens his eyes in the morning, his day is a whirlwind of tasks. He checks his email during breakfast, sends texts while commuting and juggles many meetings throughout the day. His calendar is a kaleidoscope of colour-coded appointments, each back-to-back. Even when he's with family or friends, he's constantly checking his phone, replying to messages and never fully present. His weekends are packed with errands, obligations and chores. David often talks about how busy he is, as if it's a badge of honour. He rarely takes time to relax, and when he does, he feels guilty for not being productive.

David is a fictional character, but you probably know someone like him – or maybe you see a bit of yourself in him. Many societies have glorified busyness to a point where it has become synonymous with success.[22] The busier we are, the more important we appear. This mentality is deeply ingrained in our collective psyche, stemming from the idea that idle time equates to wasted time. As a result, our lives have become a whirlwind of activities, tasks and commitments, leaving us racing against the clock. We feel compelled to constantly fill our schedules and broadcast our busyness to validate our self-worth. Sometimes we even use it as a shield against feelings of loneliness or lack of inner purpose.

Social media and the fear of missing out (FOMO) can also fuel our drive to appear perpetually busy. With endless streams of exciting updates from others, we fear being sidelined and irrelevant, leading us to broadcast our crowded schedules in a bid for inclusion and significance. Reflecting on the Covid years, you might find a tinge of nostalgia for those times when our calendars were clear and we could embrace relaxation without the shadow of FOMO.

In the workplace, appearing busy has become almost like an art form. Many job roles lack clear indicators of what it means to be productive and valuable. When the path to making a significant impact is unclear, we often instinctively resort to making an impression of being busy through swift email correspondence, scheduling and participating in meetings, and completing other visible tasks.

We often mistake busyness for productivity – if we're busy, we must be accomplishing something, right? This perception provides a false sense of accomplishment and soothes our need for validation. We have an 'illusion of productivity': we think we're productive when, in fact, we're highly inefficient in the way we get things done. Clearly, it's extremely difficult to give anything our focused attention while maintaining the appearance of busyness.

Technology, while a great enabler, has fortified the busy trap. The constant connectivity blurs the lines between work and personal life. The expectation of immediate responses to emails, messages and notifications fosters an environment where constant engagement seems not just beneficial but almost obligatory.

This isn't to say that some of us aren't genuinely overwhelmed by unrealistic demands and internal or external expectations. However, the point I want to make is that we frequently create our own busyness. To break free from this trap, reflecting on the insights from Chapter 1 may provide a pathway to navigate your daily demands. Rather than getting lost in a whirlwind of activities, prioritise those that align with your goals – Quadrant 2 tasks. Instead of juggling countless responsibilities, why not concentrate on doing a few things really well? Remember Pareto's 80/20 rule: about 20 per cent of your efforts will drive 80 per cent of your productivity and success.

When you're engaged in a task, give it your undivided attention. Experience the joy of accomplishing tasks faster and freeing up time for things that truly matter to you. This isn't just about efficiency – being fully present in interactions with loved ones helps build deeper connections.

Setting boundaries and saying 'no' can be challenging, but it's crucial. Taking time for yourself, resting and relaxing aren't indulgences; they're necessary for your productivity and well-being. Rather than viewing breaks as wasted time, see them as opportunities to recharge. True productivity and value don't stem from a frantic pace, but from balancing focused effort, strategic prioritisation and the wisdom to know when and how to rest.

The Key Takeaways

Mastering the art of focus will transform your mental performance and boost your efficiency. By learning to direct your attention deliberately, you can make the most of your 1,440 daily minutes and safeguard your mental energy. By prioritising deep concentration during your 'golden hours' and crafting an environment that fosters flow, you not only maximise your productivity but also open up more time for the pursuits and passions that truly matter to you.

- Mental fatigue following intense work is a natural consequence of the brain's need to shift gears. Understanding this can help you value rest and recovery more. The goal is to experience fatigue from deep, focused engagement on meaningful tasks, rather than from the exhaustion of constant multitasking and interruptions.

- The myth of multitasking suggests that juggling multiple tasks simultaneously boosts productivity but, in reality, it leads to diminished focus and increased errors. By embracing single-tasking – dedicating your attention to one task at a time – you enhance both the quality of your work and your overall efficiency.

- The Pomodoro Technique, with its structured intervals of focused work followed by short breaks, is a powerful tool for strengthening your ability to focus. By breaking tasks into manageable chunks and allowing brief periods for rest, you train your brain to sustain concentration for longer.

- Reaching a state of flow, where work feels effortless and time seems to disappear, is a powerful boost to both productivity and satisfaction. To experience flow more frequently, focus on aligning your tasks with your strengths and interests, create an environment free from distractions, set clear and achievable goals, focus on the process and create mental cues.

- Not all hours of the day are equally productive. By reserving your golden hours for high-concentration work, you can significantly boost your efficiency and productivity. To make the most of these valuable hours, use them for Quadrant 2 activities – those crucial but non-urgent tasks that align with your long-term goals.

- Thoughts can pop up unexpectedly and clutter your mind if not addressed. Keep a notebook handy to jot them down or use a trusted system for organisation. Additionally, applying the 2-Minute Rule – tackling tasks that take less than two minutes right away or during designated time slots – can help clear your mind and maintain focus.

- We often mistake busyness for productivity, but it's important to distinguish between genuine progress and merely staying occupied. Instead of filling your day with constant activity, focus on meaningful tasks that align with your goals. Recognise that true productivity comes from strategic effort and effective prioritisation, not from the illusion of endless motion.

3

Igniting Your Inner Drive

On 20 February 2010, something extraordinary happened at the Winter Olympics in Vancouver. Dutch speed-skater Mark Tuitert sensationally won gold in the 1500m, beating the two undisputed favourites, Chad Hedrick and world-record holder Shani Davis. For once, everything had gone well. He had skated a perfect race.

Overwhelmed with joy, he was brought to tears, struggling to comprehend the magnitude of what he'd just achieved. For nearly five minutes, he could do nothing but hold his head in disbelief. Eventually, he managed to compose himself enough to skate a few triumphant victory laps, while a sea of orange-clad Dutch fans filled the stadium with their national anthem.

Tuitert's Olympic gold didn't come easy. His path to that moment had been filled with struggles, disappointments and near misses. At the age of eighteen, he burst onto the Dutch all-round scene, winning the World Junior Championships and achieving an impressive fourth place finish in the Dutch Championship. Yet, despite being hailed as the next big star, all-round success never came.

In 2007, at age twenty-seven, he made the difficult decision to abandon all-round skating and shift his focus to shorter distances, only to face the rise of one of the greatest middle-distance skaters in history, Shani Davis. Again, he found himself battling for only an occasional podium finish.

But Tuitert never gave up. He knew his potential, believed in his abilities and was willing to put in the hard work necessary to reach his goal – win Olympic gold. That day in Vancouver, his hard work and dedication paid off. He delivered a performance of a lifetime and left the world, including myself who saw it live on TV, in awe. On the grandest of stages, perseverance, belief and sheer willpower had triumphed.

The journey of Mark Tuitert inspired me greatly. When he won his Olympic gold, I was struggling. Five years post PhD, I was yet to make my mark as an economist. I was working very hard, but success eluded me and I only received rejections from journal editors. Questions began to cloud my mind – was the struggle worth it? Would the endless hours spent in the office ever bear fruit? How much longer should I persist before throwing in the towel? It's easy to keep your motivation high when you are often winning. It's a tall order when victories are sparse.

Fortunately, I had two things in common with Tuitert: a strong determination and a concrete goal – to publish an article in a top-tier academic journal. Two years later, success finally did arrive. To this day, I vividly remember the moment I found out that my paper was accepted into one of my profession's top journals.

Of course, new challenges emerged, but that period taught me a valuable lesson: having a clear, meaningful goal is key to sustaining motivation. Yet, as I later discovered, there's more to it than that. When we truly understand how motivation works, we gain the ability to push through even when the going gets tough. It's not just about knowing our goals – it's about mastering the drive that keeps us moving forward, no matter the obstacles.

The Two Faces of Motivation

Motivation is our inner drive or desire to accomplish tasks, achieve goals or engage in activities. It's what gets us out of bed, keeps us working hard and helps us persevere through challenges. Motivation plays a fundamental role in shaping our behaviour and is influenced by a variety of factors, both internal and external.

Intrinsic motivation comes from within. It's the inner desire to engage in an activity for the pure joy or fulfilment it brings. The task itself brings personal satisfaction and pleasure, and achievement feels like its own reward. This sort of motivation can be found in pursuing hobbies, engaging in creative activities, learning out of sheer curiosity, or doing work that aligns with our deeper purpose.

Intrinsic motivation is all about doing something because we want to, not because we have to, which boosts our performance and persistence. It encourages firefighters to work longer, inspires fundraisers to make more calls and enhances the creativity of security officers.[1] In short, it's the best predictor of engagement in almost everything we do.

Extrinsic motivation, on the other hand, comes from external factors. It involves seeking rewards or recognition or avoiding punishment as the primary driving force behind an activity. Common examples include working for a pay cheque, studying to earn good grades or exercising to lose weight. Extrinsic motivation might push us to finish a task, but its fuel comes from external incentives rather than internal satisfaction. This is why people might stick to a diet to win a competition but abandon it after the prize is won. The motivation disappears when the reward is no longer in sight.

Both intrinsic and extrinsic motivation play important roles in driving our actions and in many cases, both types work together. For example, staying active can be driven by the inner desire to be fit and healthy as well as the external rewards of looking and feeling better, or fitting into that old pair of jeans.

At the heart of understanding these two types of motivation lies the Self-Determination Theory (SDT), developed by psychologists Edward Deci and Richard Ryan. SDT posits that three core psychological needs fuel intrinsic motivation: autonomy, competence and relatedness.[2]

- *Autonomy* is the need to feel in control of our actions and decisions. Activities that allow for personal choice foster intrinsic motivation because we feel empowered to engage in them. When we choose to pursue a project we're passionate about, we tend to be more invested and motivated to see it through.

- *Competence* refers to our need to feel effective and capable in our activities. When we feel skilled at what we do, we're more likely to engage with enthusiasm. When we feel competent, we're more motivated to tackle new challenges and persist in the face of obstacles.

- *Relatedness* involves feeling connected to others and experiencing a sense of belonging. When we engage in activities that foster relationships – like teamwork or community service – our motivation tends to increase because we feel a part of something larger than ourselves.

When these three needs are met our intrinsic motivation thrives, leading to greater engagement, persistence and satisfaction with our activities. Extrinsic rewards can enhance intrinsic motivation when they align with these psychological needs.[3] For instance, think about the last time you received positive feedback on a project or task you completed. That affirmation likely made you feel more competent and appreciated, which might have sparked a desire to push your boundaries further. In addition, when rewards offer a choice or enhance autonomy – like giving students the option to choose their project topics while also rewarding them for high-quality work – they can deepen engagement.

However, extrinsic rewards can also diminish intrinsic motivation when they undermine our sense of autonomy, competence or relatedness, or when they shift the focus away from internal enjoyment towards external incentives. This phenomenon is known as the *overjustification effect*. It occurs when an external reward overshadows the inherent pleasure of the task.

A classic study by psychologists Mark Lepper, David Greene and Richard Nisbett in 1973 illustrates this effect. In the experiment, children who enjoyed drawing were asked to create colourful pictures. They were divided into three groups: one group was told they would receive a reward, another received an unexpected reward and the third received no reward at all. The results were striking – children who received the expected reward were less likely to draw for fun later. The promise of a reward had shifted their focus from the inherent joy of drawing to the external reward, diminishing their natural enthusiasm.[4]

This shift happens because the reward changes the focus from 'I'm doing this because I love it' to 'I'm doing this because I'll get something out of it'. When the reward is removed, so too is the drive to continue. In essence, extrinsic rewards can create a transactional relationship with the task, making it feel more like work than play.

The interplay between our inner drive and external rewards is what propels us forward. When we feel a sense of agency, competence and connection to our goals, our motivation to pursue our projects intensifies. Yet, amidst this drive lies a crucial question that sustains our efforts: why do we want to achieve these goals in the first place?

The Power of Why

My friend Emily has long been an ultramarathon runner with an equally demanding legal career. On the weekends, she's unstoppable – pounding through miles of trail with nothing but the rhythm of her breath to keep her company. In those moments she feels truly alive, completely in sync with her surroundings. But come Monday, she trades her running shoes for court attire, stepping into a world of legal briefings, client meetings and endless paperwork. The thrill of the trail fades into the background, replaced by the often tedious demands of her high-powered job.

For a long time, Emily felt torn between her two lives: the one that fuelled her passion and the one that paid the bills. She felt like she was simply enduring the week to enjoy the weekend. But then something shifted. One day, she realised that her legal career, as draining as it could sometimes be, was what enabled her to pursue ultramarathons in the first place. Those long hours weren't just about meeting deadlines – they were what supported her running dreams, funded her adventures and provided for the life she cherished.

With this new perspective, her job started to feel different. Every legal document she reviewed, every case she worked on, wasn't just a task on her to-do list – it was part of what allowed her to live her passion. Work became less of a burden and more of a bridge, connecting her weekdays to the weekends, her career to her purpose. What changed? Emily found her 'why'.

As Simon Sinek explains in *Start with Why*, understanding our purpose transforms even the most mundane tasks into something meaningful. When we lose motivation or struggle with routine, asking 'Why am I doing this?' can completely shift our perspective. Suddenly, the grind becomes part of a bigger picture, and the day-to-day tasks serve a greater goal. For Emily, once she recognised how her work supported the life she truly loved, the two parts of her life weren't in conflict anymore – they were in harmony.

So, how can you find your own why? You can start by asking yourself three questions:

1. What are my core values and beliefs?

2. What issues or causes are close to my heart?

3. How can my talents and skills make a positive impact on the world?

Reflecting on these questions will help you identify your purpose and align your goals with your values, sparking a stronger motivation within you. When you struggle to find answers, you can try an exercise that I found particularly powerful: writing your own eulogy.[5]

Find a place where you can be alone and uninterrupted. Now imagine your own funeral, at which there are four speakers: a family member, a friend, a colleague and a member of your community. Each of them speaks about you and what your life meant to them from a different perspective. Think deeply. What would you like each of them to say about your life? How do you want to be remembered by each of these individuals? Take a few minutes to write your thoughts down.

This exercise may seem unsettling at first, but it serves as a powerful tool for self-reflection and personal growth. When I did it myself, I had an unexpected realization – none of the speakers mentioned my list of publications. Instead, they spoke about how deeply I cared about helping others create a more harmonious life, and how that had inspired them. It was a wake-up call. All the guilt I had been carrying for not publishing 'enough' suddenly seemed misplaced. I realised my energy would be better spent on the kind of writing that truly resonated with me – like this book – and that shift made all the difference.

Writing your eulogy allows you to identify your core values, discover areas for improvement and shape your future actions. If you find yourself surprised or dissatisfied with the way your current eulogy reads, don't be discouraged. This is an opportunity, not a final verdict. The story of your life is still being written, and you have the ability to shape it in the direction that feels right. Start by identifying the gaps between how you're living now and how you'd like to be remembered. Ask yourself: what changes can you make, starting today, to better align your actions with the legacy you want to leave behind?

Perhaps it's about devoting more time to relationships, focusing less on career milestones that don't resonate with you, or committing time and effort to certain causes. Small, consistent actions – like prioritising the people you care about or setting aside time for passion projects – can have a profound impact over time. The key is to be intentional. Use the insights from this exercise as a guide to shift your priorities, making sure the way you live matches the legacy you want to leave.

It's important to realise that feeling good isn't a requirement for motivation. If it were, Emily wouldn't be ploughing through legal documents, and I certainly wouldn't be sitting here, writing on a sunny Sunday while my family enjoys the outdoors. I'm not writing because I am in a great mood – I'm writing because of the impact I want to make. Besides, how many times have you felt good on a given day and still not done what you said you would do? Motivation doesn't come from feeling good; it comes from having reasons tied to your purpose and values, driving you to act despite life's obstacles. A good student studies not because they're in a good mood, but because they want to excel in their exams and secure their dream job.

Finding your why can give purpose and meaning to everything you do. It connects your actions with your core values and beliefs, providing a clear target to aim for and access to a deep well of motivation that will keep you going through life's challenges. As the Roman philosopher Seneca wisely said: 'If you don't know which port you are sailing to, no wind is favourable.'

Knowing your why sets the direction, but it's a tiny player in your brain – dopamine – that actually gets you moving. Without this little molecule, even the strongest why wouldn't be enough to get you off the ground.

The Dopamine Effect

Every Wednesday morning from October to March, I face a dilemma: stay in my warm bed or gather my bathing suit, bundle up and walk to the nearby lake. The knowledge that a group of friends will be waiting usually gives me the push I need to get up.

When we gather at the lake, we all face the same struggle: should we really subject ourselves to the cold water? As the temperature drops, our pre-swim chats grow lengthier. We procrastinate because we all know what's coming: the shock to our bodies when we immerse ourselves in the water. Eventually, one of us summons the courage to spur the rest of us into action.

Following the group, I take the plunge. The moment my body hits the water, my muscles tighten and I struggle to catch my breath. My skin feels like it's being pricked by a thousand needles. All I can think about is breathing and moving. The rest of the world fades away. It's my body's instinctive response to the extreme cold. But once the initial shock subsides, a strange sense of calm washes over me. My body adapts, my breathing steadies and, dare I say it, the water almost feels comfortable.

Once back on dry land, I hurriedly dress to ward off the cold shivers that make zipping up jackets a challenge. Sipping on hot tea, I gradually feel my body warm up again. And there's something else I feel – invigorated, alive and intensely motivated to tackle the rest of the day's activities. And that feeling lingers for hours.

Entering the icy water requires immense willpower. While it gets easier with practise, the shock to the system is always painful, no matter how often you've experienced it. Yet, it's the incredible post-swim feeling that keeps me coming back week after week. There's truly nothing like it.

As soon as I plunge into the icy water, my body responds with a rush of adrenaline, accompanied by a surge of dopamine, a neurotransmitter that plays a crucial role in motivation.[6] While many associate dopamine with pleasure, its true function lies in driving wanting and craving – the pursuit of happiness, rather than happiness itself. While dopamine is released when we experience pleasure, it's primarily released when we anticipate or long for something.

Studies on rats highlight just how important dopamine is for motivation. In a controlled lab setting, rats were trained to press a lever to receive food. When researchers blocked their dopamine, the rats still enjoyed the food if it was given to them but lost the drive to press the lever to get it. When dopamine levels were artificially boosted, the opposite occurred. The rats pressed the lever with newfound enthusiasm, working harder for the same reward – even though their enjoyment of the food didn't change. In short, less dopamine means less effort, while more dopamine means more drive.[7]

Dopamine's role in driving wanting, makes it a key factor in learning. A famous experiment with monkeys illustrates this clearly. The monkeys were trained to associate a light with the arrival of food. Initially, their dopamine spiked with the arrival of food. However, once they learned that the light signalled the arrival of food, the dopamine surge shifted – occurring the moment the light turned on rather than when the food was delivered.[8] Why? The light became the 'surprise', not the food. The experiment revealed that dopamine is highly attuned to the unexpected – to possibility and anticipation.

Like monkeys, we get a dopamine rush from unexpected surprises – a surprise gift, an unexpected compliment or more money in our bank account. This is known as *reward prediction error*, our brain's way of comparing expectations with actual outcomes. We constantly make predictions about what is happening next. When something happens that exceeds our expectation dopamine levels spike, cementing that positive experience in our memory.[9]

Even the mere possibility of a reward triggers a dopamine release. For instance, if you anticipate praise for a successful project, based on your past experience, this expectation activates dopamine, motivating you to put in the effort. When the outcome exceeds expectations – such as receiving more praise than you anticipated or a bonus – dopamine levels spike, reinforcing the behaviour that led to this success. Conversely, if the reward falls short of expectations or doesn't arrive, dopamine activity decreases, signalling disappointment. This prompts you to adjust your future expectations or actions, guiding you towards more effective strategies in the future. By responding dynamically to both positive and negative outcomes, dopamine plays a vital role in helping us learn and adapt, steering our actions to what we perceive as most rewarding. [10]

The dopamine system thus plays a central role in motivation, but its influence lies primarily in driving the pursuit of our goals rather than the achievement itself. By setting specific, achievable goals and breaking them into smaller milestones (SMART goals), we can harness dopamine's power. Each milestone creates a sense of expectation – an anticipation of the reward tied to completing it – energising us to keep going. This makes the process of working towards our goals just as motivating as reaching the final result.

To enhance this approach, try incorporating intermittent rewards, by treating yourself occasionally after reaching a milestone.[11] Unpredictability is a powerful driver of dopamine release, which is why slot machines are so addictive. The uncertainty of whether we'll win triggers anticipation, creating a dopamine surge. When the reward does arrive – a win – the brain treats it as a better-than-expected outcome, causing another dopamine surge and a stronger desire to keep going.

By mixing up when and how you reward yourself, you create a sense of novelty that keeps you invested in your goals. Maybe you reward yourself after two milestones, skip the next one, and then celebrate an especially tough accomplishment with an unexpected treat. This element of surprise keeps your brain guessing and prevents the slump in motivation that can creep in when progress starts to feel routine. Intermitted rewards help you stay engaged, energised and excited for what's next.

Another way to ensure you'll stay motivated in the long-term is by shifting your focus to enjoying the process, rather than fixating on the outcome. Associating 'winning' with the effort itself makes everything easier and more enjoyable. Remember, dopamine is tied to the anticipation of a reward, and the reward itself is subjective. If you find an activity enjoyable, your brain begins to associate it with positive outcomes, triggering dopamine release in anticipation of the reward, making you want to keep going.

Take learning to play the piano as an example. Instead of fixating on mastering a difficult piece, find joy in the process of practising. Every note you play correctly, every bar you get right, is a small victory. Tell yourself that the learning process is enjoyable and rewarding and each practice session is a step forward in your musical journey. By shifting your mindset, you train your brain to release dopamine throughout the process, keeping you motivated to continue and reinforce the habit of practice.

Dopamine plays a central role in staying motivated to reach our goals. While our brain's dopamine levels are largely influenced by our behaviours, environment and goals, there are also some lifestyle practices that can support a healthy baseline of dopamine production:[12]

- **Sunlight exposure**: Natural sunlight exposure, especially early in the morning, stimulates dopamine production.
- **Cold exposure**: You don't need to jump in a freezing lake to get the benefits of cold exposure. Just 1–3 minutes in a cold shower, if done regularly, can also be effective.
- **Tyrosine-rich foods**: These foods, such as red meats, nuts or hard-fermented cheese, provide the amino acid tyrosine, a building block of dopamine.
- **Ingest caffeine**: Caffeine, in the form of coffee, tea or something else, stimulates dopamine release in a mild, temporary manner. It also increases the availability of dopamine receptors, which enhances your brain's sensitivity to dopamine.
- **Adequate sleep**: Quality sleep helps the replenishment of dopamine receptors, which is essential for maintaining the system's sensitivity.
- **Stress management**: Chronic stress can negatively impact dopamine levels. Practice stress-reduction techniques such

IGNITING YOUR INNER DRIVE

as meditation, deep-breathing exercises, yoga or mindfulness to manage stress effectively.

- **Regular exercise**: Physical activity increases dopamine release in the brain. This increase is higher when you enjoy the activity, so it's best to search for a sport you like.

Dopamine fuels our motivation and keeps us moving forward. When we learn to harness it effectively, staying engaged and energised in our daily lives becomes easier. Yet, even with dopamine working in our favour, procrastination can still sneak in, quietly sabotaging our progress and keeping us stuck in a loop of inaction. Why is this? Let's have a closer look at procrastination and how we can break free from its grip.

The Motivation Equation

We've all been there: delaying important tasks, avoiding responsibilities and pushing deadlines to the limit. We put off something we should do, even when we know this is not in our best interest. We choose a quick reward over a long-term gain. Procrastination affects us all to some extent. In fact, during college years, a staggering 80–95 per cent of students regularly procrastinate. Even as adults, an estimated 15–20 per cent of us are chronic procrastinators.[13]

The impact of procrastination on productivity is significant. Students who submitted their thesis just before the (twice) extended deadline not only received lower grades on their paper but also performed poorly on other exams. Furthermore, the procrastinators experienced a decline in their health, suffering from increased stress and illness compared to their peers.[14]

We procrastinate for various reasons. One of the main drivers is the false belief that we need to feel inspired or motivated to start a task. Unfortunately, waiting for that elusive 'right moment' often results in things not happening at all. Our preference for immediate enjoyment over long-term rewards – *present bias* – can also lead to procrastination.[15] And when we're confronted with tasks we find daunting or decisions we fear making, we tend to kick the can down the road. Finally, some of us thrive on the adrenaline rush of last-minute work, believing we perform better under pressure.

Procrastination is not always bad. It can sometimes be harmless or even advantageous. For instance, delaying an action can allow us to gather more information, weigh our options and make a better choice. However, it becomes problematic when it's habitual and interferes with our well-being, productivity and ability to meet our goals.

It might sound obvious, but increasing motivation is the key to combating procrastination. A helpful tool is the motivation equation developed by organisational psychologist Piers Steel:[16]

$$Motivation = \frac{(Value * Expectancy)}{(Impulsiveness * Delay)}$$

When we value a task and believe in achieving positive outcomes, we naturally feel more motivated to complete it. On the other hand, impulsiveness and delay are motivation killers. Impulsiveness refers to the tendency to give in to distractions and short-term gratification, while delay represents the time it takes to accomplish a task.

How can we control these elements and increase motivation? Strategically setting SMART (Specific, Measurable, Achievable, Relevant and Time-bound) goals, a concept we briefly discussed in Chapter 1, is an effective way to enhance value and expectancy while lowering impulsiveness and delay.

Defining *specific* goals eliminates ambiguity, outlining exactly what you aim to achieve. For example, if you want to exercise more, a SMART goal would be: 'I will jog for thirty minutes three times a week.' The level of precision offers a clear roadmap making it easier to assign value and paves the way for positive expectations. A specific goal narrows your focus, making it easier to resist distractions.

Incorporating *measurable* criteria into goals allows you to track your progress and celebrate milestones along the way. If you track the pounds you've lost since you starting changing your diet, you give yourself tangible evidence of your advancement, boosting expectancy. You also know what still needs to be done, pushing you to stay on track.

Setting goals that are challenging yet *achievable* fosters a sense of competence and self-belief. This prevents the feeling of overwhelm, which can trigger abandoning tasks or delaying them. For instance, if your goal is to read more, aiming to read five books in a month could be overly ambitious and discouraging. Instead, targeting a goal of reading for fifteen minutes before going to bed is more feasible, enhancing the likelihood of success and maintaining motivation.

When goals are *relevant* – i.e. they resonate with your purpose and values – you're more likely to stay committed and engaged. It reduces the temptation to engage in behaviours that don't align with your overarching priorities. Tying tasks to your long-term aspiration can immediately boost motivation. For example, linking an exercise goal to keeping up with your kids adds meaningful value, making it easier to stay on track.

Lastly, *time-bound* deadlines create a sense of urgency. By setting a specific timeframe for completion, you're less likely to delay action because the time constraint pushes you to make progress consistently. Keep in mind that we tend to value things less when they're further away. Therefore, aiming to save £2,500 within a year is more effective than aiming to save £5,000 in two years.

Let's give it a try. Pick one thing out of the techniques you've read so far that you want to try. Suppose you want to improve your focus. A SMART goal would be to set aside twenty-five minutes (one Pomodoro) each morning to work on a single task without distractions for the next two weeks. This goal is specific (improving focus by working on one task), measurable (twenty-five minutes), achievable (a manageable time commitment), relevant (it ties into your larger objective of becoming more focused) and time-bound (for the next two weeks). This way you give yourself a clear and structured plan, which makes it easier to follow through and track your progress.

When aiming for a bigger goal, like becoming a manager, it's helpful to break it down into intermediate steps, such as completing a leadership course or gaining project management experience. For each step, you can create SMART goals, like completing a leadership course within six months by dedicating five hours per week to study, or leading two major projects by the year's end to build management experience. This approach offers clear, achievable milestones on your career path.

Since smaller goals feel more manageable and immediate, we're less likely to feel overwhelmed or succumb to procrastination. Moreover, our motivation tends to increase as we get closer to achieving a goal – a phenomenon known as the *goal gradient hypothesis*.[17] When the reward is in sight, we tend to feel more driven to reach the finish line. By breaking down larger objectives into smaller, more attainable steps, you create a sense of progress that incentivises you to continue working towards our goals.

For some, making SMART goals public can boost motivation as it introduces a sense of accountability. When others know what you're aiming for, you might be more likely to stay committed, as external feedback or even social pressure can help keep you on track. Sharing your leadership course plans with your team or a mentor, for instance, might encourage you to follow through, knowing they'll be checking up on your progress. Plus, having someone invested in your success can offer valuable encouragement and support.

Another way to increase your motivation is to find aspects of your tasks that genuinely interest you and making them more enjoyable. Add some fun to your chores by listening to a podcast or by treating yourself after completing a task. The release of

Pokémon GO sparked an increase in physical activity. This wasn't a coincidence; chasing virtual creatures makes walking outdoors much more enjoyable.

My personal favourite technique to quickly boost my motivation is swapping 'I have to' with 'I get to'. Words are powerful and, by shifting your perspective, you can transform your entire experience. I use it very often. For instance, when having to wake up early on a Sunday to write this book, the shift from 'I *have* to wake up at 7 a.m. to write' to 'I *get* to wake up at 7 a.m. to write' made a huge impact on my motivation. This small change reminded me that without a book deal and accompanying deadline, I wouldn't be writing in the first place. I encourage you to try it out. Replace 'I *have* to make dinner for my children tonight' with 'I *get* to make dinner for my children tonight'. Notice the difference it makes?

Setting SMART goals will boost your motivation and curtail procrastination. But make sure you plan realistically. We all have a tendency to underestimate the time, costs and risks involved in achieving a goal (the planning fallacy). Unrealistic expectations can lead to frustration and demotivation when faced with obstacles or delays. You can combat this by acknowledging potential challenges and allocate extra time and resources in your plans. By staying realistic, you'll be better prepared for setbacks and maintain your motivation when they do occur. 'That's all great,' you might now say, 'but how do I deal with multiple, conflicting goals?' Glad you asked.

Juggling Multiple Goals

'I have a crucial board presentation coming up next week and a stack of urgent reports on my desk. On top of that, I need to help my daughter with her homework and make it to her soccer game this weekend. Oh, and don't forget the community workshop I've agreed to lead, which requires preparing materials and practising my presentation. Plus, there's a half-finished painting in the garage meant as a birthday present that still needs to be finished. Where on earth do I begin?'

Many of us regularly experience this kind of inner conversation. We all have multiple goals and dreams that compete for our attention. It often feels like we're torn in different directions, having to choose between one thing or another. Our careers, families, personal projects and health all contribute to our happiness, but how do we navigate all our goals without losing ourselves? How can we handle these responsibilities without falling short?

Juggling multiple goals is a huge challenge we all face daily. Unfortunately, there's no easy fix. At times, you may feel overwhelmed and guilty for not being able to give everything and everyone the attention they deserve. However, there are strategies we can adopt to make our lives a bit easier.

Utility maximisation is a fundamental concept in economics. It refers to how individuals and organisations strive to use their limited resources – time, money or energy – to achieve the greatest satisfaction or benefit. For example, when deciding how to spend £40 on a meal, you could choose to dine at a fancy restaurant where a meal costs £35, leaving little room for dessert or drinks. Alternatively, opting for a more casual eatery which offers a main course for £15 allows you to indulge in dessert and a drink. Utility maximisation is about weighing these options and choosing the combination that brings the highest satisfaction within your constraints.

Now let's apply this principle to juggling multiple goals in daily life. Utility maximisation here means making deliberate choices about how to allocate your time and energy to achieve the greatest overall benefit. It's not just about achieving your goals – it's about doing so efficiently. For instance, if your goals include advancing your career, spending quality time with your children and staying fit, consider how these objectives can overlap. Instead of treating them as separate tasks, you could take your children to the park after work. This lets you bond with them while staying active.

Or you could cook healthy meals together, combining nutrition, quality time and teaching life skills. By finding such synergies, you allocate your time and energy more effectively and reduce the feeling of being pulled in multiple directions.

That said, no matter how skilfully we manage our time, we can't pursue all our goals at once. Some must take precedence based on urgency and importance. As a wise friend once put it, 'You can have it all, just not all at the same time.' This is where prioritisation becomes essential, especially our Quadrant 2 activities – the important but not urgent tasks that contribute to our long-term ambitions and personal development. The tools outlined in Chapter 1 can help you identify and schedule these tasks.

Even with careful planning, conflicts between goals are inevitable, and compromise often becomes the best solution. For instance, imagine you've been offered a chance to take on a high-profile client at work, but your family is eagerly awaiting a summer vacation. If you accept the client, you might sacrifice precious family time; if you decline, you forgo a career-boosting opportunity. A compromise could involve negotiating a flexible work arrangement – agreeing to take on the client but working remotely during the summer holidays. This way, you can balance career advancement with family time, meeting both goals partially. Recognising compromise as the wisest approach can also help alleviate guilt for not fully achieving either goal.

It might not come as a surprise that utility maximisation becomes easier when setting SMART goals. These provide clarity and focus, helping you allocate resources effectively and maintain momentum. For instance, if your goals include improving fitness, learning a language and honing time-management skills, breaking each into specific, measurable steps allows you to track your progress and prioritise accordingly. By doing so, you ensure steady advancement in all areas without feeling overwhelmed.

Finally, a practical way to make progress towards multiple goals without feeling overwhelmed is *habit stacking*. This method, introduced by James Clear in his book *Atomic Habits*, involves linking new habits to existing ones by leveraging established routines. Instead of trying to create completely new routines from scratch, which can be challenging and mentally taxing, you build on existing habits already ingrained in your daily life. For example, learn a new language by listening to a language learning podcast while biking to work.

Maximising utility doesn't mean running ourselves ragged; instead, it's about achieving the right balance among our goals to boost overall satisfaction while staying within our limits. When juggling multiple goals, keep in mind that it's okay not to have everything perfectly aligned all the time. Life is inevitably a balancing act with its constant ebbs and flows. While we balance our goals, we'll also need to prepare ourselves to face the inevitable failures and setbacks.

Dealing with Failures and Setbacks

In 1995, basketball legend Michael Jordan suffered a devastating defeat in the NBA semifinals. Despite having victory in sight, Jordan made two crucial mistakes under immense pressure: first he missed a shot, then a defensive lapse allowed the opposing team to score. The Chicago Bulls were eliminated from the playoffs, leaving both the team and fans devastated.

Rather than letting this setback discourage him, Jordan used it as motivation to improve himself. He later admitted that he wasn't physically prepared for the intensity of the playoffs after returning from baseball. Driven by a strong desire to reclaim his position, he pushed himself harder than ever before. After that moment, he never lost in a playoff series again.

Find inspiration in Michael Jordan's story, as you navigate your own challenges and setbacks. Success lies not in avoiding mistakes, but in how we respond to them. Every missed shot, every error, presents an opportunity for growth, learning and building resilience. Failures and setbacks are inevitable in life. In fact, those who haven't failed haven't ventured outside their comfort zone. Whether it's a career setback, personal disappointment or an unexpected turn of events, it's our capacity to handle these challenges that will ultimately shape our lives.

Instead of viewing failures as insurmountable roadblocks, try to shift your perspective and see them as stepping stones to success. A setback also presents an opportunity to gain new insights, fine-tune strategies and emerge stronger. Take a moment to analyse the factors contributing to the setback. What lessons can be drawn from it? Assess your actions, decisions and external influences. This process of reflection gives you valuable insights for the future.

We hold the power to shift our perspective on any situation. We don't need to enjoy client complaints or tolerate excessive workloads, but we can alter our interpretation of the situation as being inherently good or bad. Even a seemingly adverse situation can transform into a positive experience when we extract value from it or use it as fuel to propel ourselves forward.

Rather than wasting energy on things beyond your control, identify areas where you can make a difference and focus there. When we direct our efforts towards taking action and finding solutions, we empower ourselves to make positive changes. While we cannot force others to change, we can always choose how we respond. While this may seem frustrating, it's actually quite liberating and empowering – it channels our energy where it matters most. We'll return back to this in Chapter 9.

Shifting our focus from chasing perfection to acknowledging progress is key to cultivating a positive outlook and encourages ongoing growth. Treat every effort you put into something as a step forward and start harnessing the power of the word 'yet'. By shifting our self-talk from 'I can't do this' to 'I can't do this yet', we embrace that any current inability is temporary, not a permanent roadblock to success. This mindset shift also brings an additional benefit as we just saw: our brain releases dopamine when we find joy in the process, enhancing our mood and motivation to keep going.

Finally, and above all, always practise self-compassion when dealing with difficult situations. Treat yourself with the same kindness and understanding that you would offer a friend going through a tough time. Surround yourself with a supportive circle of friends, family or mentors. Sharing experiences and seeking guidance from those who truly care about you can offer valuable insights and emotional support when overcoming challenges.

Failures and setbacks are an inherent part of life. Success isn't defined by the absence of failures, but by our ability to overcome them. If you never take the shot, you'll never score. As we navigate these challenges, cultivating willpower and tenacity becomes essential. These traits not only help us bounce back, but also fuel our drive to keep moving forward despite obstacles.

Staying the Course

Standing at the foot of the Torres del Paine in Patagonia, I gazed up at the rugged silhouettes of two of its iconic peaks. I was excited. Today, I would finally climb the mountain and soak in one of Patagonia's most breathtaking vistas. With a spring in my step I joined our group as we began the ascent, eager to tackle the mountain and take in the awe-inspiring views ahead.

But as we climbed, the wind picked up and dark clouds began to gather. After two hours of relentless trekking – halfway up the mountain – our guide called us together and suggested we turn back. The clouds, he explained, would obscure the Three Torres by the time we reached the summit, reducing the view to nothing more than shadows in the mist. Disappointed, I turned around and retraced my steps, realising all my effort had been for nothing.

The next morning, we returned with renewed determination. Just like the day before, the trail was steep and unforgiving. Hours slipped by, and my muscles – still tired from the previous day – began to protest, each rocky ascent testing my resolve. Yet, beneath the fatigue, a quiet voice urged me on, reminding me to stay focused on the goal: the spectacular view that lay ahead.

Then, just when it felt like the climb might never end, I rounded a bend – and the world seemed to shift. There it was: the stunning green-blue glacial lake, shimmering like a jewel in the sunlight, with the Three Torres standing proudly behind it, fully visible. In that breathtaking moment, the struggle of the ascent melted away, and I was reminded that the greatest rewards often come when we're willing to persevere.

We all know that when we're truly motivated, we find the strength to persevere, even when the going gets tough. Think of the times when you fully committed to something – whether it was finding your life partner, learning to play guitar or helping your child to graduate high school. When your 'why' is clear, it becomes easier to push past obstacles, knowing that the reward is worth the effort. For me, flying halfway across the world to witness the Three Torres made quitting unthinkable, even when I had to hike up the mountain twice.

It's quite easy to stay motivated when the goal is clear and the reward is just around the corner, like that stunning vista at the top. But how do we keep going when the summit is out of sight, when the payoff feels distant or when setbacks cloud our path? Our ability to resist temptations, overcome challenges and stay focused on the long game depends on how well we manage ourselves.

When we talk of self-control, it helps to distinguish between *trait self-control* and *state self-control*. Trait self-control refers to a person's ability to regulate their behaviour and impulses across various situations over time. It's a stable part of someone's personality and is also referred to as conscientiousness or grit. Individuals with high trait self-control are generally better at managing temptations, delaying gratification and focusing on long-term goals. It's a highly valued trait because it's strongly connected to better outcomes in health, wealth, relationships and academic achievement.[18]

In contrast, state self-control – also known as willpower – is a temporary exertion of control in specific situations, like resisting dessert at a party. This type of self-control fluctuates based on factors such as fatigue, stress and motivation. Psychologist Michael Inzlicht's process model of self-control suggests that failures of state self-control occur not from depleted energy but from shifts in motivation and attention over time. As we exert self-control, we lose interest in tasks we feel we must do and become more focused on things we want (immediate gratifications), making it harder to resist temptations.[19]

The two types of self-control are fundamentally different, and someone who excels in trait self-control doesn't necessarily have high state self-control. In fact, individuals with high trait self-control don't spend more time resisting temptations; instead, they tend to experience fewer temptations that need controlling.[20] This could be due to their strategic avoidance of situations that might lead to temptation or because they're less influenced by the allure of immediate rewards.[21]

So, how can we enhance our ability to stay committed to our goals? A great starting point is to implement strategies that help us resist temptations when they arise, effectively strengthening our willpower in those moments. We can learn from the children in Walter Mischel's famous marshmallow test.[22] In this study, kids faced a choice: eat one marshmallow immediately or wait fifteen minutes for two. Those who successfully resisted the temptation often distracted themselves by engaging in activities like singing or playing games. They also employed reappraisal techniques, imagining the tempting marshmallow as a puffy white cloud instead of delicious candy. We can adopt similar 'out of sight, out of mind' and reappraisal tactics to bolster our self-control in the moment.

Another effective strategy is 'if-then' planning, also known as *implementation intentions*. Research by psychologist Peter Gollwitzer shows that creating specific, actionable plans for handling potential challenges can greatly boost self-control. For instance, setting an intention like, 'If I feel the urge to snack, then I will drink a glass of water first', provides a clear and simple course of action that helps curb impulsive behaviour. By anticipating triggers and defining our actions in advance, this method strengthens our ability to manage impulsive behaviour when it counts.[23]

Building habits and routines can significantly reduce the need to exert self-control. By automating healthy behaviours – such as exercising, studying or maintaining a balanced diet – we minimise the mental effort required to resist temptations because the actions become second nature. When motivation dips, these established habits help us remain consistent without having to rely solely on willpower. In Chapter 7, you'll find effective strategies to build good habits.

These self-control strategies can help us resist temptations and achieve short-term goals, like fitting into a wedding dress or running 10k for a charity, but the evidence that they work sustainably over many months or years is less encouraging.[24] Furthermore, learning to resist temptations doesn't necessarily help us persevere in the face of challenging situations. For more lasting change, it seems more beneficial to focus on enhancing our trait self-control or conscientiousness. The good news is that we can improve this trait, and such changes tend to be longer lasting.[25]

Where do we begin? One promising avenue seems to lie in targeting a specific region of the brain called the anterior mid-cingulate cortex (aMCC). This area functions as a control hub for decision-making, helping us align our choices with our long-term goals. It also plays a key role in inhibitory control, helping us resist impulsive actions and prioritise behaviours that offer meaningful, lasting benefits.[26]

Multiple studies underscore the critical role of the aMCC in our ability to persevere.[27] Damage to this area impairs planning and the capacity to exert mental effort, while greater volume and activity of the aMCC strongly predict individual differences in grit and persistence. Research has shown that direct electrical stimulation of this region increases the 'will to persevere' in patients. Similarly, formerly obese individuals who successfully maintained weight loss exhibited heightened aMCC activation when resisting tempting food. Remarkably, 'superagers' – people who retain sharp cognitive abilities well into old age – tend to have larger and more active aMCCs, suggesting its role in sustained mental and physical resilience.

This naturally raises an intriguing question: can we strengthen the aMCC through our daily habits? Although the degree to which the aMCC can be altered through behavioural training is still uncertain, emerging research suggests that engaging in new and challenging activities may enhance its volume and function. For instance, older adults who began aerobic exercise three times a week for six months showed improvements in aMCC volume, whereas those who focused solely on stretching and toning did not. This highlights the potential of regular, effortful activity to 'train up' the aMCC.[28]

Meditation and mindfulness practices also offer promising avenues, as they have been associated with structural and functional changes in the midcingulate cortex (MCC), supporting the idea that this part of the brain can adapt through focused effort.[29] Moreover, practising self-control can enhance our capacity for self-regulation, potentially by increasing the strength of the aMCC.[30] Engaging in small, deliberate acts of willpower ('micro sucks') – like doing twenty burpees after a 10k run, choosing an apple over a chocolate bar, resisting the temptation to hit the snooze button or finishing a shower with cold water – give you the opportunity to strengthen your self-regulation.

Personally, I've found this approach incredibly effective. Viewing each small act of willpower as an opportunity to build my perseverance makes it easier to resist distractions, like the temptation to check my phone during a boring seminar. These incremental challenges might not seem particularly groundbreaking, but cumulated over time they can gradually help us improve our self-regulation abilities.

The Key Takeaways

Motivation is crucial to achieving what you want in your life. It is not a fixed state but a continuous process that requires constant attention and effort. By actively harnessing your motivation, you can make the most of your time and preserve your mental resources. Through thoughtful goal setting, harnessing the power of dopamine, turning challenges and setbacks into opportunities and bolstering resilience, you can enhance your motivation for all you want to accomplish.

- Motivation comes in two forms – intrinsic and extrinsic. While external rewards can spark motivation, it's the internal drive, the passion and satisfaction from the task itself, that fuels long-term success. According to self-determination theory, autonomy, competence and a sense of connection are essential to feeling intrinsically motivated.

- Understanding the 'why' behind your actions is key for unlocking deeper motivation and purpose. When you know why you're pursuing a goal, even the toughest challenges become more manageable. To clarify your why, try writing your own eulogy. Reflecting on how you want to be remembered helps you align your goals with what truly matters.

- Dopamine plays an essential role in motivation by driving your desire to pursue rewards and achieve goals. It's the brain's way of reinforcing behaviours by creating anticipation and excitement around positive outcomes. Harness dopamine effectively by breaking big goals into smaller more manageable milestones, rewarding yourself intermittently to maintain momentum and learning to enjoy the journey.

- Procrastination isn't always negative, but it becomes an issue when it prevents you from reaching your goals. To combat it, try to increase the perceived value and expectancy of tasks while reducing impulsiveness and delay. Setting SMART goals is an effective way to achieve this. For a quick motivation boost try swapping 'I have to' with 'I get to'.

- Juggling multiple goals involves finding a balance that maximises overall satisfaction while staying within your limits. Understanding when to prioritise and when to compromise makes it simpler to navigate conflicting objectives. Try to identify overlaps in your goals and use habit stacking to accomplish more in less time.

- Success isn't about avoiding failures but about how you bounce back from them. Instead of viewing setbacks as roadblocks, try seeing them as opportunities for growth and improvement. Embrace the power of 'yet' to turn challenges into progress and remember to be kind to yourself as you navigate tough times.

- Your ability to resist temptations and stay focused on long-term goals hinges on your self-control, which can be categorised into trait and state self-control. State self-control can be strengthened through strategies like 'out of sight, out of mind', reappraisal, and if-then planning. A promising approach to improve trait self-control is strengthening the anterior midcingulate cortex (aMCC) by embracing new challenges and incorporating 'micro-sucks'.

PART 2

Elevate Your Brain: Strategies for Cognitive Enhancement

In the first part of this book, we focused on reclaiming our most valuable resources: time and energy. We explored practical strategies to take control of our schedules, cut through distractions and align our daily actions with our core values and long-term goals. By applying these principles, we've laid the groundwork for a more productive, intentional life.

Now that we've established a solid foundation, it's time to turn our attention to the engine behind all of this – our brain. How we manage our mental energy matters, but equally important is how we exploit and strengthen our cognitive abilities. After all, sharpening our brain not only helps us become more productive but also opens the door to lifelong learning and creativity.

Often, we overlook our brain's strengths because we aren't fully aware of them. For instance, many of us rely on rote memorization to learn new information without realising that we remember things much more easily when visualising and connecting concepts. This lack of awareness means we often don't fully tap into our brain's potential. By exploring and understanding our brain's inherent strengths and weaknesses we can enhance our cognitive performance and achieve better outcomes.

In this part, we'll dive into the mechanics of boosting our brain power. We'll explore techniques to supercharge our memory (Chapter 4), optimise our learning (Chapter 5) and spark our creativity (Chapter 6). We'll also learn how to keep our brain agile and sharp, so it can perform at its best (Chapter 7).

As we explore these topics, keep in mind that there is no universal solution. Each of us is unique, and what proves effective for one person may not work for another. Embrace the process, experiment with different approaches and discover what best aligns with your individual needs and preferences.

4

Memory Magic

Jim Kwik's words from a few days ago still echo in my mind: 'There is no such thing as a good or bad memory, only a trained or untrained one.' Since enrolling in his *Superbrain* course, the phrase has quickly become my personal mantra. Now on day five of the thirty-day programme, I eagerly power up my laptop, excited to dive into the next lesson. With the pandemic limiting my daily activities, Jim's dynamic and engaging classes are a welcome escape from the monotony of the day.

Today, Jim sets out to teach us ten key brain foods: avocados, blueberries, broccoli, coconut oil, eggs, leafy greens, salmon, turmeric, walnuts and dark chocolate. He's already made it abundantly clear that rote memorization isn't the way to go, so I am curious to see what techniques he has in store. He unveils the 'body method', a strategy that uses different parts of our body to store information. We're instructed to choose ten body parts and mentally place a food item on each, visualising them as vividly and absurdly as possible.

Before I know it, I envisage avocados splattering on my head, the soft pulp trickling down my face. My ears jingle with the weight of gigantic, juicy blueberry earrings. Broccoli tendrils sprout out of my nostrils and cover my face like a verdant mask. From my mouth shoots a torrent of eggs. My neck glistens with a coat of slick coconut oil, setting a slippery stage for the leafy greens pirouetting on my shoulders. A generous salmon dangles from my neck, while my hands are fully covered in golden turmeric. A belt of chunky walnuts cinches my waist and my feet are snug in boots, crafted entirely of decadent dark chocolate.

Much to my surprise, twenty minutes later I can effortlessly recall the ten brain foods in order, forwards and backwards. Even the following day, I can still recite the list with startling clarity. Evidently, a straightforward memory technique has the power to significantly enhance my recall capabilities. And up to that point, nobody had bothered to teach me that technique. What else is there to discover about my memory, I wondered.

The Compounding Value of Memory

As a first-year economics student, I learned about compound interest. It's the interest calculated on both the principal and the accumulated interest from previous periods. In essence, it's interest earning interest and it leads to exponential growth of our savings or investment over time. Here's how it works: say you invest £100 at an annual interest rate of 5 per cent compounded annually. After the first year, you'll earn £5 in interest, bringing your total to £105. In the second year, you'll earn 5 per cent interest on the entire £105, resulting in £5.25 in interest, and a total of £110.25. The longer you keep going, the more quickly your savings will grow. After ten years, you'll have earned £155.14, a return of 55 per cent on your initial investment!

Interestingly, the concept of compound interest is a useful analogy for how memory works. Every time you learn something new, your brain forms a memory by linking that new knowledge to what you already know, creating a web of connections. The more memories you accumulate, the greater the network of associations you build. Just as compound interest accelerates the growth of your savings over time, your ability to learn and retain new information improves as your knowledge network expands. With each new piece of knowledge, you build more links in your mental network, making it quicker and easier to learn and remember additional information.

Think about the last time you learned a new language. At first, each new word's contribution to your knowledge bank is small. But, as time progresses, the words interconnect and build upon each other. Soon enough, you're stringing sentences together, confidently ordering food in a restaurant or asking for directions. Each additional word you commit to memory fosters more neural connections, making further learning and memorization progressively easier. This is the magic of a good memory – it's like a spiderweb, the bigger it gets the more it catches. And the more it catches, the bigger it grows.[1]

Some may suggest that technology, readily available at our fingertips, negates the need for a strong memory. Why make an effort to remember when information is just a click away, right? With tools like Google and generative AI providing prompt answers, and smartphones keeping tabs on everything from meetings to milestones, committing facts to memory appears almost unnecessary. Moreover, apps and devices can sometimes process and analyse data in ways that outpace our natural abilities.

However, the rise of technology doesn't devalue a good memory – instead, in my view, it enhances its importance. When faced with a problem or task, our memory serves as an internal compass, guiding us to the most relevant information based on past experiences and accumulated knowledge. It helps us quickly pinpoint key sources, saving valuable time and boosting productivity. Instead of sifting through endless results online, a well-trained memory allows us to cut through the noise and access what we need.

Moreover, a strong memory bolsters our ability to critically evaluate and synthesise the information retrieved from tech tools. When delving into complex topics, it's not enough to simply gather data – we need to interpret it. Memory allows us to connect seemingly unrelated ideas, assess the credibility of sources and integrate new knowledge into what we already know. Technology may give us the raw data, but it's our memory that transforms it into meaningful insights, drawing connections that lead to a deeper understanding.

It's also worth noting that information stored in our memory is far quicker to retrieve than anything we can look up. Furthermore, when we recall something from memory, we're tapping into a deeper understanding of the concept, as it's been processed, internalised and connected to knowledge we already possess. Research even shows that when we look things up, we tend to remember where we found the information rather than the information itself.[2] This reliance on external sources shifts our mental effort from learning to simply locating, which makes retrieval more time-consuming.

Finally, relying solely on technology is a bit like always opting for the elevator. While convenient, we miss out on the workout it provides. Regularly challenging our brain to store and retrieve information keeps it sharp and agile – it's like taking the stairs for our mind. Just as physical exercise builds endurance, the mental effort of memorization strengthens our cognitive abilities. Over time it can enhance our problem-solving skills, creativity and ability to think critically and remember important facts – like someone's name.

A robust memory, like compound interest, has the potential for exponential learning and growth. While technology can be a great enabler, the power of a strong memory remains unparalleled. And the good news is that it can be strengthened at any age. But how does our memory actually work?

Memory Mechanics

Imagine being in a bustling farmer's market on a sunny Saturday morning. Your eyes capture the vibrant colours of the fresh produce, your ears pick up lively conversations and your nose detects the aroma of freshly baked bread. As you navigate through this sensory wonderland, let's explore how your brain transforms these fleeting moments into lasting memories.

MEMORY MAGIC

As you stroll among the market stalls, the various sensory inputs are temporarily stored in your sensory memory, the first stage of our memory system. Sensory memory holds information for a very short duration – think milliseconds to a second. It acts as a temporary holding area, capturing everything around you but giving your brain just enough time to decide what's worth paying attention to.[3] If it's not deemed important, the sensory data fades away almost instantly. This avoids the brain from becoming overwhelmed.

The selected sensory information then moves into short-term memory, where it can be held for about 20–30 seconds, sometimes a bit longer – just enough time to use or process the information further. Here we actively process all the relevant sensory information, plus the information that we recall from long-term memory, to think about the input we just received. Think of it as your brain's scratchpad, helping you keep track of everything that matters in that moment.

Perhaps you've found a stall that sells beautiful sunflowers. Your short-term memory grabs that detail – the location of the stall and the price of the flowers – and holds it just long enough for you to decide whether to buy them or keep exploring. You pull in a memory from last week when those same sunflowers brightened up your kitchen. This interplay between new sensory inputs and long-term memories helps you make informed decisions on the spot.

Because information is being actively processed, short-term memory is also called working memory. Strictly speaking, the two terms do not completely overlap, but for our understanding of the memory process this doesn't matter.[4] The capacity of our short-term memory is strictly limited. It was long thought that it could hold seven things, give or take two.[5] However, it's now widely accepted that it can hold even less – only four pieces of information.[6] The capacity can, however, appear larger when information is grouped or chunked together.

Information in short-term memory quickly decays, unless we

keep rehearsing it. And because of its limited capacity any new sensory input that the brain deems important will replace the information already in it. If you get distracted by a friend calling your name, your attention shifts and your brain quickly replaces the sunflower detail with thoughts of moving towards her. This constant updating ensures that our brain remains focused on the most immediate and relevant information.

Our short-term memory acts as a conduit to long-term memory. Information in short-term memory can be encoded for long-term memory storage in a process known as *consolidation*. This involves strengthening what is called the *memory trace*, making it more stable and durable over time. Not every piece of information in short-term memory will move into our long-term memory. Most of the things that pass through our brain don't need to be remembered any longer than the moment or two we spend perceiving them and, if necessary, reacting to them.

For information to be stored in long-term memory, it needs to be rehearsed or made more memorable by making meaningful connections between the new information and existing knowledge. When your friend called your name, you momentarily lost focus on the sunflowers as your short-term memory had to adjust quickly. However, if this encounter with your friend led to a memorable conversation after which you bought the sunflowers, then that information would enter your long-term memory.

In our brain, a memory is nothing more than a unique network of neurons active at the time something happened. Neurons are nerve cells that can send and receive information; there are roughly 128 billion of them.[7] They communicate via electrical and chemical signals that they send to each other through synapses – the junctions where neurons connect; a process facilitated by the release of neurotransmitters. Via this process, neurons form networks or patterns in the brain.

How the initial memory is stored is a complicated process and involves various regions of the brain, but two regions are particularly important: the hippocampus and the cortex. The hippocampus is the initial storage for memories. When you experience or learn something, this part of the brain helps to bind together the different elements of the experience (the happiness you felt when you met your friend, the colour of the flowers and the smell of freshly made bread) in a coherent whole. It creates a cohesive memory by forming a network of activated neurons that represent the event. The hippocampus thus helps consolidate short-term memories into long-term memories.

Some of the memories stored in the hippocampus are then gradually transferred to the cortex for long-term storage. The hippocampus stores information as event memories or sequences, but when the information is consolidated to the cortex you only keep the information that is critical. When you learned that London is the capital of the UK, the fact itself is stored in your cortex, but the moment you learned the information is not; it's not critical so your brain lets go of it. This process helps you create a knowledge network with information that is relevant to you. You can think of it as an expansive library where all your knowledge, experiences and skills are stored.[8]

While memory consolidation also occurs when we're awake but resting, sleep plays a fundamental role in this process. The hippocampus has a limited storage capacity and during sleep, especially the deep stages of non-REM sleep, it's cleaned up. Important memories – such as the conversation you had with your friend – are transferred to the cortex for long-term storage, while trivial ones – like the sandwich you had for lunch – are thrown away. This process prepares the hippocampus for new storage the following day.[9]

Although we cannot control the memory sorting process during sleep, our daytime behaviour can influence which memories get moved to long-term storage. Important things we've encoded properly, especially those we repeated throughout the day, are more likely to be transferred. Also, information we take in just before sleep is more likely to be consolidated as it's still fresh.

Sleep also helps to reinforce memories and integrate the newly acquired information with pre-existing knowledge. During sleep, the hippocampus reactivates the neural network associated with the newly acquired information. This replay strengthens the synaptic connections and thus the memory. This process is best performed 'offline' as otherwise new information would interfere.[10]

REM sleep – the most active sleep stage characterised by vivid dreams – seems to facilitate the integration of new memories with existing ones, often in unexpected ways. Brain scans suggest that during REM sleep, different parts of the brain that handle complex thinking work together in a way that helps connect memories that aren't closely related.[11] This might explain why we often wake up with fresh insights after a full night's sleep. Additionally, REM sleep also aids in processing emotional memories, which can help reduce the intensity of those emotions.[12]

Some studies suggest that a good night's sleep after learning a new procedural task – like playing a song, riding a bike or typing on a keyboard – helps us perform better on that task the following day. During practice, the routine is initially stored in the hippocampus, but it's consolidated into the cortex overnight, making it easier to access and apply the next day, which enhances the skill. However, it's not entirely clear whether this improvement is due to the effects of sleep itself or simply because the brain and body have had time to recover from the exhaustion of training.[13]

What about naps? Daytime naps can enhance memory function, though the effects are generally small. Factors such as age, nap duration, timing or habitual napping don't seem to play a major role.[14] While napping can be useful up to a point, it cannot substitute for the advantages of having sufficiently long and high-quality sleep.

Sleep is important for memory consolidation, making it essential for optimal learning. Moreover, as we'll explore further in Chapter 7, sleep has various other vital functions. When it comes to sleep, you get very little benefit from cutting corners. The best indicator for adequate sleep is simply feeling fresh and alert throughout the day. In Chapter 7, you'll find valuable strategies to improve your sleep.

Now that we understand how memories are formed, let's explore how they're retrieved. You might be surprised to discover that recalling a memory isn't as simple as hitting 'play' on your mental video – it's more like piecing together a puzzle, with unexpected twists along the way.

Memory Retrieval

Just like many of you, I vividly remember the day the planes crashed into the Twin Towers. I was in Amsterdam, mid-afternoon, working at my desk that overlooked one of the canals. Sharing my office with two fellow PhD students, we were in the throes of our work when the horrific news broke. One of us caught wind of the tragedy through a news update and immediately informed the rest of us. We huddled around his computer, witnessing the second plane's impact live.

My office mates probably hold different recollections of that day. Still, I stick to my story. This is how I remember it, so it must be true, right? Emotionally charged events like 9/11, tend to produce what psychologists call *flashbulb memories* – vivid, detailed recollections of where we were and what we were doing when we heard the news. These memories stand out, clear and precise, leading us to believe they're flawlessly accurate. Yet they aren't.

We tend to have great confidence in our flashbulb memories, but the details are often highly unreliable. For instance, studies conducted after the 9/11 attacks demonstrate substantial changes in people's accounts over time. People were asked to recount their experiences immediately after the event and then again at increasingly longer time intervals. Despite their confidence in their memories, the details often shifted, revealing inconsistencies and errors.[15]

This phenomenon illustrates the complexities and errors in memory retrieval. Our memories are not perfect recordings of past events. They're not simple replays, but elaborate rewrites – the product of a constructive process influenced by numerous biases and distortions. When we recall a specific event, our brain doesn't just pull out a neatly organised file containing all the details. Instead, it pieces together the memory by assembling different elements – images, sounds, emotions and contextual cues – from various brain areas, while filling in the gaps with inferences and pre-existing knowledge. Over time, these reconstructions can become distorted, influenced by subsequent experiences, conversations and even media coverage, creating inaccuracies in our recollection. As it turns out, even our most significant memories are not perfect recordings.

To make matters worse, it's possible that entire events in our mind have never happened. Elizabeth Loftus, whose work has been fundamental in understanding that our memories are reconstructed and not stored in some sort of mental library, showed this in one of her most famous studies. Participants received a booklet with four childhood stories – three true and one fabricated about getting lost in a mall. Some participants later recalled the false event as real, demonstrating how suggestion can create false memories.[16] It underscores the malleability of memory, with important implications for eyewitness testimony and therapy.

Our memory system is thus unreliable and error-prone. While this can be a challenge in our personal relationships – you might remember aspects of your wedding day differently than your spouse – these imperfections also serve important functions. The fact that we don't remember everything perfectly, helps us integrate new information and adapt to changing environments. As contradictory as it might sound, we don't have a memory for remembering the past but to be prepared for the future.[17]

In a constantly changing world, holding on to every detail would be a hindrance rather than a help. Imagine you had to remember every little detail about a red traffic light: its exact shade, the specific intersection, the time of day you saw it, the make and model of every car that passed by. This overwhelming amount of information would clog your memory and make it difficult to process new experiences or react swiftly to new situations. Instead, by remembering the essential concept that a red traffic light means stop, your brain can efficiently use this information across different contexts.

Moreover, this ability to generalise from abstract memories is crucial for learning. When you encounter a new traffic signal that is unfamiliar in appearance but still shares key characteristics with a red traffic light, you can infer its purpose. This flexibility means your knowledge is not static; it evolves as you experience new situations, allowing for continuous learning and updating.

Consider cooking a new recipe. Instead of remembering every individual recipe you've ever made in detail, you retain the core techniques and principles: chopping, sautéing, boiling. This foundational knowledge allows you to tackle new recipes confidently, recognising patterns and applying familiar methods to new ingredients and procedures.

Our imperfect memory also helps us move past conflicts. Forgetting the precise details of an argument allows us to forgive and reconcile more easily. If we remembered every slight and disagreement perfectly, including the emotions it invoked, it would be much harder to maintain long-term relationships and function as a social species. By letting go of the minutiae, we can focus on the positive aspects of our relationships.

Having an imperfect memory is thus often perfectly suited to our needs. However, the larger our repository of general knowledge, such as facts, concepts and meanings, the easier it becomes to rapidly update and expand our understanding of the world around us. This enables us to quickly grasp new information, make informed decisions and engage in meaningful conversations. Before we jump into improving our memory, let's pause to consider why we forget in the first place.

The Disappearing Act

It's a quiet Friday evening, the kind that calls for nothing more than sinking into the cushioned comfort of my couch. Remote control in hand, I scroll through the titles in search for the perfect movie. I settled on *Drive*, drawn in by the fact that my favourite actor, Ryan Gosling, plays the main character, the Driver, and the promised action and intense drama.

The movie opens with a tense, fast-paced chase. The Driver manoeuvres his car with expert precision, leaving the police baffled in his wake. The intensity grabs me instantly and, pleased with my choice, I settle in and immerse myself into the story. But as the movie progresses, a glimmer of familiarity begins to flicker. At first, it's just a passing sensation, like déjà vu lingering at the edges of my mind. I brush it off, too caught up in the unfolding story.

Then, there it is – the unforgettable elevator scene. If you've seen the movie, you'll know the one I mean: the Driver and his neighbour Irene share a slow-motion, passionate kiss; a rare moment of tenderness amidst the tension. But just as quickly, the mood shifts. The Driver spots a hitman and in one brutal move, he attacks, violently ensuring Irene's safety but shattering the illusion of his gentle nature. Suddenly it dawns on me, I've seen this movie! How could I have forgotten? And why does my brain choose this moment to awaken this buried memory?

Memory lapses occur almost daily. We've all experienced moments of walking into the kitchen and forgetting why we went there. Or the times we struggle to recall a name or a piece of information that we should know. Forgetting is so common that you probably rely on numerous methods to help you remember important information, like keeping a birthday calendar in the toilet or scheduling important events on your phone.

But what is forgetting, really? Forgetting is the natural process by which information stored in memory becomes inaccessible or fades away. There are various ways in which we can forget information. It could be that the information was never stored in long-term memory. Or it was stored but the connection between neurons has been lost along the way. Or, as was the case in my movie-watching episode, the connection between neurons was still there but not very strong and it was only activated when there was a cue – the elevator scene.

EBBINGHAUS FORGETTING CURVE

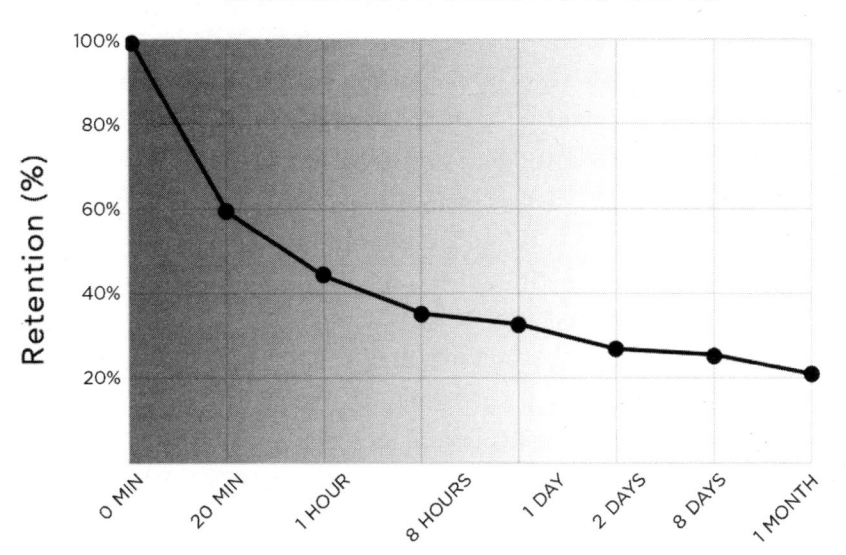

Retention (%) vs Elapsed Time Since Learning: 100% at 0 min, ~60% at 20 min, ~45% at 1 hour, ~35% at 8 hours, ~33% at 1 day, ~27% at 2 days, ~25% at 8 days, ~21% at 1 month.

Psychologist Hermann Ebbinghaus pioneered research on forgetting in the late nineteenth century.[18] Through meticulous self-testing, he explored the nature of memory decay over time. His groundbreaking work involved memorising nonsense syllables and tracking recall at various intervals. Ebbinghaus found that forgetting declines logarithmically, with a sharp drop post-learning, followed by a more gradual decline over time. A small amount of the information then stays in memory for a very long time. He called this phenomenon the *forgetting curve*. His insights laid the foundation for modern memory theories, profoundly shaping our understanding of how we remember and why we forget.

The forgetting curve doesn't necessarily imply permanent loss or erasure of information from long-term memory. Rather, it highlights the difficulty of recalling information at various points in time. While some memories that were stored in long-term memory get lost over time, other information remains in long-term memory, albeit in a potentially weakened or less accessible state.

The gradual decline in memory over time can be attributed to several factors. One explanation, known as *decay theory*, suggests that it's simply due to a lack of use. Memories are strengthened through repetition and rehearsal, so if we don't think about or revisit a memory, the connections associated with it may weaken. This is actually a good thing. Making quick decisions would be more difficult if a memory that hasn't been used for years is reactivated as quickly as a memory that is used daily.[19]

Sometimes we forget because new information interferes with old memories, making them harder to retrieve. This is known as *interference*. Remembering last night's dinner is usually straightforward. However, recalling a meal from three weeks ago on a random Tuesday presents a greater challenge. The cascade of meals since then are clouding that memory. Unless that dinner marked your fortieth birthday, in which case you will easily remember it. Unique events tend to stick in our minds. Milestones that stand out as special moments, like your high-school graduation, marriage or the birth of your first child, are much more likely to be remembered.

At other times, like in my recent movie-watching experience, memories linger beyond reach due to a lack of appropriate triggers. Despite initial details such as the movie's title, its lead actor Ryan Gosling and a brief synopsis, my recollection remained elusive. It wasn't until a specific scene unfolded – the elevator moment – that the memory resurfaced. This particular scene – a masterclass in visual storytelling – is highly memorable due to its raw emotion, understated intensity and abrupt change in tone.

There are a number of other factors that can play a role in forgetfulness. As we just learned, sleep plays an important role in memory consolidation, so a lack of quality sleep makes it more likely we forget what we've learned or experienced. Intense or chronic stress and anxiety can also cause lapses in memory, as our brain's focus shifts away from encoding and retrieving information to survival. This is why we often struggle to remember details of moments when we are feeling overwhelmed or anxious. Finally, as we grow older, we tend to forget more due to cognitive decline.

Forgetting is a natural part of life, and it's normal, even beneficial, to forget things over time. However, there are several strategies we can utilise to boost memory retention and solidify information in our brain. This is where we'll turn next.

Relying on VAC

A significant portion of our cognitive abilities, including our capacity to remember, is influenced by genetics.[20] Still, everyone is able to improve their memory and this often requires a different kind of thinking. Many of us were taught in school to use rote memorization – repeating information until it sticks. Perhaps you remember repeating the elements of the periodic table over and over again, struggling to memorise them despite your best efforts. While repetition can aid memorization, much more effective strategies are available.

The principle underlying all memory techniques is that our brains don't remember all types of information equally well. For evolutionary reasons, our brains excel at visual and spatial memory. Our hunter-gatherer ancestors relied on memory to recall the whereabouts of food sources, identify predators and navigate home after a three-day hunt. Those with superior visual and spatial memory could find food, track prey and navigate better, increasing their chances of survival and reproduction. Over time, this shaped the strong visual and spatial memory systems in the human brain.

While we possess a magnificent capability to recall visual imagery and spatial information, we often stumble when it comes to abstract information, random facts, lists of words, numbers and names. This is because, without a concrete reference, our brain finds it hard to encode, store and subsequently recall such information.

Memory techniques work by converting hard-to-remember information into forms that our brain can more easily latch onto. Ultimately, memorising is not a photographic but mostly a creative process. When we actively process and structure information, and link it to existing knowledge, retention becomes easier. Applying the mnemonic VAC – Visualise, Associate and Chunk – is a powerful way to boost our memory skills:

Visualise

Remember the last time you were engrossed in a novel? Perhaps you read Elena Ferrante's *My Brilliant Friend*. You may have pictured Lila as a striking, dark-haired girl with eyes brimming with defiance and intelligence. Whereas you may have imagined Elena as slender, scholarly and quiet, with a gentle gaze absorbing the world around her. You probably imagined them sitting together in (your version of) a bustling marketplace of 1950s Naples, talking, laughing and shedding tears.

When reading a novel, we instinctively construct mental images, converting written words into a multisensory experience. We use our creativity and imagination to create these pictures, thereby engaging the visual processing centres of our brain. This enhances memory encoding and makes it more likely that we recall the characters, places and events. The deeper we're immersed in the narrative, the better our chances of recalling it later.

In the 1970s, psychologist Lionel Standing conducted pioneering experiments that revealed the remarkable capability of our brain to remember visual information. Thousands of images were presented to the participants, each displayed for just a brief moment. Astonishingly, these participants could later identify the images with startling accuracy.[21] A more recent study repeated the experiment but this time with 2,500 highly similar images. Participants still demonstrated excellent recall.[22]

When studying textbook material or abstract concepts, we often don't engage our visual processing centres, making it much harder to recall the information. This principle applies equally to auditory information; when we hear content without visualising it, recall can be challenging. However, once we start visualising the information we can significantly boost retention. Furthermore, information tends to be more deeply processed when we create the images, again increasing chances of recall.

You can make your mental images more 'sticky' by bringing information to life. Make them as vivid, colourful, energetic and bizarre as you can, rather than mundane, dull and black-and-white. There is a logic to it. We all easily forget ordinary life events, yet emotional, extraordinary, incredible, unbelievable or amusing experiences tend to linger in our mind for a long time.

When bringing information to life you can use the mnemonic ISEEOU ('I see you') as a guide:

I = Illogical
S = Senses
E = Energy
E = Emotion
O = Outstanding
U = Unusual

The more dramatic, bizarre and multisensory your image, the easier the recall. For example, to memorise that the 'S' in ISEEOU stands for 'Senses', picture yourself holding a giant S-shaped strawberry (the choice of fruit starting with an 'S' is no coincidence). You feel its smooth, cool surface in your hand, breathe in its ripe aroma, and as you bite into it, the juicy flavour bursts onto your tongue. This vivid, multisensory experience makes the word 'Senses' far more memorable by directly engaging your own senses, forming a powerful mental connection. You can try it yourself with the other words.

For abstract concepts, it can help to find analogies or metaphors and visualise those. Take the idea of time management, for example. You can picture it as a glass jar and your daily tasks as different-sized stones. The important tasks – your Quadrant 2 activities – are big rocks, while smaller, less crucial tasks are pebbles. To manage your time well, you need to place the big rocks in the jar first; if you fill it with pebbles first, there won't be room for the big rocks. Visualising this analogy helps reinforce the importance of prioritization in time management.

Another method to create an image for the unimaginable is to visualise a similar sounding or punning word in its place. Consider the abstract concept of gravity. Instead of picturing the invisible force pulling objects towards the Earth, you can visualise a 'Gravy-Tea' party, where people are gathered around a table with a large pot of gravy in the centre. The gravitational pull of the gravy draws utensils, plates and even people towards it, creating a playful representation of the concept of gravity's attraction.

Excellent mnemonists stand out due to their knack for conjuring up elaborate mental images on the spot, crafting scenes so uniquely vivid they're impossible to forget. You might think, 'This isn't how I usually think' or 'I'm not that creative'. This isn't the way I used to think either and I never considered myself a particularly creative person, but you can train yourself to start memorising like this. That being said, we do differ in our ability to visualise images in our mind's eye. You can test your own ability by taking the Visual Vividness Imagery Questionnaire (VVIQ).[23]

Start by challenging yourself to remember something simple without writing it down. Then advance to more complex concepts. Experiment and see what works best for you. For me, abstract ideas often pose a challenge, but I've found that generative AI can be a helpful tool to visualise such concepts. However, simply prompting AI to come up with an image that represents the idea or word you want to remember isn't enough. You need to vividly imagine that image in your own mind, otherwise it won't stick. Some of us naturally excel at creating quirky or bizarre mental images, but, with practice, everyone can boost their visualisation skills. Give it a shot – you might surprise yourself.

Association

Imagine I show you two pictures with a person's face. When I show you the first picture, I tell you the person's last name is Baker. When I show you the second picture, I tell you the person is a baker. A couple of days later, I'll show you the pictures again and ask what you can recollect about the pair. You likely draw a blank on Mr Baker's name, but you remember that the second person bakes for a living. This phenomenon is known as the Baker/baker paradox.

Why does this happen? It's due to context. Contextual cues play an important role in how our brain processes and retains information. When we hear that someone is a baker, our minds automatically conjure up a wealth of related images, smells and experiences. We might visualise a cosy bakery with lines of fresh bread or picture a white baker's hat. These associations create a memory trace, helping us to recall the baker more easily.

The surname Baker, on the other hand, is tricky to memorise as it lacks significant associations in our mind. Our only link is the person's face, and that link is tenuous and tends to dissolve quickly. Devoid of context, the name becomes just another piece of information among myriad others we encounter, making it more prone to being forgotten.

The Baker/baker paradox highlights the power of context and association in improving memory retention. The richer and more connected the information, the better we remember it. Basically, we want to turn capital 'B' Bakers into lowercase 'b' bakers. Several techniques can help:

- **Mnemonic devices**: These memory aids associate new information with familiar concepts, making it easier to remember. The brain best remembers things that are repeated, rhythmic, structured and easily visualised. Mnemonics can take various forms – here are some popular types:
    - *Acronyms*: Creating a word out of the first letters of the items you want to remember, like ROY G. BIV for the colours of the rainbow (Red, Orange, Yellow, Green, Blue, Indigo, Violet).
    - *Rhymes and alliteration*: A rhyme scheme or alliterative sentence makes information more memorable, such as 'i before e, except after c'.
    - *Acrostics*: Create a sentence where the first letter of each word corresponds to the list, like 'Please Excuse My Dear Aunt Sally' to remember the order of algebra operations (Parentheses, Exponents, Multiplication, Division, Addition and Subtraction).
- **Personal experiences**: Tying new information to your personal experiences or interests creates strong hooks as you establish a deeper connection. For example, if you're learning about historical events, try to connect them to events or experiences in your own life to make the information more personally meaningful.

Association is all about linking new information to what's already stored in our long-term memory. By creating meaningful connections between what we need to remember and familiar concepts or experiences, we'll improve our ability to recall the information.

Chunking

In 1982, psychologists Bill Chase and Anders Ericsson shattered a longstanding belief about the limitations of memory with a groundbreaking experiment on an undergraduate student known as SF. They sought to discover if a person's memory could be improved with practice. SF spent hours each week at their Carnegie Mellon lab, repeating a simple memory test – the digit span test. He was asked to repeat a sequence of digits presented orally, with the length of the sequence gradually increasing. Initially, he could only retain about seven digits, but two years later, he could recall a staggering eighty digits.[24]

How did he do it? SF was an avid runner, and he decided to group digits into race times. For instance, the number sequence 3,484 became 3:48.4, the world record for the mile, and 2,711 translated into 27:11, the world record for the 10k. Instead of memorising an abstract string of numbers, SF recalled familiar and meaningful units of information. By compartmentalising or 'chunking' the information, and associating it with information stored in his long-term memory, he dramatically improved his memory performance.

By breaking down information into smaller, more manageable pieces, chunking makes it easier for the brain to remember. It reduces the number of items to remember by increasing the size of each item and gives the brain a hook by tying the chunk to something meaningful.[25] Chunking works by leveraging the brain's natural ability to process and remember information in meaningful patterns. When we organise information into chunks, we establish mental structures that facilitate encoding and storage in our long-term memory, effectively allowing us to extend the capacity of our working memory.

For instance, it will be hard to remember the letters YADLUFITUAEB, but if you look carefully, you see that they can be chunked into two words – 'BEAUTIFUL' and 'DAY' – which are easy to remember. Similarly, the sequence 149220021989 is hard to remember, yet if chunked into 1492, 2002 and 1989 they represent three important dates in European history (discovery of America by Christopher Columbus, the introduction of the euro in twelve European countries and the collapse of the Berlin Wall).

So, the next time you are trying to remember items, try forming groups and look for ways to relate them in meaningful ways.

What do the items share in common? Connect these clusters with things from your memory for better recall.

When it comes to chunking – and to our memory more broadly – what we already know determines what we're able to learn. You can take meaningless bits of information, run it through a filter that applies meaning to it and make that information much stickier. By practising chunking and incorporating this technique in your learning habits, you will likely find that you are able to remember more.

Now that we've seen that relying on VAC can greatly increase our ability to recall information, let's move to another crucial memory tool: organisation.

Organise to Remember

In a surprising turn of events that seemed as surreal as the images he conjured up in his mind, Joshua Foer went from being a journalist merely reporting on the world of competitive memorising to winning the US Memory Championship. By his own admission an ordinary guy with no extraordinary cognitive abilities, he triumphed over the nation's most skilled mnemonists.

What happened? Foer's journey began with an assignment to explore the little-known world of memorisation contests. As he watched competitors memorise full decks of cards, recite lengthy poems flawlessly and demonstrate other mind-boggling memory feats, he wanted to know more. What was the secret of these mental athletes? Did they always have such outstanding memories? The surprising answer: no. Most of them were ordinary individuals who had trained their minds using the age-old principles of memorisation.

Drawn by an irresistible challenge, Foer decided to test his own limits. His goal? To compete in the upcoming USA Memory Championship. Over the next year, he delved into the world of ancient memory techniques once used by great minds like Cicero and mediaeval scholars. Through rigorous training, he learned to quickly turn numbers into unforgettable images and employ the 'method of loci', an age-old, very powerful memory technique.

On the day of the championship, all his efforts paid off. He made it to the final and faced the ultimate challenge: memorising two decks of cards. With intense focus etched on his face, he converted each card into a vivid image within his memory palace – his childhood home in Washington, DC. It was a mental marathon, stretching his focus and creativity to their limits. As he placed the final card in the palace, it marked a silent triumph. He had demonstrated to the world that, with dedicated practice and the right memory techniques, even the most ordinary individual can achieve extraordinary results.[26]

Foer's impressive achievement underscores an important aspect of memory: the power of organisation. Placing information into mental 'folders' or spatial frameworks can greatly improve our memory. As we discussed earlier, we remember by connecting new information to things we have already stored in our long-term memory. When information is associated with familiar locations or categories, it becomes even more memorable and easier to retrieve. We create stronger memory traces and reinforce neural connections, thereby enhancing long-term retention.

It also facilitates retrieval by providing cues or prompts that trigger memory recall. When you need to access information, you can mentally 'navigate' through the folders or locations to find it. This organization also reduces interference between items; when information is grouped into distinct categories or locations, it's less likely to become confused with unrelated material, resulting in more accurate memory retrieval.

Organising new information thus aids retention and retrieval and there are various methods available to us:

Body method

The body method, which I was using at the beginning of this chapter, is a pretty straightforward technique. You use different body parts as storage for new information. I used ten storage compartments, but you can easily expand it as needed. By linking information to a familiar object – your body – you boost recall efficiency.

To practise this technique, it's easiest to start with nouns, like the brain foods. Nouns are easier to visualise, making them simpler to handle and store. Give it a shot by storing your next shopping list and see how it goes. Before heading off to the supermarket, scan your body from head to toe and check if you can recall the full list. If an item didn't stick, go back and reinforce the connection using the ISEEOU mnemonic. It helps to visualise the image clearly in your mind.

If you want to get creative, you can also use the body method to remember abstract or conceptual information. If the information seems unimaginable, you can again try substituting a similar-sounding or punning word. Your storage space doesn't have to be limited to your body; a familiar object like your car works too, as long as it has enough compartments. With multiple objects, you can create countless memory files in your brain for long-term storage.

Storytelling

Our brain loves stories – with characters, conflicts and resolutions. This isn't just coincidence; it's rooted in our evolutionary past. Storytelling was vital for our ancestors, helping them share crucial information about their surroundings. Narratives were key to passing down survival strategies and cultural values, making them fundamental to communal living. In fact, storytelling is likely the oldest mnemonic device we have. Stories are far more likely to be remembered and successfully retrieved compared to mere statistics.[27]

By creating a storyline that incorporates key details or concepts we like to remember, we create hooks for our memories. Stories provide context and meaning to information, transforming abstract facts into vivid, memorable experiences. The narrative provides structure to the information making it easier to retrieve

MEMORY MAGIC

later on. Furthermore, storytelling engages multiple areas of the brain. When we hear or read a story, we visualise the scenes, empathise with the characters and anticipate the outcomes. This multisensory engagement helps solidify the memory, as it involves more neural pathways and creates a stronger memory trace.

To illustrate, I've created a story for you. If you spend five minutes on it, you can experience the power of storytelling. First read the story and try to visualise it. Then read it again. Pay extra attention to the words in bold. Now try to recall the story from memory and only read it as a check. In the final round, try to tell the story from memory and only check when you're stuck. Now close the book and write down the words in bold.

On a bustling market day, a mischievous dog knocked over a **fire hydrant**, sending a burst of water skyward and soaking a brightly coloured **balloon** that was tied to a nearby stall. As the balloon wobbled precariously, a pharmacist's cart tipped over, scattering a bottle of **lithium pills** across the cobblestone street. The pills rolled and tumbled, landing in a pile of fresh **berries** being sold by a vendor. Suddenly, a wild **boar** burst onto the scene, drawn by the scent of the berries. It charged through the market, causing vendors to leap out of the way. The boar's rampage ended when it collided with a barbecue pit, sending **charcoal** briquettes flying. From the chaos a **knight** emerged carrying an oversized **oxygen** tank for reasons only he knew. Trying to restore order he slipped on a tube of **toothpaste**, which had fallen from a nearby stall, sending him skidding across the market square. His wild slide came to a stop beneath a flickering **neon** sign where he lay dazed and confused.

How did you manage? If you followed my instructions carefully, you will have been able to recall most of the bold words in the right order. You remembered ten words – but not only that. You remembered the first ten elements of the periodic table. The ten words in bold are keywords for the ten elements:

fire hydrant	hydrogen	**charcoal**	carbon
balloon	helium	**knight**	nitrogen
lithium pills	lithium	**oxygen tank**	oxygen
berries	beryllium	**toothpaste**	fluorine
boar	boron	**neon sign**	neon

Method of loci

The method of loci (sometimes called the memory palace or journey method) is considered the most powerful memory technique. Perhaps not surprising, 90 per cent of exceptional memorisers use this method.[28] It's similar to the body method, but we use places (loci) to store information. The technique dates back over 2,500 years and it's credited to the Greek poet Simonides of Ceos.[29]

The method of loci utilises our exquisite spatial memory to structure and store information that otherwise lacks structure. The principle is simple: pick a space you know well and mentally place the things you want to remember there. These spaces can be anything – your home, office building, a stroll through a town or stops along a railway. They can be real or imaginary, indoors or outdoors, big or small, as long as they're familiar and have an order linking one location to the next.

If you have never used the method of loci, it's best to start with a place you are intimately familiar with: your home. Wander through your home and select twenty (or fifty if you're up for a challenge) key points, like your front door, your bed or the bathroom toilet. Then create a logical route between them. You can start with your front door, the next point might be the doormat, etc. Once you have a route with ten stops, visualise a journey from one to the next. Then move on to the next ten, until you have the number you want. When you've visualised all points and committed them to memory, write them down.

Now let's store some information in your memory palace. Put the ten keywords that represent the first ten elements of the periodic table in your memory palace. See the fire hydrant in front of your door, a big balloon tied to your doormat, etc. To retrieve the images, all you need to do is take a mental stroll through your home. You can also try it backwards; it shouldn't make a difference. If you revisit the journey later today and again tomorrow, and perhaps again a week from now, your memories will solidify.

Neuroscientist and memory athlete Boris Konrad offers some valuable tips to ensure an effective mental journey. He advises making each point unique to avoid confusion. You can use a table in the kitchen and one in the living room as separate points, but not three doors in the hallway. Always use the same route in a space and make it logical. Keep a limit of ten points per room and aim for twenty to fifty points in one mental palace.[30]

While creating mental palaces and linking images to them does require practice, time and effort, the method of loci is incredibly powerful. You can use it to store anything from key points in a lecture to important details from a meeting or a recently read text. And here's another compelling reason to give it a try: recent research shows that practising the method of loci enhances memory for both seasoned memory athletes and beginners alike.[31]

Investing in the method of loci is a personal choice that can offer significant rewards, though it's a more advanced technique that may not suit everyone. In contrast, the memory technique for remembering people's names is surprisingly straightforward. And the benefits speak for themselves.

Memorable Names

As soon as the news broke, the air was brimming with joy – finally we were allowed to mingle outdoors again with more than two people. The local park quickly came alive with groups of friends gathering together, full of happiness and excitement. Nature had joined the party, giving us a beautiful sunny day. Embracing our newfound freedom, my friends and I relished in playing games and sipping wine.

Then, a familiar voice called my name. Seated beneath the old oak tree was a friend, accompanied by someone I didn't know. She introduced her as Angela. I've never been great with names, but I'd just mastered the technique to remember them. This was the perfect chance to put it to good use.

As I'd learned, the secret to remembering names lies in association. In Angela's case, it was rather simple. I quickly visualised Angela with grand, angel-like wings, appearing as a heavenly figure straight out of a Renaissance painting. As the image settled, I repeated her name. Thanks to the striking imagery, her name became etched into my memory. Still to this day, I remember her.

Remembering names is not just about making a good impression or avoiding awkward moments; it plays an important role in nurturing lasting connections. Whether navigating the corporate world, looking to stand out as a student or making connections at social gatherings, your capacity to remember names reflects the importance you attribute to those you encounter. People are more open to your message when they sense your genuine interest. Remembering someone's name is a powerful way to demonstrate your engagement.

You may think you're not capable of remembering names, but that's a fallacy. There's no such thing as having a 'good' or 'bad' memory for names; it all comes down to the strategy you use. Kevin Horsley, an international grandmaster of memory, summarises this strategy in a mnemonic – CCCC, which stands for Concentrate, Create, Connect and Continuous Use:[32]

Concentrate

The first step is the most crucial one. When meeting someone new, give them your undivided attention. If you don't pay attention, you can't encode the information. Often, when you forget a name, it's because your brain was preoccupied with other thoughts or distractions. Instead, make a genuine effort to concentrate on the person in front of you, their name and their face.

When you hear someone's name for the first time, repeat it. This not only confirms you heard it correctly but also aids in retention. If the name is difficult or unfamiliar, ask for the spelling or inquire about the name's origin.

Create

The second step involves creating a mental image that links to the person's name. Abstract names are hard to remember, as our brain doesn't have a hook to hold on to. Furthermore, auditory memories are never as solid as visual ones. It becomes much easier to remember the person's name when you make an image out of it, like I did with Angela. This is where creativity comes into play.

Think of a visual association or a funny image that somehow reflects their name. The more bizarre the connection, the more memorable it becomes. For instance, imagine a person named Max wearing a 'maxi' skirt, or picture David as a slingshot-wielding warrior ready to face Goliath. These visual associations forge a memorable link in your mind.

Connect

The third step involves creating a connection between the image and a distinct physical feature. For example, if Max has long hair, picture him wearing a maxi skirt woven from his own hair. Or maybe you've met a woman named Rose with bright red lipstick. Imagine her blowing a cloud of rose petals every time she speaks. These vivid associations help solidify the connection between the name and the person in your memory.

Another approach is to tie the image to something you know about the person. For instance, if Lily loves hiking, picture her walking along a trail surrounded by a stunning field of lilies. If you find it difficult to link your image with a physical feature or something you know about the person, you can focus on just one approach. Either stick with the image you've created or rely on their distinctive feature. Both methods will help you remember their name, although creating a strong visual image is generally the more effective strategy.

Continuous use

The final step involves continuously using the person's name in conversation, both during your first meeting and in subsequent interactions. This not only ingrains their name in your memory but also shows that you value them as an individual. Try to strengthen the association during the course of the day or evening.

If you want to excel at remembering names, I found it very helpful to create a list of common names and associated images. For example, I visualise Mark wearing a T-shirt emblazoned with a bright green 'check' mark, John I picture in a tennis outfit (referencing John McEnroe) and Stuart is stewing artwork in a pot. You have about thirty seconds to come up with an image as that's how long the name will be available in your short-term memory. So the more images you have ready in your mind, the easier it will become to remember the names of new people you meet.

Mastering the art of remembering names requires practice, but it might be worth the effort. As the American writer and lecturer Dale Carnegie once said, 'A person's name is to that person the sweetest and most important sound in any language.'

The Key Takeaways

Memory is far more than just recalling facts. It's the foundation that allows you to learn, adapt and navigate the complexities of life. A strong memory helps you retrieve critical information, acquire new abilities and make knowledgeable decisions. A strong memory functions like compound interest, growing its value exponentially over time as you accumulate more knowledge. By exploiting your brain's strengths and sidestepping its weaknesses, you can boost your memory potential.

- Short-term memory, which holds information temporarily, acts as a gateway to long-term memory, where information is stored more permanently. Sleep is important as that is when the brain processes and organises information learned throughout the day. Prioritising sleep is one of the best things you can do to improve memory.

- You quickly forget information shortly after learning it, with the most significant decline happening within the first day. This forgetting happens because information doesn't reach long-term memory or is affected by memory decay over time and interference from other information. Regular review and active engagement with the material can help combat this natural forgetting process.

- Your brain excels at remembering visual information. By creating vivid mental pictures of the information you want to remember, you significantly enhance your ability to retain and recall that information. To bring information to life you can use the mnemonic ISEEOU ('I see you') as a guide.

- The likelihood of remembering something increases significantly when you can attach a reference point to it. Your brain excels at remembering information through associations. By linking new knowledge to familiar concepts or experiences – turning capital 'B' Bakers into lowercase 'b' bakers – you enhance your ability to retain and recall information.

- Chunking helps you organise information into bite-sized, manageable units, making it easier for your brain to process and remember. By grouping items together and looking for ways to relate them in a meaningful way, you can improve both retention and recall.

- Techniques like the body method, storytelling and the method of loci boost memory retention by organising information. The method of loci – visualising a familiar place and linking each piece of information to a particular location therein – is particularly powerful.

- Remembering names becomes easier using the 4 Cs strategy: Concentrate on the name when first hearing it; Create a mental image or association with the name; Connect it to something familiar or memorable; ensure Continuous use by repeating the name in conversation and practice.

5
Learning How to Learn

My grandmother, or 'oma' as I called her, was an extraordinary woman. Born in 1907, she witnessed many changes in her life. When she was a child, washing was still done by hand, TVs hadn't been invented and transportation was largely by foot, bicycle or horse and carriage. By the time she passed away in 2011, at the remarkable age of 104, the world had changed beyond anything she could have imagined in her youth. She had witnessed the birth of commercial aviation, watched as humans landed on the moon and experienced the rise of the internet and mobile phones.

Despite these monumental changes, throughout her life oma remained adaptable, curious and keen to learn. Already in her nineties, she bought a computer and asked one of her children to teach her how to send an email. It wasn't easy at the beginning. The internet was an alien concept and the hand-eye coordination required was challenging for her. Unfazed, she persisted and mastered this new skill. Even so, she preferred sending me handwritten letters, believing that nothing could replace their warmth and personal touch.

Oma didn't allow herself to be left behind, instead she embraced new inventions and societal shifts with curiosity and, in most cases, enthusiasm. Even at a very old age, oma's mind remained sharp, her spirit young and her heart open. She taught me that learning is not something reserved for the young or limited to formal education. There is always room for acquiring new knowledge, adapting and embracing change at any stage of life. I guess it wasn't a coincidence that she was a teacher by profession.

Some of my grandmother's genes clearly passed onto me. As an economics professor, I have dedicated my life to studying, learning and teaching. Like her, I plan to keep learning well into my later years. But when I realised that my memory techniques weren't as effective as I once thought, it made me question my entire approach to learning – and I suspect I'm not alone. Despite years of formal education, many of us are left with degrees but little understanding of *how* to learn effectively. The good news? Learning is a skill that can be mastered at any stage of life.

The Malleable Brain

Since 1865, London's iconic black taxi drivers have been required to pass a test called 'The Knowledge'. To become fully licensed, they must memorise all 25,000 streets in the city and prove their ability to navigate flawlessly between any two points. The test not only requires efficient route planning but also the ability to recall every landmark on route. Aspiring cab drivers typically spend three to four years driving around on mopeds, learning the city's every nook and cranny. Only 50 per cent of hopefuls pass.

'The Knowledge' is considered one of the most challenging memorization tests in the world. The difficulty lies in the fact that the streets of London have no discernible pattern. Aspiring taxi drivers must meticulously create a mental map, as there is no reliable system to remember the order of the streets.

Curious about the impact of learning 'The Knowledge' on the brain, neuroscientists Eleanor Maguire and Katherine Woollett, followed a group of seventy-nine aspiring cabbies over the course of four years. Before their training, the group showed similar performance on memory tests and had comparable hippocampus sizes. However, post-training, those who passed 'The Knowledge' stood out with improved memory performance and increased volume of their right posterior hippocampus, a part of the brain known to be involved in spatial navigation.[1] Essentially, memorising all the streets in London rewired the brains of the London cabbies.

When we learn something new, a new neural pathway is formed in the brain. The more we repeat the experience, the more it becomes ingrained in our brain's wiring. This process, known as tuning, strengthens connections between neurons and allows signals to travel faster. Consequently, these well-tuned connections become more efficient at carrying and processing information, making them more likely to be used in the future.[2] Or as neuroscientists like to say: 'neurons that fire together, wire together'.[3]

To maximise efficiency, the brain strengthens neural pathways that are frequently used while selectively eliminating those that are rarely activated. This pruning process allows the brain to get rid of what's unnecessary, old and stale, and replace it with new, more useful pathways.

As we acquire fresh knowledge, our neural networks become more complex and interconnected, enhancing our existing capabilities. Think of this process as walking through a field of tall grass. The well-trodden path you usually take represents the knowledge you regularly apply – it's familiar, effortless and instinctive. Your brain has well-established neural connections for this information, just like the clear trail through the grass.

Venturing off this path to forge a new one mirrors the experience of learning something new. It can be challenging at first, as the tall grass resists your progress and you must exert considerable effort to push through. Similarly, your brain must work hard to form new neural pathways when dealing with unfamiliar ideas or mastering a new skill.

Just like a new trail forms in the grass with persistent walking, your brain strengthens new connections through consistent practice and repetition. Over time, the unfamiliar becomes familiar, and the challenging becomes second nature. Instead of one path, you have now created two paths that are interconnected.

The capacity to learn and adapt is strongest during childhood. A child's brain is incredibly malleable and naturally primed to learn and absorb new information effortlessly. Early childhood plays a pivotal role in brain development as our experiences during this time shape how our brains are wired.[4] It takes about twenty-five years for the human brain to reach its full adult structure and function. After the age of twenty-five, our brain becomes less plastic, making it harder to learn new skills and adapt to novel experiences. Nevertheless, as neuroscientists have discovered, the adult brain is capable of change. It can generate new neurons, forge fresh connections between neurons and enhance the efficiency of neural communication.

We are thus never too old to learn. While changing specific neural pathways formed during childhood learning is more challenging and requires effort, there's a silver lining. Unlike children who often learn because they're told to do so by their parents or educators, as adults we have the advantage to pursue learning aligned with our own personal objectives. Intrinsic motivation, as we saw earlier, is a powerful driving force. Self-directed learning tends to be much more effective than coerced education.

However, there will be times when learning feels laborious, and you may feel hard-pressed to continue. In those moments, it can be beneficial to pause and reflect on why you embarked on this learning journey in the first place. Reminding yourself of your personal objectives can rekindle your intrinsic motivation. Are you learning to advance your career, fulfil a passion or acquire a new skill for personal enjoyment? By reconnecting with your 'why', you can find renewed energy and purpose, transforming that struggle into a source of inspiration.

Building Blocks

When I first set out to understand how the brain learns, I felt like I was diving into an ocean without knowing how to swim. The sheer volume of alien concepts like 'neurons', 'synapses' and 'schemas' was overwhelming, and I couldn't connect the dots. Each piece of information seemed isolated, floating around without any clear structure or meaning. It was as if I was trying to assemble a jigsaw puzzle without having seen the picture on the box – it was slow and frustrating work.

I remember sitting at my desk, surrounded by textbooks and articles, feeling completely stuck. Each new concept demanded so much effort to understand because I didn't have a solid grasp of the basics. My brain had no framework to anchor this new knowledge, making the learning process feel disjointed and tedious. Once I learned the basic structure and function of the brain, things started to make more sense. I could integrate new information more easily. It was as if I had sorted the puzzle pieces into groups, making it easier to see how they connected. The learning process became not only faster but also much more enjoyable.

Why does this happen? Our brain is a complex network consisting of billions of neurons (the nodes) that communicate through synapses (the connections). When we learn something new, neurons fire and form new synaptic connections. However, without any prior knowledge, these connections have no anchor points, making it difficult for new information to stick. If you're trying to learn about quantum physics without any background in physics, each concept feels foreign and isolated. You have no framework to relate 'wave-particle duality' or 'quantum entanglement' to anything familiar, making the process slow and laborious.

This is where *schemas* come into play. While cognitive scientists don't seem to agree on the exact definition, in essence schemas are mental models formed in our long-term memory that help our brain organise and interpret information. They act as frameworks that allow us to categorise new information in relation to what we already know.[5]

The process of forming a schema involves a series of interconnected steps. We first assimilate the new information into our existing schemas. If the new information doesn't quite fit, our brain accommodates by adjusting old schemas or creating new ones. Our brain then organises this information into intricate networks, forming complex schemas that aid us in understanding and predicting our world.

For instance, a child who knows what a dog is might initially label a wolf as a 'dog' because they both have four legs, pointed ears, sharp teeth and a bushy tail. Once her parents explain that a wolf is different from a dog, she forms two distinct schemas. The dog-schema includes characteristics like being domesticated, friendly, varied in size and breed, living in houses and barking. Meanwhile, her wolf-schema might include traits like being wild, living in forests, howling instead of barking and eating grandmothers. Once she grows older and realises that *Little Red Riding Hood* is a fairy tale, she'll adapt her wolf-schema again.

The strength of our schemas is reinforced through repeated exposure and practice. The more we encounter and use certain information, the more robust the corresponding schemas become. These well-established schemas provide a framework for organising new information, making it easier to identify patterns, draw connections and generate insights.

If we encounter new information that aligns with existing schemas we also remember it better. When researchers asked participants to remember a rubber duck in two different scenarios – one placed in a bathroom and another one in a toy store – they consistently remembered the duck in the bathroom better because it fit neatly into their existing bathroom schema. In contrast, a rubber duck doesn't align as well with the typical items found in a toy store, making it harder to recall.[6]

Schemas are crucial for learning. When we try to learn something that is new for us, like a new language, we cannot activate any schemas yet. We can only store information in our brain that fits in the hippocampus. Storage in the hippocampus is small, as we saw in Chapter 4, and it is only cleared when we sleep. Learning is therefore slow and tedious. But once we have prior knowledge about the language, we have some schemas stored in the cortex and it becomes much easier to integrate new information and adapt existing schemas when necessary.

While schemas serve as building blocks for knowledge, they can also become barriers if not updated or if we stay closed to new perspectives. Schemas can lead to overgeneralizations and stereotypes that block us from seeing the unique attributes of a person or situation.[7] They can stifle learning as our brain focuses on what fits and ignores what doesn't, a phenomenon known as *confirmation bias*.[8] We will explore this in greater detail in Part 3, but first, let's look at how developing expertise depends on building and refining schemas.

The Road to Excellence

In 1938, Adriaan de Groot, a Dutch psychologist and chess master, wondered what set grandmasters apart from lesser players. After analysing the decision-making processes of various players during a chess tournament, he discovered that a grandmaster's advantage lay not in being better at planning ahead or having the ability to consider more possible moves. What set them apart was their ability to swiftly identify the right move and discard inferior options.

Intrigued by his findings, de Groot conducted a second experiment. This time, he briefly showed players a chessboard, tasking them to memorise and recreate it. The result: grandmasters could almost flawlessly recall the positions of the pieces, whereas less skilled players only remembered a handful of them. Instead of seeing thirty-two separate pieces, grandmasters instantly recognised strategic patterns – like the Panov attack or the Queen's Gambit. Like SF, the Carnegie Mellon undergraduate we met in Chapter 4, they chunked pieces together to recall their positions more easily.[9]

Later research showed that skilled chess players didn't just form chunks, but also extracted much more information from them. Years of practice had equipped them with a mental library of countless chess configurations. This allowed them to quickly assess the board, recognise patterns and determine their next move with remarkable speed and accuracy.[10]

These and other studies demonstrate that experts don't rely

so much on stronger analytical skills – chess-masters are equally bad at remembering random arrangements of chess pieces as novices. Their advantage comes from an organised store of knowledge acquired through practice. Similarly, veteran firefighters don't deliberate in the throes of a crisis; they draw from related experiences and intuitively decide how to best approach the fire.[11]

Within their fields, experts see the world differently, noticing things that non-experts overlook. They process information quickly, focus on the most relevant details and instinctively know what to do with it. What's the secret to building such a knowledge library? It boils down to one thing: continuous learning and practice.

How long do we need to practice before becoming an expert? While 10,000 hours is often cited, this number oversimplifies reality.[12] Certain areas of expertise are inherently more complicated and the level of competitiveness in a field can raise the bar for how much effort is needed. Additionally, individual differences mean some people may require more practice than others.[13]

Swedish psychologist Anders Ericsson, who extensively studied expertise and human performance, found that how you practice matters far more than the number of hours spent. Experts don't just repeat what they already know; they actively push their limits, working on challenging tasks and targeting their weak spots. For example, professional musicians focus on the most difficult sections of a piece, and elite figure skaters dedicate more time to perfecting the most difficult jumps and spins.[14]

This is called *deliberate practice*; a method of learning that centres around focused, intentional practice aimed at improving specific skills. Unlike regular practice, which might involve repetition without a clear goal, deliberate practice requires clear goal setting, immediate feedback and constantly challenging yourself just beyond your current abilities. It won't come as a surprise that deliberate practice is demanding and requires sustained effort over a long period.[15]

The extent to which deliberate practice accounts for individual differences between experts and novices remains a topic of debate.

Ericsson holds the view that deliberate practice explains a great deal, while others argue that natural talent, intelligence and the age at which one begins also play important roles.[16] Regardless, everyone agrees that there's no shortcut to becoming an expert. It demands dedication, passion and resilience, but when you love what you're doing, the journey becomes rewarding in itself.

Whether you're striving to become an expert or simply looking to pick up a new skill, your approach to learning can make all the difference. And if you're anything like me, chances are you've never encountered the techniques we're about to explore.

The Learning Lab

On a quiet Sunday morning, I snuggled up on the couch. It was one of those early spring days and the warmth of the sunlight seeped through the window caressing my skin. On the side table a steaming mug of freshly brewed coffee accompanied me in this moment of tranquillity and solitude.

On my lap was the book *A Mind for Numbers* by Barbara Oakley; a present that had been sitting unread on my bookshelf. A friend had bought it for me when I told her about my quest to unravel the secrets to effective learning. With her recommendation ringing in my ears, I flipped open the book and began to read.

Diving into its pages, I came across an intriguing concept: 'the illusion of competence'. As Oakley explained, merely reading a text creates a deceptive impression that it's imprinted in our brain.[17] A theory I found hard to believe. After all, I'd always heavily relied on repetitious reading as my method of study.

Yet, gripped by curiosity, I decided to run a little test on myself. I shut the book and attempted to recall what I'd just read. To my dismay, the crisp, clear text that had made perfect sense minutes ago was now a blurry memory. Suddenly, the 'illusion of competence' wasn't a theoretical concept anymore. It was an uncomfortable reality I faced on that sunny Sunday morning.

That day marked a turning point in my approach to learning.

I realised it was time to evolve beyond my old habits and outdated study techniques and adopt superior strategies instead. I discovered three main learning habits – active recall, spaced repetition and active learning – that can significantly improve our ability to retain what we've learned.

Habit 1: Active recall

Active recall is a powerful learning technique that involves actively retrieving information from memory rather than simply passively reviewing it. Instead of just rereading or highlighting text, it requires engaging with the material by recalling key concepts, facts or ideas from memory. This process strengthens neural connections and boosts memory by forcing the brain to actively retrieve and reconstruct information.

Practising active recall leads to deeper learning, better long-term retention and improved comprehension, compared to passive study methods.[18] By regularly testing ourselves through active recall, we can reinforce our understanding of the material, identify gaps in our knowledge and develop stronger memory recall skills over time.

While a powerful technique, I find using active recall challenging and regularly face an internal tug of war: shall I continue reading, hoping for the information to stick, or pause for a short recall that might reveal I've retained very little? Sometimes I use it; other times I don't. Active recall is more effortful than passive reading, but I've found a few strategies that make the process easier:

- **Segment your reading**: Try breaking your reading into 25-minute slots followed by a short recall session (remember the Pomodoro Technique!) This practice can gradually become a habit executed while taking a sip of water or going to the bathroom.

- **Be selective when highlighting**: When you keep underlining or highlighting sparse, it's easier to recall key ideas.

It helps to start by identifying main ideas before making any marks. Limit yourself to highlighting at most a sentence, preferably less, per paragraph. Overdoing it can inadvertently feed the 'illusion of competence' as the hand's movement can trick you into believing you've understood something you haven't.[19]

- **Doodling**: Drawing something in the margins that reflects the key concept you're trying to remember can aid recall. It takes time and you might find it hard to think of an image, but it can be worth a try to see if it works for you.

Habit 2: Spaced repetition

You've likely experienced this: you read a book or studied hard for a test, only to realise a few days later that you've forgotten most of it. As we discussed in Chapter 4, this is a common experience known as the forgetting curve. We tend to forget around 50 per cent of what we've learned after just one day, and by the end of the week, only about 25 per cent remains. It can be incredibly frustrating to put in the effort to learn something, only to have it slip away so quickly.

Fortunately, spaced repetition offers a powerful solution to combat the forgetting curve. Rather than cramming all the material into one intense study session, spaced repetition involves revisiting the information at strategically spaced intervals, allowing for better retention and long-term memory formation.[20] Most language-learning apps, like Duolingo, are built on this very principle.

There doesn't appear to be any strict rules about timing, but spaced repetition seems most effective when the first review takes place shortly after the initial learning session – ideally within a few hours or a day. This first step is critical because without it, our natural metabolic processes will cause the memory trace to fade. Subsequent reviews should then be spaced out over increasingly longer intervals – days, weeks and even months – allowing the memory to strengthen while reducing the effort required for relearning. The exact timing will vary depending on the complexity of the material and your individual learning pace, so it's worth experimenting to find what works best for you.

Spaced repetition is so effective because it fortifies the neural connections tied to the information. By prompting our brain to reactivate the memory just before it's about to fade, each review session essentially 'resets' the forgetting curve, strengthening the memory trace with each pass. This technique also allows us to focus on what hasn't been retained yet, connecting it to what's already stored in long-term memory. Especially when combined with active recall, it's one of the most effective strategies for learning.[21]

Habit 3: Active learning

The third habit that makes learning more effective is active learning – a type of learning where we actively engage with the material rather than simply memorising or observing it. It involves taking notes, asking questions and participating in discussions. Extensive research has shown that students learn more when they are actively engaged in the classroom than they do in a passive lecture environment.[22] We can apply this outside the classroom too.

When we are actively engaged, we're more likely to remember what we've learned because we are not just passively absorbing information, but actively processing and integrating it with our existing knowledge. Here are some strategies that I've come across that you can consider adopting:

- **Self-quizzing**: You can test your knowledge by creating flashcards or quiz questions based on the material you're learning. When you quiz yourself regularly, you reinforce memory retrieval and can identify areas that require further review.

- **Teaching others**: Explain what you've just learned to a friend, family member, colleague or even yourself. Teaching others requires you to organise your thoughts, articulate ideas clearly and ensure your understanding is comprehensive. Sharing what you've learned with others is like learning it twice.

- **Note-taking**: When done right, note-taking can greatly enhance the chance that you remember what you've learned. Shortly, we'll discuss tools for efficient note-taking.
- **Concentrate on meaning**: Focus on understanding the underlying concepts rather than just memorising facts. By relating new information to what you already know, you can create a deeper, more meaningful connection that enhances retention.[23]
- **Seek feedback**: It can help to ask for feedback on your understanding of the material from peers, mentors, or online communities. Incorporating such feedback can help to refine your learning approach and address areas of weakness.

Much like the other skills we've explored, learning is a skill that can be developed. Anyone can refine their learning and studying ability. By adopting one, two or all the learning habits, you'll find that you become a stronger, more capable learner. And if you're ready to take it a step further, there's more you can do.

The Efficient Learner

In the iconic white tent of *The Great British Bake-Off* contestants face the ultimate challenge of baking under pressure. Each week, bakers are given a series of tasks – a signature bake, a technical challenge and a showstopper. They must manage their ingredients, tools and, most critically, their time, to create bakes that not only taste delicious but also look impeccable.

Upon receiving their assignment, each contestant plans their steps meticulously, knowing that every moment and movement counts. To achieve the desired texture and flavours, each ingredient is measured with precision, mixed together to attain the perfect consistency and then baked at the ideal temperature for the exact amount of time.

With the clock ticking, choosing the right balance of speed and precision is paramount. The most successful bakers are those who can seamlessly move between tasks, allowing doughs to rise as custards cool, and have the agility to adjust on the fly if things don't go as planned. The victors are not only highly creative bakers, but also masterful time managers and resilient problem-solvers.

The Great British Bake-Off is a masterclass in economic efficiency. Resources have to be used optimally in order to yield excellent results. Similarly, achieving the best learning outcomes requires us to use our resources – time, energy and intellect – as efficiently as possible. Besides utilising the learning strategies we just explored, there are some other things we can do to boost our learning efficiency:

Attention

Paying attention is crucial for effective learning. It's the difference between simply hearing information and truly absorbing it. By actively focusing on what we're learning, our brain is able to take in, understand and retain new information more effectively. Attention acts as a spotlight, brightening the critical details needed to fully comprehend the information.

Interestingly, our brain is surprisingly adept at picking up relevant information even without our conscious awareness. For example, have you ever been engrossed in conversation at a party but still managed to hear someone speak your name from across the room? This is known as the *cocktail party effect* – a remarkable demonstration of our brain's alertness to specific, relevant information even amidst numerous distractions.[24]

Still, to truly optimise our learning, proactive attention is key. By giving our undivided attention to what we're studying, we allow our brain to allocate cognitive resources more efficiently. Therefore, minimising distractions really helps – whether it's turning off your phone and email, finding a quiet space or investing in noise-cancelling headphones. Attention isn't just a tool for learning; it's the foundation.

Neural hooks
A while back I stumbled upon RIOPY, a French-British pianist and composer who is somehow able to express intricate emotions and narratives without uttering a single word. I find his music intensely beautiful and it puts me in a relaxed state in which I can focus very well. Ever since I discovered his music, it's been my constant companion when writing.

As with so many things, scientists don't seem to agree on whether music is helpful or a distraction while learning. It seems to depend on the type of music – music that is loud or with lyrics tends to be more distracting – and on individual characteristics, like age.[25] However, for me, the serene piano music works wonders. It calms my mind, while tuning out other noises that I find disruptive.

More than that, the music acts as a powerful cue for my brain to switch to 'focus mode'. By consistently playing the same music during intense work sessions, I've conditioned my brain to link this particular music to deep concentration. To make the 'focus-cue' stronger, I also apply the same hand cream with a distinctive fragrance every time a focus session is about to begin. Similar to Pavlov's dogs responding to a bell, I've conditioned myself to respond to music and smell.

Playing the same music and smelling the same scent doesn't only provide mental cues; it also bolsters recall of information, a phenomenon called *context-dependent memory*. Context refers to the circumstances or setting in which information is learned. This includes the physical environment, emotional state or the sensory contexts such as smell or music. By linking specific contexts with information, we effectively 'tag' our memories with environmental cues. This makes it easier to retrieve those tagged memories when we encounter similar conditions or emotional states in the future.[26]

The phenomenon was illustrated in 1975 by psychologists Duncan Godden and Alan Baddeley who asked divers to memorise a list of words. Some were asked to do this underwater, others on land. Interestingly, divers who learned and recalled words in the same environment – either underwater or on land – remembered significantly more words than those who switched environments.[27] Many other studies have demonstrated this context-effect also in more common surroundings. So, if you want to boost your recall, consider studying in the same environment where you'll need to remember the information. This simple strategy can make a surprising difference when it's time to retrieve what you've learned.

Stress
The human body is designed for survival, and stress is a part of that survival mechanism. Whenever danger strikes, our body springs into action, flooding our system with stress hormones like cortisol and adrenaline. The result is an acceleration in heartbeat, blood pressure and energy levels, prepping us up for the 'fight or flight' response.

Stress also triggers a shift in our brain functioning. Our emotional centre, the amygdala, goes into overdrive while our decision-making and self-control unit, the prefrontal cortex, steps back to let instinctual responses take over. This process ensures that we can quickly evaluate the situation and decide how to react. It's essential for survival: when a lion is approaching, you don't want to be contemplating your dinner options.

While stress plays a crucial role in our lives, prolonged exposure can wreak havoc on both brain and body. Chronic stress keeps our bodies in a perpetual state of alarm, flooding us with stress hormones. This exacts a toll on our health, contributing to cardiovascular problems, weakened immunity and disrupted sleep patterns, to name a few.[28]

Inside the brain, chronic stress leads to important changes. It inhibits the growth of new cells in the hippocampus, the brain's memory centre, and causes the prefrontal cortex to shrink. Meanwhile, the amygdala – which plays a key role in processing emotions – grows larger and becomes more active.[29] These neurological changes impair clear thinking and can lead to memory problems, difficulty managing emotions and heightened levels of anxiety and depression over time.

While chronic stress is undeniably harmful, acute stress – short-lived stress triggered by specific situations – can actually boost cognitive performance when experienced in moderation. The relationship follows an inverted U-shape: very little or a lot of stress results in worse performance compared to moderate stress levels.[30] Picture an impending exam or major deadline. Too little stress breeds complacency, often resulting in procrastination and ineffective preparation. Conversely, excessive stress overwhelms, triggering panic, anxiety and a scattered mind incapable of focusing effectively. In contrast, moderate stress acts as a catalyst, motivating us to organise our time efficiently and rise to the challenge at hand. It fosters a sense of urgency that drives focused effort and can enhance performance.

When stress hits – a sudden realisation that a crucial deadline looms just three days away – our brain shifts gears. Executive control steps back as the amygdala takes charge. Our focus sharpens, processing speeds up and everything else seems to fade away. The amygdala, in its heightened state, makes us more attentive to the material and ensures information sticks. But there's a trade-off. With executive control functions sidelined, our cognitive flexibility and decision-making abilities take a hit. It's a short-term disruption, though. Once the initial wave of stress subsides, our executive control functions gradually return, often with renewed clarity.[31]

The acute stress response thus acts as a catalyst, spurring us into action and pushing us forward. The challenge lies in regulating the stress response – keeping it in check so our brain can naturally restore balance. This obviously is often easier said than done. When you are already feeling stressed and see the clock ticking away while you're staring at a blank page, it's hard not to get more stressed. However, recent research offers hope. Neuroscientists discovered that it's possible to train people to downregulate the amygdala or upregulate the executive control network. These findings hint at our ability to actively control our stress levels more than we previously thought.[32]

How can we leverage the benefits of acute stress without letting it overwhelm us? While further research is needed, focusing on our breathing looks like a good place to start. Various breathing techniques seem effective in reducing stress and promoting a sense of calmness and well-being:[33]

- **Deep belly breathing**, or diaphragmatic breathing, involves breathing deeply into the abdomen rather than shallowly into the chest. Sit or lie down comfortably with your spine straight. You can close your eyes to enhance focus. Place one hand on your chest and the other on your abdomen. Inhale deeply through your nose, allowing your abdomen to rise as you fill your lungs with air. Keep your chest relatively still. Exhale slowly through your mouth or nose, letting your abdomen naturally fall. Repeat for several minutes, aiming for a slow and steady rhythm.

- **Box breathing**, or equal breathing, is a controlled pattern where each phase – inhale, hold, exhale, hold – is equal, typically lasting four seconds each. Sit or lie down comfortably with your spine straight. Inhale deeply through your nose, counting to four as you fill your lungs. Focus on expanding your abdomen, not lifting your shoulders. Hold your breath for four seconds to allow oxygen absorption. Exhale slowly through your mouth or nose for four seconds, fully emptying your lungs. Pause for another four seconds before beginning the next cycle.

- **4-7-8 breathing**, or relaxing breathing, is similar to box breathing but now you inhale for a count of four, holding the breath for a count of seven and exhaling slowly for a count of eight. Repeat the cycle three more times, for a total of four breath cycles. This completes one round of 4-7-8 breathing.

Preparing yourself adequately before facing a stressful situation can make a world of difference. Arriving early not only gives you time to settle in but also allows for a moment of quiet reflection or a leisurely stroll outside. These moments can be invaluable for calming nerves and collecting your thoughts before the intensity ramps up. Try listening to soothing music as you mentally prepare. It's a simple yet effective way to create a serene space amidst potential chaos. Anything that can amplify jitters or fuel unnecessary stress — even that extra cup of coffee — is best to be avoided. Opting for herbal tea or simply hydrating with water can help to keep your mind clear and your body balanced.

As we'll explore in more detail in Chapter 9, our mindset about stress also plays a pivotal role in how we experience and manage it. How we perceive stress determines whether it becomes a hindrance or an ally. When we perceive stress negatively, it tends to manifest as a heavy burden. But when we see it as a potential motivator and enabler, it can become a powerful tool for growth and achievement.[34]

A key step towards shifting your mindset is to actively reframe your thoughts. Instead of focusing on daunting thoughts like, 'I'll never meet the deadline' or 'This is too much', try to create a more empowering narrative. Reflect on past successes in similar situations, affirm your ability to tackle challenges with a methodical plan and break tasks down into manageable steps. By consciously shifting your thoughts from doubt and overwhelm to optimism and resilience, you can alter your stress response into a positive force.

Everyone's experience with stress is unique, making it crucial to find strategies that work best for you. During particularly stressful periods, ensure you take regular breaks and get ample rest to prevent stress from becoming chronic. A good indicator of effective stress management is the ability to sleep well after a stressful day.

If stress becomes persistent or overwhelming, consider seeking professional help to receive personalised coping strategies and therapeutic interventions tailored to your specific needs.

Sticky Notes

For a long time, my iPad served mainly as a device for leisure activities like playing music, catching up on the news, scrolling through my social media feed or streaming movies while travelling. Considering its price tag, I began to regret the purchase due to its seemingly limited use. However, buying an Apple pen dramatically changed this. Nowadays my iPad and pen are indispensable work tools.

I've always been an avid note-taker. In pursuit of efficiency, I transitioned years ago from traditional pen and paper to note-taking on my laptop. The digital method seemed superior, as the typed notes could be swiftly organised and searched, which presented a significant advantage over the scattered physical notebooks I was using for my various research projects and tasks.

Switching to digital note-taking definitely made retrieving my notes easier, but I suspected it negatively affected my ability to recall the information. Buying my Apple pen prompted me to test this hunch. I found an app that facilitated digital notebook creation and in combination with my pen I recreated my old pen-and-paper setup. The first time I tried it was at a seminar and I freely doodled away. Afterwards, I noticed how much more I remembered from that seminar. Since then, I've fully returned to handwritten notes.

Interestingly, research corroborates my experience. Psychologists Pam Mueller and Daniel Oppenheimer tracked the learning progress of two groups of students – one taking notes on their laptops and the other writing them down by hand. Those who wrote their notes by hand showed a better grasp and retention of the study material than their laptop-using counterparts. The improvement in comprehension was mostly related to conceptual questions. Both groups performed equally well when it came to recalling facts. This suggests that the act of handwriting notes might engage cognitive processes that enhance deeper comprehension and learning.[35]

The distraction potential when taking notes on laptops is well-known but this study showed that even if laptops are exclusively used for note-taking, learning can get hampered. The reason being that when notes are typed, they tend to mirror the speaker's words more than handwritten notes. This kind of mindless dictation is accompanied by 'shallower' information processing, which reduces the likelihood of recall. When we write notes by hand, we tend to be more actively involved, facilitating deeper information processing.[36]

When done right, note-taking not only captures key information for future review (external storage) but also aids comprehension and retention through encoding of the material. Here are some strategies you can consider to make your notes stick better:

- **Choose the right tools**: Typing notes may be preferable for meeting minutes or concrete action points. However, for deeper processing, handwriting, either on paper or its digital equivalent, seems superior. Many note-taking apps these days can swiftly convert handwritten content to typed letters and have search functions.

- **Identify your purpose**: The goal of taking notes during a lecture is very different from note-taking during a weekly meeting with your team. By being clear on your intention with your notes, it's easier to distinguish between information that's relevant to you and information that's not.

- **Focus on key points**: Effective note-taking is about capturing crucial information, not transcribing verbatim. If you're not already doing so, consider training yourself to identify and prioritise key points and main ideas.

- **Develop shorthand**: A shorthand system of your own symbols, abbreviations or acronyms for common phrases or recurring terms accelerates note-taking and reduces writing time.

- **Use visuals**: Your brain excels at remembering visuals and a picture can say more than 1,000 words. In particular, if you are a visual learner, adding pictures to your notes can greatly boost recall. Using different fonts, colours, frames or arrows helps to organise individual pieces of information and establish relationships among them.

- **Review and reflect**: You might be keen to quickly move on to the next thing, but reviewing notes shortly after learning reinforces memory consolidation and helps fill in any gaps in comprehension.

- **Experiment with note-taking methods**: Various note-taking methods have been developed. Each have their own pros and cons and differ in their suitability for various types of content. Have a look online to find one that fits your needs best.

Effective note-taking is a personalised process that should align with your individual learning preferences and goals. Experiment with different techniques and adapt them to suit your unique needs and circumstances. And remember, we can only write down what we pay attention to, so consider keeping distractions, like your phone, out of reach during meetings, lectures or presentations.

Effective note-taking shapes what we retain. But how we read influences what we absorb in the first place. And speed is not all that matters.

Reading, Fast and Slow

About four decades ago, psychology professor Donald Homa received an intriguing request from the American Speed Reading Academy. A specialist in memory and linguistic visual perception, his expertise was sought to validate an exceptional feat. Two students had reportedly mastered the art of reading at a staggering speed of 100,000 words per minute. This was not only ten times more than their peers, but also a whopping 300 times more than an average college graduate would read (200–400 words per minute). Keen to examine this phenomenon, Homa agreed to conduct controlled tests in his lab.

The students were given the challenge of reading an entire college-level textbook, and then prove their comprehension through a multiple-choice test. They adeptly swept through the text in less than six minutes, with reading speeds between 15,000–30,000 words per minute. However, they failed the test on all three attempts. Evidently, they could read fast but without much comprehension. Homa concluded that, 'the only extraordinary talent exhibited by these two speed-readers was their extraordinary rate of page-turning'.[37]

While we cannot draw strong conclusions from a study with only two participants, other studies echo Homa's findings. The notion of speed-reading as a quick fix to consuming information doesn't hold up under scientific scrutiny.

In today's digital age, we often find ourselves bombarded with information – emails, reports, social media updates, books, magazines, just to name a few. Keeping up with this constant stream of information can feel overwhelming, but it's often needed for staying informed and connected. So the question is, how can we process all this information efficiently?

Successful reading is more complex than merely recognising words quickly. It involves understanding the text's intended meaning, the connections between words and deciphering the implications that are not directly stated. Efficient reading is a balance between reading speed and comprehension.

Speed-reading proponents and courses often promise a significant boost in our reading speed without compromising comprehension. They suggest strategies like absorbing more words with fewer eye movements and quieting our inner reading voice. However, decades of research, recently reviewed by a team led by the late psychologist Keith Rayner, a leading expert in reading, reveals that these two methods don't help improve reading efficiency.[38]

Firstly, our retina isn't good at distinguishing light and dark areas beyond its central focus, which makes comprehending text in our peripheral vision challenging. Basically, it's not biologically nor cognitively possible to understand a whole block of words or lines of text in one glance. Experiments have repeatedly shown that the peripheral vision of speed-readers is not superior to that of normal readers.[39]

Secondly, while silencing our inner reading voice can speed up our reading, it comes at the cost of decreased comprehension. Inner speech (subvocalization) seems to play an important role in identifying and understanding words. Thus, trying to eliminate subvocalization is not necessarily going to help.

What about speed reading apps? Most of these present words one at a time in a constant spot, allowing users to control the speed. The idea, known as 'rapid serial visual presentation', is to fixate the reader's gaze and eliminate eye movement. These apps also eliminate regression – brief looks backward to reread certain words. However, as users increase the text speed, their comprehension levels tend to dip. Furthermore, regression tends to support comprehension rather than causing a problem for reading. Just like the traditional speed-reading methods, science doesn't back up the promise of these apps.[40]

What the research shows is that there is a trade-off between speed and accuracy. Language processing, not the ability to control eye movements, is the primary determinant of reading speed. Our ability to identify and understand words, rather than our ability to see them, limits our reading.[41] Consequently, it's unlikely that we can double or triple our reading speed while still being able to understand the text as well as if we'd read it at normal speed.

Still, some people can read exceptionally quick and still maintain comprehension. The skill that these people seem to have acquired is an exceptional ability to effectively skim. Effective speed-readers appear to be intelligent people who already know a great deal about the topic they are reading about; they are able to successfully skim the material at rapid rates and accept the lowered comprehension that accompanies skimming. They also seem to have honed the skill of deducing reasonably accurate inferences about the text from partial information and their preexisting knowledge (a process called *extended inferencing*).[42]

From what I can tell, an easily mastered technique that guarantees both high reading speed and comprehension doesn't exist. However, there are strategies that can enhance reading efficiency. The key is recognising that different reading goals require different approaches. A skilled reader is adaptable, adjusting their pace based on the material, time of day, environment and focus level. It's unrealistic to expect to read technical material as quickly as fiction. Setting a clear reading goal helps determine the necessary comprehension level and the maximum achievable speed.

Being flexible with your reading speed within a single text is also beneficial. Some parts may be easy to grasp, allowing you to breeze through without pausing on every word. Conversely, when encountering new terminology or complex concepts, a slower pace is necessary to ensure understanding. This variation is common, and by adjusting your pace accordingly, you can maximise speed without sacrificing comprehension.

If complete, detailed comprehension isn't the goal, skimming might do the trick. Start by scanning the text for headings, paragraph structure or keywords to quickly identify relevant information. Once you've found those key areas, shift to a more focused reading. Pay particular attention to the beginnings and endings of paragraphs, as these often hold the most important points. Skimming can also help you decide whether a text is worth diving into or whether it's better set aside. It's a very useful skill for managing an overwhelming amount of reading, as long as you're willing to trade a bit of accuracy for speed.

Here are a few other tools that I came across that you could try out to boost your reading speed while maintaining comprehension:

- **Stay focused**: Maintaining focus and concentration enhances your comprehension. Reading below your natural pace can leave your mind bored and prone to wandering off. Compare it to driving. When driving slowly, it's easy to get distracted by your surroundings; when in a race car, your full focus is required. The Pomodoro Technique can help maintain focus. Set a 25-minute timer and aim to continue reading at your normal (or slightly faster) pace until the timer rings.

- **Use a visual pacer**: Moving your finger or a pen along the text as you read can help increase reading speed. It helps to maintain focus by providing a reference point and active engagement with the text. By encouraging a steady and rhythmic movement of the eyes it provides a metronomic guide. It can also prevent unnecessary regression.

- **Skim before reading**: This gives you an overview of the text's structure, main ideas and key points, helping to organise your thoughts. It enables you to activate your prior knowledge and make connections. Both processes create neural hooks, making it easier to understand and retain information when you read the text in depth.

- **Ask questions**: Asking questions about the text improves your engagement with the material. This helps to maintain focus as your brain doesn't like open loops and will start searching for answers. Confusion often experienced during skimming can be helpful as it can spark questions that the brain wants answers to.

- **Push your limits**: Regularly challenging your reading speed while maintaining comprehension can strengthen your 'reading muscle'. If you find yourself coasting (reading slower than your actual pace), push yourself to increase your pace. You'll likely find it actually enhances your understanding.

Ultimately, what matters in reading speed is how quickly you can identify a word, a process that speeds up with familiarity. Thus, the secret to increasing speed is to read more. Practising reading is admittedly time-consuming but becomes easier when you turn it into a habit. Reading – either digitally or on paper – just 20–25 minutes each day will allow you to finish a book in one to two weeks, on average, which will greatly enhance your reading ability. Great readers read often. Now you know their secret.

One Size Does Not Fit All

There I stood on the podium, hands slightly damp with anticipation, adjusting the microphone in preparation for my talk. I observed the sea of curious and expectant faces in the dimly lit auditorium. I was about to present my latest research on the impact of the global financial crisis on small businesses. Presenting to my peers wasn't new to me, and I found it rather exhilarating.

With a deep, steadying breath, I launched into my presentation. My meticulous preparation anchored me, driving away the initial butterflies. Clicking through my slides, I carefully outlined my methodology, findings and conclusions, my voice steady and relaxed.

After my presentation ended, I returned to my seat, feeling the familiar knot of anxiety tighten in my stomach. I knew what was about to come – the critique from my peers. A respected researcher in my field ascended the podium and began her discussion of my work. I listened intently and nodded along as she highlighted its main conclusions.

But as she started dissecting my methodology, keeping up became more challenging. Her words seemed to blur together, leaving me feeling somewhat lost and confused. My mind was racing to keep up with her critique. What had she said about the sample I used? And what was her suggestion for addressing potential confounding factors? I tried but struggled to grasp the finer points of her feedback.

As the floor was opened to questions from the audience, a wave of apprehension flooded me. I anticipated thoughtful questions from my colleagues, but I feared I couldn't fully understand them, let alone deliver coherent replies. Sure enough, as the questions began to pour in, I found myself struggling to comprehend their meaning. My mind felt foggy and my thoughts scattered as I attempted to process the many questions.

Summoning all my expertise and knowledge, I steadied myself and made the best attempt to provide insightful responses. As the Q&A session ended, I breathed a sigh of relief. Yet, the nagging feeling of falling short lingered; the feeling that I'd failed to clearly communicate my ideas. It was only on the following day, when I revisited the discussant's slides and reflected on the audience's questions, that I managed to formulate concise responses and articulate my thoughts with the clarity that had eluded me in the heat of the moment.

For a long time, I mistook my struggle to respond to questions and feedback for a lack of intelligence, which only aggravated my imposter syndrome. However, I eventually discovered this wasn't true at all. Through various brain-training tools, I discovered that while I excel at visual processing tasks, I struggle with auditory processing tasks, suggesting that my brain is less adept at quickly interpreting and responding to auditory information. It made me realise that my struggles were not a reflection of my intelligence, but rather a manifestation of how diverse our processing abilities can be.

A conversation with Uta Noppeney, a professor of neuroscience and expert in sensory processing, shed more light on my experience. She explained that our ability to understand speech in noisy environments can diminish as we age. It becomes more challenging to separate the source we're interested in from extraneous noises, requiring significant cognitive effort. Consequently, we have less brain power left to understand the complex information sent our way. The ability to discern speech in noisy environments tends to be harder for non-native language speakers.

These insights were a game-changer for me. We all excel in some areas, while in others, we may face challenges. Some of us are quick problem-solvers, others may have a flair for words and some may exhibit exceptional spatial abilities. Recognising our cognitive strengths and weaknesses is an important step towards harnessing them to our advantage.

To truly grasp how diverse we can be, I've found the Cattell-Horn-Carroll (CHC) theory of cognitive abilities particularly insightful.[43] This theory, one of the most widely accepted models of human intelligence, offers a detailed, hierarchical structure of our cognitive abilities. It integrates decades of research and offers a nuanced view. According to the CHC theory, intelligence is not a single entity but a diverse palette of abilities organised into three levels.

On top of this hierarchy, we find *General Intelligence* or 'g'. This represents a broad cognitive capability that influences our performance in various tasks. It gives us a rough measure of our overall cognitive ability.

Moving down the hierarchy, we encounter ten *Broad Abilities*, which further dissect our cognitive strengths. These include our capacity to solve novel problems (fluid intelligence), our proficiency in literacy-related tasks (reading/writing ability), and our ability to use learned knowledge (crystallised intelligence), hold and manipulate information over short periods (short-term memory) or perform simple cognitive tasks quickly (processing speed), to name a few.

At the bottom level are *Narrow Abilities*, the specific skills that fall under the broad categories. These narrow abilities are highly specialised, highlighting the precise ways in which our brains shine or could use some sharpening. Phonetic coding –

which falls under the broader category of auditory processing – is one example. It's a skill that allows us to recognise and manipulate sounds of speech, which is crucial for language development, reading proficiency and effective communication.

The CHC theory highlights the diversity of our cognitive abilities. For instance, you might excel at recognising patterns and have strong spatial awareness, yet find quick decision-making challenging. Conversely, someone else might have exceptional auditory processing skills, enabling them to quickly absorb spoken instructions, but struggle with visual-spatial tasks like map-reading. Tests like the Woodcock-Johnson IV and the Wechsler Adult Intelligence Scale (WAIS-IV) can help you gain a clearer understanding of your unique cognitive profile. By identifying your strengths and weaknesses, you can leverage your abilities more effectively and navigate your learning journey with greater self-awareness and acceptance.

The Key Takeaways

Learning is a lifelong journey that doesn't depend on age or experience. Continuous acquisition of new knowledge and skills helps you grow in both your personal and professional lives. Effective learning isn't just about exposure to information; it's about how you engage with it. Techniques such as active recall, spaced repetition and active learning significantly enhance your ability to retain and apply new knowledge. By recognising your cognitive strengths and weaknesses, you can tailor your learning strategies for optimal results.

- Neuroplasticity – the brain's incredible ability to reorganise and form new neural connections throughout life – is key to learning. This dynamic process helps you adapt to new experiences and acquire new skills. Although it's most pronounced in childhood, neuroplasticity continues to play a vital role in learning and adaptation throughout your life.

- Schemas help you learn by organising and interpreting new information based on what you already know. They act as mental frameworks, making it easier to process and remember new concepts.

- To become an expert, it's not enough to simply practise; it's important to engage in deliberate practice. This means consistently working towards specific goals, pushing yourself beyond your comfort zone and seeking constructive feedback.

- Effective learning strategies like active recall, spaced repetition and active learning boost your ability to retain and apply new information. Active recall reinforces memory by encouraging retrieval of information, while spaced repetition spreads out review sessions for better long-term retention. Active learning implies engaging in hands-on activities, like self-quizzing, teaching others or note-taking.

- Learning efficiency can be improved by minimising distractions when learning. Creating 'neural hooks' aids focus and retention. Try listening to the same music, using a particular scent or studying in the same space. Such associations help your brain link new information to familiar cues, enhancing memory and recall.

- While chronic stress is undeniably bad, acute stress, in moderation, can be a powerful motivator, enhancing cognitive performance and focus. Effective stress regulation involves recognising stress triggers, employing calming techniques like deep breathing and positive reframing, and adopting a mindset that stress can enable you to perform better.

- Effective note-taking boosts information retention. Consider writing by hand for better recall and using visual aids like pictures, colours and frames to illustrate complex ideas and relationships among them. Regularly reviewing and revising notes helps to reinforce understanding and memory.

- There isn't a unique and easily learned behaviour where both reading speed and comprehension are high. It helps to adjust reading pace depending on the text. Techniques like using a visual pacer, skimming before reading, staying focused and reading regularly can significantly boost both speed and comprehension over time.

- There is no one-size-fits-all approach to learning as we all possess distinct cognitive abilities. By gaining insights into your unique cognitive profile, you can strategically harness your strengths and address your weaknesses. Effective learning involves identifying your cognitive preferences, applying personalised strategies and adopting a mindset that embraces diverse learning paths.

6

When Creativity Strikes

In the early 90s, two young, ambitious economists crossed paths at Harvard University. Joshua, an expert in labour economics, had been trying to unravel the effects of education, minimum wage laws and military service on people's earnings. Meanwhile Guido, a whizz in econometric models, had devoted his time to refining methodologies that underpinned the empirical work in labour economics and beyond.

Joshua was wrestling with a challenging conundrum. His research had revealed that individuals who were drafted were less likely to take up higher education – an intriguing discovery that begged the question: how much of this was the direct result of the draft and how much was due to other factors?

Intrigued by the intellectual challenge, Joshua and Guido decided to join forces. Leveraging their unique strengths and perspectives, they delved into the heart of the problem. Traditional methods proved to be useless, leading only to dead-ends. After each failed attempt, they persisted, challenging each other to outgrow their existing paradigms.

Then, on a seemingly ordinary day, after another fruitless meeting, the pair decided to regroup at a nearby coffee shop. Guido, being locked away in his office for hours, welcomed the refreshing breeze as he made his way to the cafe. Surrounded by nature he relaxed and allowed his mind to wander. Unprovoked, his thoughts circled back to something Joshua had said earlier. And then things suddenly made sense – the solution was not deeply buried within economics, but hidden in plain sight within the field of statistics.

He could hardly contain his excitement as he hurried towards the café to share the revelation with Joshua, who immediately saw the breakthrough too. A surge of elation washed over them as they realised they had finally cracked the puzzle that had confounded them for so long. Two unrelated insights from different fields combined had formed the answer.

Their collaboration and relentless pursuit had given birth to a revolutionary methodology that would profoundly impact the field of economics. They discovered a way to measure cause and effect in real-world situations, helping economists better understand how things like education or policy changes truly impact people's lives. In 2021, Joshua Angrist and Guido Imbens, along with David Card, were awarded the Nobel Prize in Economics for their groundbreaking work.

As Guido shared this story with me one rainy afternoon in Amsterdam, I was struck by how much it mirrored everything I'd learned about the creative process. Creativity isn't a stroke of luck, but the result of deliberate mental effort. It involves a rhythmic dance between focused thought and allowing the mind to freely wander. Creativity thrives on viewing situations from different angles and an openness to blend old ideas in novel ways. It's about harnessing the power of collaboration, persisting through challenges and recognising that failure is an integral part of the creative process.

And then, often when you least expect it, magic happens. You've enriched the world with something new, something previously unimagined. Such is the beauty of the creative process.

Creative Sparks

In the 1940s, a curious Swiss engineer named George de Mestral found inspiration in an unexpected place. After taking his dog out for a walk in the Swiss Alps, he noticed that the dog's fur and his own pants were covered in burrs. Intrigued by the persistence of these natural hitchhikers, he decided to take a closer look. Under the microscope, he discovered that the burrs had tiny hooks that allowed them to latch onto fabric and fur.

Inspired by this mechanism, de Mestral began experimenting with creating a synthetic fastening system that mimicked the burrs' gripping action. After countless experiments and modifications, he successfully invented Velcro. The name cleverly combines the French words 'velours' (velvet) and 'crochet' (hook), signifying the two components that make it work.

De Mestral's invention revolutionised the way we fasten things, from shoes and clothing to astronaut suits, medical devices and household products. A simple walk in the Alps and a curious mind led to an invention that affected almost everyone's life. Sometimes, the best ideas are right under our noses, waiting to be discovered.

At its heart, creativity involves looking at familiar things through a different lens and creating something original and worthwhile. It involves connecting disparate ideas in novel ways, seeing patterns where others might see chaos and imagining what could be instead of merely accepting what is. Creativity encourages us to think outside the box, uncover innovative solutions and adapt to ever-changing circumstances.

It might not come as a surprise that memory and creativity are intrinsically linked. Memory, the repository of our experiences, emotions and knowledge, is the wellspring from which creativity draws. When we engage in creative pursuits, we delve into this storehouse, pulling out bits and pieces from different shelves, and assembling them in new ways. Memory enables us to recognise patterns, identify problems and draw upon past successes and failures to bolster our creativity. Engaging in creative activities, in turn, fortifies our memory by stimulating new connections and pathways in the brain.[1]

In today's rapidly evolving world, creativity is more crucial than ever. It equips us with the flexibility to adapt and devise innovative solutions in our personal and professional lives. With technology automating many routine tasks, creativity is a valuable asset that differentiates us from machines. Moreover, with the growing influence of AI – capable of generating creative outputs – it is even more essential for us to cultivate and nurture our own creative abilities as it allows us to harness the strengths of both human ingenuity and AI innovation.

But beyond practical value, creativity can also add a magical touch to our lives. It can rekindle our childlike sense of wonder and imagination, promote self-expression and foster connection through shared experiences. In short, creativity can add colour and depth to our lives. As Albert Einstein aptly said, 'Creativity is intelligence having fun.' Unfortunately, there are plenty of misunderstandings about what creativity truly involves. So before we move on, let's debunk the biggest ones.

Misconceptions About Creativity

Before becoming a writer, I comfortably placed myself in the 'not the creative type' category. My drawings looked more like abstract experiments with uneven lines and awkward shapes, the kind only a parent would proudly hang on the fridge. Singing wasn't much better – I'd wince at the sound of my own voice even when singing 'Happy Birthday'. As for acting, if there were a prize for delivering the most stiff, unconvincing performance, I'd have a shelf full of trophies.

But here's what I've learned: creativity isn't confined to paintbrushes, musical instruments, dramatic monologues or inventing Velcro. It's so much broader, encompassing every ingenious solution and novel idea that makes us stop and think, 'Why didn't I think of that?' Creativity comes to life in how we solve problems at work, in the unique recipes we whip up in the kitchen and in the quirky ways we might tell a story to amuse our friends. It's the gardener visualising a flower display on a barren plot. It's the teacher finding a new way to make a seemingly boring topic fresh and exciting for their students. It's the parent spinning an engaging bedtime tale. Creativity resides in all of us, permeating every aspect of our lives.

The idea that creativity also encompasses small, incremental changes that slowly but surely improve our lives is encapsulated in the Japanese philosophy of Kaizen. Kaizen, which means 'change for the better', encourages continuous, small improvements in the workplace and our personal lives. It's about looking at how things can be done better by identifying inefficiencies, brainstorming solutions, implementing small changes and then analysing the results. Creativity viewed in this spirit is a daily practice accessible to everyone, crafted through the subtle art of noticing and improving.

A widespread misconception is that creativity is an innate talent – you either have it or you don't. While genetics and upbringing influence creative potential, it's also a skill that can be honed and cultivated through practice, appropriate techniques and exposure to a diverse range of experiences. Creativity may come more naturally to some, but everyone can acquire some creative skill. Besides, we don't all need to become the next Mozart, Einstein or Picasso.

Creativity is also not a spontaneous act. While moments of inspiration can strike seemingly out of nowhere, these insights tend to be the result of deliberate effort and a methodical approach to problem-solving and idea generation. Creativity very rarely happens spontaneously; it requires discipline, persistence and the willingness to iterate and refine ideas over time. It's a process of trial and error, learning from mistakes and persistently pushing boundaries until the desired outcome is achieved.

Finally, there's a misconception that creativity declines with age. Studies show that creativity actually increases until we reach middle age and then starts to gradually decline. But, when researchers give people all the time they need, the drop in creativity with age almost disappears. This suggests the issue isn't a reduction in creativity, but slower processing speeds and decreased working memory as we age. When there's no rush, older adults do just as well on creative tasks. Creativity doesn't really go away with age – it just manifests at a different pace.[2]

With those myths out of the way, it's time to uncover how we can extract valuable insights and truly harness our creative potential.

The Wandering Mind

You've likely been there. You're immersed in your work, wrestling with a challenging problem. You've exhausted all angles, explored every avenue, yet the solution remains elusive. Just when you're about to throw in the towel, a breakthrough occurs. Not at your desk, but while you're washing dishes. A solution, unlike anything you considered during the day, yet somehow related. A fresh, creative combination of previously considered alternatives.

This isn't merely a lucky coincidence. It's a common way we derive insights, facilitated by the effective collaboration of the two main networks in our brain: the central executive network and the default mode network, which we discussed briefly in Chapter 2. When faced with a challenge, our central executive network springs into action, fortifying our attention, augmenting our working memory and enhancing our decision-making prowess. It ensures we dissect the problem, scrutinise every facet and thoroughly evaluate potential fixes. Yet, when a solution remains out of reach, it's time for the default mode network to take over.

The default mode network, or mind-wandering mode, activates when our brain is at ease and isn't focused on a specific task. Our thoughts start to wander, bouncing between past memories to future dreams, untethered by the constraints of focused reasoning. It's during these mental strolls that our brain starts piecing together the puzzle in novel ways, drawing from a well of memories, emotions and knowledge, leading to an 'Aha!' moment that can feel both surprising and obvious.

This dynamic collaboration between the two networks seems to fuel most creative pursuits. It's like an imaginative artist and a critical curator joining forces. When we let our minds meander, we uncover ideas that might have otherwise remained buried. The executive control network then hones these rough ideas into practical, implementable plans.

Interestingly, when we engage in creative thinking, the default and control networks, who usually do their own thing separately, start talking to each other more.[3] Our capacity to come up with original ideas can be predicted by how well the two networks are integrated.[4] Creativity therefore seems to emanate from a skilful integration of the default and control networks.

While it's still unclear whether the connection between these networks can be strengthened, we can certainly enhance our ability to conceive novel ideas and solve problems by allocating time for daydreaming.[5] Combining such periods of deliberate mind-wandering with phases of intense focus helps to ensure that our ideas don't merely remain whimsical thoughts but become valuable solutions.

When I embarked on my own creative pursuit – writing this book – I thought it would be wise to follow in the footsteps of successful writers. In line with the importance of engaging both the default and central executive networks, they all seem to do the same: dedicating a part of the day to focused writing and another part to mental relaxation. Charles Dickens, for instance, wrote from 9 a.m. to 2 p.m. In the afternoons, he often went for long strolls through London. These walks, he believed, fuelled his creativity and helped him weave his tales.[6]

I followed suit and was amazed at how this routine benefitted my writing. Mornings were devoted to writing, getting text on paper. This was followed by a few hours of mental relaxation where I'd go for a walk, run or swim. It was fascinating to experience how often new storylines or ideas spontaneously popped into my head during these breaks.

While it's often not possible to drastically alter our daily routines, introducing moments of deliberate mind-wandering can yield a significant creativity boost. Simple tasks like walking the dog, doing laundry or taking a warm shower can all stimulate the default network, enhancing your creativity.[7] Especially when you've hit a roadblock on a problem, stepping back and allowing your mind to wander can prove particularly useful.[8]

Innovative solutions tend to spring from a blend of focused thinking and relaxation, reminding us that at times progress requires letting go and seeing where our thoughts may lead us. And other times it requires us to abandon the familiar and chart a new course.

Directing Creative Thought

London's Hyde Park hummed with energy as fans filled the grounds for Bruce Springsteen's long-awaited show. The sun dipped low, casting a warm glow across the sea of eager faces, just as the first chords of 'No Surrender' echoed through the park. The crowd surged, a shared thrill rippling through the air, signalling the start of a night that promised to be anything but ordinary.

As I looked around, the sheer happiness was palpable – people dancing without a care, singing along as loud as they could, laughter mingling with the songs. The stage lights danced, with Bruce Springsteen and the E Street Band shown on the big screens. The scents from the nearby food trucks filled the air, adding to the sensory feast.

Then, among this whirlwind of sights, sounds and smells, a familiar face caught my eye – a friend I hadn't seen in ages. Excited, I made my way through the throng of people, eager to reconnect and share this magical moment with her.

Spotting my friend amid the crowd of Hyde Park may seem like a simple act, but, in reality, it's a remarkable feat of our brain. As I scanned the crowd, my brain sifted through a myriad of visual cues – facial features, expressions, subtle nuances in light and context – comparing them swiftly with faces stored in my memory. Once a match was found, recognition triggered the appropriate emotional and social responses.

The speed and efficiency with which our brain can do this is truly astonishing. Despite being bombarded with various other sensory inputs, it can swiftly identify a familiar face in a sea of strangers. This demonstrates our brain's exceptional pattern-recognition capabilities – finely honed to identify and respond to key signals in our environment, enabling us to make rapid decisions based on past experiences.

Much of this pattern recognition occurs subconsciously. Our brain is constantly processing sensory inputs even when we're not consciously focusing on them. This enables us to swiftly make sense of our surroundings, alerting us to familiar patterns or anomalies demanding our attention. It's a vital survival mechanism, aiding us to respond effectively to potential threats or rewards.

Conscious pattern recognition, on the other hand, involves active focus and analysis. This comes into play when we need to solve problems, absorb new information or make decisions based on complex data. For example, when studying for an exam, we intentionally look for patterns to help understand and remember key concepts. Similarly, in professional settings, analysing data to inform strategic decisions requires conscious effort to recognise and interpret patterns.

While both subconscious and conscious pattern recognition play important roles in our cognitive functioning, they pose a challenge to our creative process. Recognising patterns enables us to draw upon past experiences and form associations that can serve as the bedrock for creative thinking. However, the same mechanism can lead to predictable outcomes, while creativity requires linking things in novel and unexpected ways.

Overcoming the brain's natural inclination to seek out the familiar can be challenging. When asked to think of unconventional uses for ordinary items, like a brick, newspaper or a paper clip, many of us can only come up with the most obvious uses of the objects.[9] But there are ways to defy our brain's innate pull towards familiarity and cultivate ideas that deviate from conventional patterns. This involves a specific kind of thinking.

Imagine this scenario: a doctor faces a patient with an inoperable malignant tumour. A type of ray can destroy the tumour if intense enough but would also harm healthy tissue. At lower intensities, the rays don't harm healthy tissue but won't affect the tumour either. What is the solution?

This dilemma is known as Duncker's radiation problem. It's a classic cognitive psychology task used to study *functional fixedness* – our tendency to see objects and concepts solely in their conventional roles.[10] The solution involves directing multiple low-intensity rays from different angles to converge on the tumour, with each ray being sufficiently weak to avoid damaging the surrounding healthy tissue. Reaching this solution requires breaking free from traditional thought patterns and look at the problem from multiple perspectives. It necessitates engaging in what is known as *divergent thinking*.

Divergent thinking involves generating multiple unique ideas or solutions to a problem. It focuses on exploring a wide array of possibilities, forging unconventional connections and thinking outside the box. It's characterised by creativity, flexibility and open-mindedness. Instead of zeroing in on a single correct answer, divergent thinking facilitates the exploration of diverse perspectives and potential outcomes.[11]

Convergent thinking, on the other hand, involves narrowing down options to find a single, correct solution to a problem. It's about focusing on a specific well-defined problem and diligently evaluating possibilities until the best solution is found. Convergent thinking aligns closely with logical reasoning and analytical problem-solving.

Both convergent and divergent thinking are vital components of the creative process, as creativity requires that an idea is not only novel but also useful.[12] Divergent thinking fuels the generation of new and innovative concepts, encouraging experimentation and exploration of unconventional possibilities. It's particularly valuable in the early stages of the creative process when brainstorming and idea generation are critical. However, it's in the later stages that convergent thinking lends its strengths, refining and evaluating ideas to identify the most promising solutions. The ability to switch between these modes of thinking is what often drives the most successful creative projects.

We tend to favour one thinking style over another, influenced by a mix of cognitive abilities, personality traits and environmental factors like education, training and cultural background. Understanding your personal preference helps you to identify your strengths and weaknesses in creative thinking.

Several tests measure divergent thinking, with the Torrance Test of Creative Thinking (TTCT) and the Alternate Uses Task (AUT) being among the most well-known.[13] The TTCT includes various tasks that assess fluency, flexibility, originality and elaboration. The tasks might involve completing unfinished figures, generating alternative uses for everyday objects or creating imaginative stories based on prompts.[14] In the AUT, individuals are given a common item, such as a brick or shoe, and must list as many different uses for it as possible within a time limit. This task tests the ability to make unexpected connections.[15]

To evaluate convergent thinking Mednick's Remote Associates Test (RAT) is most commonly used. Participants are presented with three unrelated words, like 'cocktail', 'dress' and 'birthday', and must identify the common associate (in this case: 'party'). The total number of correct answers determines their level of convergent thinking.[16] While the RAT is a valuable tool for assessing convergent thinking, it has important limitations. It relies heavily on verbal skills and cultural knowledge, making it less suitable for non-native speakers or individuals from diverse backgrounds. Additionally, the test may overlook other forms of convergent thinking that involve different problem-solving skills.

Self-reflection can also shed light on your preferred thinking style. Think about how you solve problems and approach creativity.

If you tend to generate many ideas and like exploring different solutions, you likely prefer divergent thinking. Enjoying activities like brainstorming, creative writing or art projects, further suggests a propensity for divergent thinking. Conversely, if you're drawn to solving puzzles, applying logical reasoning or basing decisions on evidence and analysis – meticulously evaluating options to find the best solution – you're probably more of a convergent thinker.

If you find it hard to assess your own preferred thinking style, ask friends, family members or colleagues for feedback on your problem-solving and decision-making approaches. They may provide valuable insights into your thinking style based on their observations of how you approach different situations.

I favour convergent thinking, thriving on logic and precision. This serves me well in my academic research, allowing me to tackle research questions in a structured and systematic way. I can sift through complex data and, like a detective, zoom in on the clues that matter, discarding what's irrelevant and piecing together a coherent conclusion. However, I find myself at a disadvantage when creativity or unconventional ideas are necessary. My predilection for linear, logical pathways hampers my ability to explore the full spectrum of possibilities, sometimes overlooking novel insights that could lead to a breakthrough.

Understanding your preferred thinking style can empower you to develop strategies that allow you to tap into both convergent and divergent thinking. Ultimately, strengthening your ability to oscillate between divergent and convergent thinking will give your creative thinking a boost.

If you want to strengthen your convergent thinking, practising structured problem-solving techniques can be beneficial. Methods such as creating pros and cons lists or using decision trees allow for a systematic way to analyse options and guide you towards the best solution. We'll explore decision trees in more detail in Chapter 9. In contrast, enhancing divergent thinking requires exercises that promote the free flow of ideas and imaginative solutions. Let's look at some practical methods to nurture this skill and boost our creative thinking.

Boosting Creativity

Overnight, my commute had morphed into a creative expedition. Philip Bond, my brain coach – whom I'll introduce to you more extensively in the next chapter – had moved me to the next stage of my brain training: boosting my creativity. The previous day we had engaged in a lively conversation about the Alternative Uses Task over lunch. Philip instructed me to do this task daily by selecting a common object and thinking about as many uses as possible. The key, he emphasised, was to reimagine the object's various aspects, like its dimension, material or weight. To further spark creativity, he encouraged me to ask, 'What is the form, and what is the function of this object?' From there, I was to explore ways to keep the form but change the function or change the function while keeping the form.

So the following day, while biking to work, I pondered alternative uses for my bike bell. At first my ideas were not particularly imaginative: a house doorbell, a dinner bell, an attention-getting device for teachers. Yet, when I let go of the notion of the bell as an 'attention grabber', my ideas took a creative turn: a cat toy, a musical instrument, an espresso cup, a cabinet handle. Shrinking the bell yielded fresh concepts: a decorative dress button, a zipper pull, a charm bracelet pendant. Expanding its size birthed the ideas of a lampshade, a flower pot, a shower head, even a makeshift shield. And when I envisioned the bell as either feather-light or very heavy, it transformed into a swimming buoy, a paperweight, a doorstop and a training aid.

Initially, thinking beyond the obvious uses was challenging. However, once I allowed myself to view the object from different perspectives, the floodgates of creativity burst open. I overcame the 'stickiness' of my previous experience and knowledge and was able to think outside the box. Besides the technique just described, various other techniques can help jolt the brain out of its usual patterns and provoke new ways of thinking that can boost our creativity and problem-solving abilities:

Brainstorming

Perhaps the most well-known creative thinking technique, brainstorming involves generating a large number of ideas in a short period, often in a group setting, without initially evaluating their feasibility or relevance. The key principles of brainstorming include deferring judgement (to encourage free flow of ideas), striving for quantity over quality (under the assumption that a high number of ideas increases the chances of innovative solutions) and building on others' ideas.

The effectiveness of brainstorming lies in its collective approach to problem-solving. By leveraging the diverse perspectives, knowledge and experiences of multiple individuals, brainstorming can lead to more varied and innovative ideas than those generated when we work alone. It also promotes a sense of collaboration and ownership of the solutions among team members, which can improve morale and engagement.

However, brainstorming is not without its challenges, particularly when it comes to group dynamics. For instance, social loafing can occur, where some contribute less in a group setting. Additionally, stronger personalities might dominate the session, potentially overshadowing quieter members who might have valuable insights. There's also the risk of 'production blocking', which happens when only one person can speak at a time, hindering the free flow of ideas. A way to overcome such group dynamics is to modify the brainstorming process into brainwriting: everyone writes down their ideas first and then attaches them to a board for discussion.

Random input

The random input technique involves picking a random word (or object or image) and trying to relate it to your problem. This breaks your usual thinking patterns, paving the way for more creative solutions. By tapping into your subconscious it sparks new ideas that logic alone might not generate. Since your brain is great at finding patterns and connections, it will make a link, no matter how unrelated the input seems to the issue at hand.

Edward de Bono, who created this technique, offers some advice on how to maximise its effectiveness.[17] The input must be random, chosen by chance, like picking a word from a dictionary or a book. A noun usually works best. Commit to the chosen word or image, even if it seems too far-fetched. Opting for an easier word tends to reduce the effectiveness. Don't rush; the first idea might not be the best. And consider different aspects of the random word. For instance, 'umbrella' could inspire ideas based on its shape or function, like circular designs or waterproof materials.

This simple technique is great for generating fresh ideas, especially when starting from scratch. Faced with a blank page, there are no cues to trigger your brain's associative thought processes. A random prompt provides that much-needed starting point.

Six Thinking Hats

Another technique developed by Edward de Bono, looks at problems from six perspectives, represented by 'hats'.[18] Each hat signifies a different thinking mode:

- *White Hat*: Focuses on facts, figures and objective information.
- *Green Hat*: For creativity, brainstorming and generating new ideas.
- *Yellow Hat*: Looking at the benefits and values of the ideas.
- *Black Hat*: Identifying difficulties, weaknesses and potential problems.

- *Red Hat*: Intuition and gut feelings about the ideas.
- *Blue Hat*: Drawing conclusions and setting objectives.

The idea is to set aside specific time periods for each hat, focusing exclusively on that mode of thinking and temporarily setting aside the others. By systematically shifting between different hats, it becomes easier to explore various aspects of a problem or decision, leading to more well-rounded solutions and insights. For creative thinking, De Bono suggests using the hats in the sequence above, but they can also be used in a different order.

The technique is particularly valuable in situations requiring comprehensive analysis, such as strategic planning, problem solving, decision-making and brainstorming. It can be used individually and in groups, where it can boost participation, reduce conflict and ensure all views are considered. To some, who prefer more flexible or intuitive approaches to creativity, this technique might feel too rigid or formulaic. Additionally, there is a risk of oversimplification as the complexity and nuance of certain issues might be overlooked. Despite this, when applied thoughtfully, the Six Thinking Hats can be a powerful tool.

SCAMPER technique

The SCAMPER technique developed by Bob Eberle in the 1970s, is another powerful tool for creative thinking and problem solving. The acronym stands for Substitute, Combine, Adapt, Modify (also Magnify and Minify), Put to another use, Eliminate and Reverse, offering a framework for exploring new possibilities by altering existing products, services, processes or ideas.[19]

To apply SCAMPER, you can use targeted questions to guide your thinking. For example:

- *Substitute*: 'What can I substitute to make an improvement?' Consider replacing one component of your idea with another that may offer enhanced benefits.

- *Combine:* 'How can I combine two ideas to create something new?' Look for ways to merge different concepts or products to generate innovative solutions.

- *Adapt:* 'What changes can I make to adapt this for a different audience?' Think about how you might adjust your idea to better serve a new group of users.

- *Modify:* 'What can I modify to improve performance or usability?' Explore ways to change features or functions for better results.

- *Put to another use:* 'Can this product serve a different purpose?' Consider how your idea might be repurposed for alternative applications.

- *Eliminate:* 'What can I eliminate to simplify the process?' Identify any unnecessary elements that could be removed to enhance clarity or efficiency.

- *Reverse:* 'What if I reversed the order of operations?' Think about how changing the sequence of steps could lead to new insights.

The effectiveness of this technique lies in its simplicity and directness. It guides your brain through a structured yet open-ended exploration of creative alternatives. This helps overcome mental blocks revealing new pathways for innovation. By breaking down the creative process into manageable components, SCAMPER makes the daunting task of 'thinking outside the box' more accessible and less intimidating.

SCAMPER is versatile, suitable for individuals or groups and can be used across virtually any discipline or field. However, as SCAMPER primarily focuses on modifying existing products, services or ideas, it's less effective for generating completely new approaches or concepts.

Mind mapping

Mind mapping is a visual technique, developed by Tony Buzan in the 1960s, used to organise and represent information in a hierarchical and interconnected manner. It involves creating a diagram that starts with a central idea or topic and branches out into subtopics, ideas and associations. Mind maps are often used to brainstorm, plan and structure thoughts, making complex information more accessible and easier to understand.

By visually organising information around a central concept, mind mapping can facilitate the discovery of new connections and insights that linear thinking might overlook. Incorporating colours and images makes the process more stimulating, which aids memory and idea generation. Actively looking for ways to connect different branches or sections of your mind map increases the likelihood of discovering new creative insights. Furthermore, revisiting and refining your mind maps can spark new ideas or reveal previously unnoticed connections.

Dream journal

Have you noticed the thoughts and ideas that appear just as you're about to fall asleep? Or the emotions you feel when you wake from a dream? There's a wealth of inspiration in the transition between wakefulness and sleep. Salvador Dalí famously embraced this creative potential with his 'slumber with a key' technique. He would nap while holding a key, and as he began to drift into sleep, the key would slip from his hand, clattering onto a plate below. The noise would wake him, giving him the chance to capture the fleeting thoughts, images and ideas that surfaced from his subconscious.[20]

Recent research supports this idea, showing that the first stage of non-REM sleep (N1), may be an ideal state for creative thinking. As we transition from wakefulness into sleep, the body relaxes and brain activity slows. During this brief sleep stage, often accompanied by hypnagogic imagery – vivid, often surreal and fleeting dream-like visions – the brain becomes less constrained by logic and more open to abstract, free-flowing ideas. In this state, unusual associations and creative insights have the space to emerge.[21]

To tap into this boundless imagination, you can try Dalí's method or something similar. You can enhance the impact through targeted dream incubation (TDI), a technique where specific thoughts, ideas or images are introduced to guide the content of your dreams. By focusing on certain stimuli just before sleep, you can 'plant' themes in your dreams. For example, you might listen to specific sounds, look at particular images or concentrate on a thought you want to explore. This approach can boost creativity even more than relying on N1 sleep alone.[22]

While the effectiveness of keeping a dream journal is less clear, it can offer a way to capture the surreal, unbounded ideas that your mind generates during asleep. The abstract and often bizarre nature of dreams, free from the constraints of rational thought, can inspire innovative solutions to problems, offer new perspectives and provide a treasure trove of material for creative projects. To make the most out of a dream journal for boosting creativity, consider these tips:

- Write immediately upon waking to capture the freshest details.
- Avoid censoring; record everything, even if it seems nonsensical.
- Reflect on your dreams for compelling ideas or images.
- Use the journal as a brainstorming tool when you're stuck.

Creativity, like any skill, flourishes with practice. By nurturing and expanding our imagination, we can boost our ability to generate novel ideas and tackle problems from new angles. This opens a world of possibilities, ripe for exploration and transformation by our unique vision. And when we bring others into the mix, collaboration can amplify these possibilities, turning individual sparks of creativity into a blazing collective fire.

Power of Collaboration

As I cycle down the vibrant streets of London's Shoreditch, the colourful murals and street art set a creative tone for the day. I park my bike and walk towards a house with warm reddish-brown brickwork and large sash windows. Approaching the black front door, I admire the charm of the street, where historical architecture meets modern artistic flair. With a sense of anticipation and excitement, I reach for the knocker. I am about to interview Tim Walker, one of the most successful photographers of his generation.

Tim opens the door with a warm and inviting smile, his dog enthusiastically greeting me. As I walk into his office, I am struck by the stark contrast between the serene simplicity of his workspace and the vibrant colours and elaborate scenes in his photographs. Renowned for his highly imaginative and fantastical imagery, Tim masterfully constructs images filled with surreal elements and elaborate set designs. Yet his office, with its exposed brick walls, large wooden table and comfy sofa, has an undeniable rustic charm. Bathing in the soft, natural light seeping in from the windows, the space emanates tranquillity, comfort and warmth.

As we settle in, savouring our freshly brewed coffee, I ask Tim about his creative process. Each image, he reveals, starts with a seed – a sentence from a book, a scene on TV or even a random conversation. 'Inspiration can come from anywhere,' he confides, 'it's about intuitively recognising its potential.' These seeds are scribbled down and stored in his 'ingredients cupboard', where they germinate until the moment feels right to nurture one into fruition. Like a magnet, other ideas gravitate towards this chosen seed, fuelling its growth, until around ten images, quotes or sketches coalesce into a rich visual narrative.

But the magic doesn't end there. Tim taps into a network of creative allies who enrich his vision with their unique perspectives. This cross-pollination of ideas opens up new possibilities, allowing him to explore angles he might not have considered on his own. Through this collaborative process, his vision expands, breathing life into his work in unexpected ways. The result is a captivating photograph that not only reflects Tim Walker's artistry but also underscores the transformative power of collaboration.

Collaboration can be a powerful creative force. When people come together to work on a project, they bring their unique backgrounds, insights and ideas to the table. This diversity creates a fertile ground for innovative ideas and solutions that wouldn't emerge in solo efforts. It's like mixing paints; together, collaborators unlock colours and nuances that are impossible to achieve alone.

The creative process is iterative, requiring testing, adjusting and refining ideas. Working together facilitates input from various angles, revealing blind spots and strengths that might be overlooked by a single perspective. With diverse perspectives at play, a collaborator can offer insights that transform the original ideas into something even more impactful.

Additionally, collaboration can offer a motivational boost. Much like how a group of friends committing to a fitness challenge can lead to better results for each individual, banding together in a creative endeavour nurtures a shared sense of purpose and accountability. The challenges and successes experienced as a team foster a sense of connection and belonging, enhancing our drive to keep going.

However, the path of collaborative creativity isn't always smooth. Hurdles such as conflicting ideas, communication barriers and different work styles are common challenges. While sometimes easier said than done, the key to navigating these obstacles lies in fostering a culture of open communication, mutual respect and shared goals. It's essential to remember that criticism – whether offered or received – is not personal; it's about understanding, problem-solving and co-creating. At times, if differences remain unresolved, it may be best to part ways so everyone can pursue their own creative journeys.

When collaboration thrives, it becomes a powerhouse of creativity. The collective power of diverse minds not only fosters innovative and well-rounded solutions but also makes the creative process more engaging and fulfilling. However, even when surrounded by the support and energy of others, moments of self-doubt will creep in. A powerful antidote to this is lowering the stakes.

A Work in Progress

Writing this book, my first, was a life-changing process. As a scientist, I was well-versed in the structure and style of academic writing, but the world of creative wordsmithing was unfamiliar territory. Yet, here I was, attempting to breathe life into abstract concepts through storytelling.

I genuinely enjoyed the writing process, but as often happens when we try something new, the voice of self-doubt regularly appeared. It became particularly strong when I shared my first draft with my editor and friends. Until then, I could live in the comforting illusion of 'all is well', despite knowing perfectly well there was room for improvement. Their feedback, albeit positive and extremely helpful, suddenly made me question everything about my book. 'Was I skilled enough to write a relatable, engaging and useful book?', 'Would anyone be willing to buy it?', 'Could I tolerate scrutiny or criticism from the public and on social media?'

As the pressure mounted, my creativity stifled, resulting in a writer's block. Just at that moment, as by divine intervention, I stumbled upon Rick Rubin's book *The Creative Act*. Rubin, a famed American record producer, is known for his knack in inspiring artists to venture into new creative realms. His book provides a wealth of inspiration for anyone engaging in a creative pursuit.

Rubin believes the key to overcoming crippling self-doubt is to lower the stakes. We often place our creation on a lofty pedestal, believing it defines us. However, as Rubin points out, a more accurate point of view is that it's a small work, a beginning. Every piece of work is merely a stepping-stone; a small but vital part of a larger journey. Our mission is to complete the project so we can move on to the next one.[23] Embracing his philosophy, I began to view my book as an evolving work and a stepping stone for future projects. This new perspective became my secret weapon in combating my self-doubt.

All of us grapple with self-doubt, and it's not necessarily a bad thing. While we might wish it away, it can actually be a useful tool on our creative journey. Self-doubt can prompt us to critically evaluate our work, identify areas for improvement and strive for excellence. It can push us to refine our skills, venture beyond our comfort zone and dare to experiment with new ideas.

Self-doubt, when we embrace it, also cultivates humility and openness to feedback, encouraging us to learn from our mistakes and improve our creations. By accepting it as a critical part of the creative journey, we can channel it positively, fostering resilience and perseverance, which can then lead to creative breakthroughs.

When grappling with self-doubt, practising gratitude can be helpful. Acknowledging the privilege of being able to create and appreciating our unique journeys encourages us to be kinder to ourselves. Instead of fixating on perceived imperfections, we can celebrate the progress we've made. Additionally, surrounding ourselves with supportive peers and mentors can help counteract the negative effects of self-doubt.

It also helps to keep in mind that failure is an essential element of creativity. It acts as a springboard for learning and innovation. Each misstep reveals insights that success alone cannot provide, paving the way towards unexpected breakthroughs. Moreover, it builds resilience and adaptability – essential traits for navigating the ebb and flow of creative work. As Thomas Edison famously said: 'I haven't failed; I've successfully found ten thousand ways that won't work.'

While excessive self-doubt can be debilitating, when acknowledged, managed and channelled productively, it can enrich the creative process. Accepting rather than suppressing self-doubt helps mitigate its disruptive influence. It helped me to remind myself that doubting my work is different from doubting myself.

In the end, self-doubt is not something to fear or avoid, but to be embraced as a natural part of the creative journey; it is a tool for growth and self-discovery. When your inner critic raises its voice, take a deep breath, acknowledge its role in the creative process and keep creating. All creatives face self-doubt; it's how we handle it that counts. As Tim Walker eloquently put it: 'Sometimes you win, other times you learn.'

The Key Takeaways

Creativity is a fundamental part of your ability to innovate, solve problems and enrich your life. It isn't a magic trick, but the result of a disciplined mind that can focus yet allow itself the freedom to wander. Creativity springs from viewing situations through various lenses, blending familiar ideas in new ways. It's a journey that benefits from collaboration, persistence against adversities and embracing failure as a vital part of the process. Creativity resides in all of us. It's a skill that flourishes with continuous practice and a curious outlook towards the world.

- Many people believe that creativity is a rare gift bestowed upon a lucky few, but, in reality, it's a skill everyone possesses and can develop with practice. Creativity doesn't flourish when left completely untethered, it thrives within constraints and through structured effort. It also doesn't go away with age; it just manifests at a different pace.

- Balancing structured work with periods of relaxed, unfocused thought fosters creativity by bridging the default network's imagination with the central executive network's problem-solving abilities. Introducing deliberate moments of mind wandering can enhance creative output by allowing thoughts to roam freely. Afterwards, creative ideas can be refined and structured through focused effort.

- Creativity thrives on both convergent and divergent thinking. Convergent thinking refines ideas through focused analysis, while divergent thinking generates a wide range of possibilities. Balancing these processes is essential for innovation, as convergent thinking refines the creative output of divergent thinking into practical solutions.

- Utilising tools such as brainstorming, random input, Six Thinking Hats, SCAMPER and mind mapping can boost creativity by providing structured frameworks for idea generation. These methods promote divergent thinking. Consider integrating these techniques into your creative process or tap into the creative power of the transition between wakefulness and sleep.

- You can supercharge your creativity by teaming up with others. Through open conversations and sharing ideas, you inspire fresh insights and refine concepts together. Embracing collaboration allows you to tap into diverse talents and experiences, unlocking ideas and solutions that might not emerge in solo efforts.

- Self-doubt is a natural part of the creative journey and can be harnessed as a positive force. Embracing moments of doubt challenges you to push boundaries, refine ideas and search for feedback. Similarly, failure might feel like a setback but it's also an essential component of the creative process. Each failure provides valuable lessons, moving you closer to an innovative breakthrough.

7

The Brain Gym

On an otherwise ordinary Tuesday afternoon, my journey to boost my cognitive abilities took an unexpected turn. I was having lunch with Philip Bond, a man that my boss, Andy Haldane – then the chief economist of the Bank of England – had once described as, 'the smartest person I know'.[1] It didn't take long to see why. Philip wasn't just well-read; his intellect seemed limitless, with a mind that was both sharp and endlessly curious. What struck me most wasn't the depth of his knowledge, but how effortlessly he could access it. Whether discussing economic theory or an obscure historical fact, he seemed to pull up the right information instantly, like a highly tuned search engine.

In the heart of London's financial district, our lunch turned into an engaging, hours-long conversation about the brain's remarkable ability to adapt and transform. We discussed how this potential could be harnessed to boost cognitive abilities, with Philip sharing the strategies he'd developed to refine his intellectual skills. His effortless recall left me wondering just how much untapped potential my own brain might hold.

Midway through our lunch, I found myself opening up about my ongoing struggle with imposter syndrome. Philip asked the question I'd asked myself a million times: 'Why do you have imposter syndrome?' I offered him the same reply that I'd consistently given myself: 'I don't know.' Then, unexpectedly, he offered to become my brain coach. His aim? To help me unlock new cognitive heights and, perhaps, chip away at that imposter syndrome. And without a second thought, I seized the opportunity.

So began my exciting journey into the world of cognitive training. Under Philip's guidance, I started daily mental workouts – first just half an hour, then gradually longer. The results were incredible. In merely a month's time, my mind was sharper, my working memory stronger and my thinking faster. Three months on, I found myself in the top 1 per cent of several working memory tests, outperforming 99 out of 100 peers. There were other welcome surprises, too. My focus and problem-solving skills got a boost, my ability to store and retrieve information improved and my creativity flourished.

What started as an ordinary lunch unfolded into a journey of cognitive growth I'd never imagined possible. I hadn't realised the full potential of my brain until I decided to push its limits. Before meeting Philip, I never thought about my brain the way I think about my body: capable of strengthening and getting fitter with exercise. Now, I know better.

There are plenty of ways to boost our brain's performance. It's not just about cognitive training like I did with Philip; physical exercise, healthy food, sleep and meditation also play important roles. But before diving into the details, let's first explore how we build habits – because making positive practices a regular part of our lives will enable us to improve our cognitive function far more easily.

Building Habits

As a teenage girl, I was captivated by a small jewellery store in our village and was often irresistibly drawn to its shimmering allure. Gazing through the windows, my eyes would soak in the necklaces and earrings I longed to call my own. Unfortunately, their steep prices were far beyond my modest teenage budget, making it impossible to buy anything. So, a few times a year, I would take the train to the nearby city, where more affordable jewellery stores awaited. It required time and effort, but there I could purchase the sparkling treasures I so desired.

The lack of an affordable jewellery store in my village created a barrier between me and my desire to accessorise. Buying bracelets, necklaces and earrings required time, effort and the cost of a train ticket. Such barriers, known in economics as *frictions*, are ever-present in our daily lives. Consider the time it takes commuting to work or school, the effort involved in buying a new car or the cost of switching phone providers. Interestingly, frictions also play a vital role in shaping our habits.

Habits are automatic behaviours that we engage in, triggered by specific cues in our environment. Having a shower every morning, putting your keys in the same spot when coming home or opening the door when the doorbell rings, are all habits. Habits streamline our daily routines, conserving our mental energy for more complex tasks. By repeatedly performing the same behaviour in a similar setting, our brain forms connections that facilitate easier execution over time, a process known as *habituation*.

A habit consists of three parts: the cue, the routine and the reward. The cue triggers the action, the routine is the behaviour itself and the reward is the pleasing outcome reinforcing the habit. For instance, our morning coffee ritual is a habit – waking up (cue) leads to brewing and drinking coffee (routine), encouraged by the ensuing alertness (reward). Over time, this sequence becomes a habit.

Our subconscious selves are constantly developing habits that allow us to effortlessly repeat past actions. Once a habit is established, we react automatically instead of making conscious decisions at every step. As a result, habits play a key role in shaping and guiding much of our behaviour. In fact, around 43 per cent of our actions are habitual, influencing everything from personal hygiene and work tasks to sports and leisure activities.[2] That's why changing behaviour requires us to adapt our habits; relying solely on strong intentions and willpower isn't enough to make lasting changes.[3]

So, how can we cultivate good habits and discard our bad ones? In her book *Good Habits, Bad Habits*, psychologist and leading habit researcher Wendy Wood explains that habit formation relies on three key elements: reward, repetition and context. By understanding each component, we can devise effective strategies to develop the habits we desire:

Reward

Habits don't just magically occur; a reward is needed to spark the initial effort. Rewards are crucial because they provide the positive reinforcement needed to solidify new habits. As we saw in Chapter 3, rewards trigger the release of dopamine, a neurotransmitter responsible for wanting and craving, which strengthens the habit loop. In essence, a habit is a mental shortcut leading us back to a reward we've previously enjoyed.

For rewards to effectively mould habit formation, they need to be unexpected and immediate. Unexpected rewards lead to a reward prediction error and amplify dopamine release. This etches the details of the rewarding experience into our memory, prodding us to repeat the behaviour. If the reward falls short of expectations, dopamine levels drop, signalling to the brain that the behaviour may not be worth repeating.

The reward must also appear quickly after the action. Immediate rewards – receiving praise from your boss after a job well done – give your brain swift feedback, reinforcing the connection between the behaviour and the positive result. A pay-cheque bonus arriving two weeks after your performance, however, may not serve as a potent reward as the brain struggles to link the action with the positive feeling.[4]

Given this timing, the most effective habit-building rewards are those embedded within the action itself. For instance, if you're trying to develop a reading habit, the immediate relaxation and immersion in a captivating story can function as intrinsic rewards. Extrinsic rewards, like enjoying a piece of chocolate right after finishing a chapter, can work as an external incentive, giving the reading habit a boost. Be careful though, as we saw in Chapter 3, over-reliance on extrinsic rewards can overshadow intrinsic ones, dampening your innate motivation.

Repetition

In a classic study, researchers tracked the gym-going habits of ninety-four members at a newly established UK gym for three months. They wanted to know how people stick to working out. Despite all members paying a fee to join, only a mere 29 per cent ended up using the gym consistently for three months. These members weren't initially more committed or keen on exercising. What set them apart? They went regularly to the gym for at least five weeks, allowing them to form a gym habit. With the established habit, going to the gym became an automatic response and they kept going, independent of the strength of their initial intentions.[5]

While the study didn't reveal the specific strategies these individuals used, those who persisted mentioned feeling in control of their exercise routines and confident in their ability to workout regularly. This suggests they effectively planned their exercise, making it easier to stick to their commitments – for example, by going to the gym every Monday night right after work.

The key to habit formation lies in repetition. By consistently performing a behaviour in response to a specific cue, we strengthen the neural pathways in our brain that support the habit. This conditioning eventually automates the behaviour, lessening the mental effort required to perform it. Each repetition of the habit loop (cue, routine, reward) reinforces the behaviour, contributing to it becoming second nature. The more we repeat a behaviour in the same context, the more robust the habit becomes.

When have we repeated an action often enough for it to become a habit? Perhaps surprisingly, it's the insensitivity to reward that determines if something is a habit. As Wendy Wood explains: 'The only way to know for sure if an action is habitual is to test what happens when the reward changes. If we persist even when we don't value the reward as much or it's no longer available, then it's a habit.'[6]

Context

We form habits when our actions repeatedly bring us more pleasure than our neural systems expect. However, context plays a pivotal role in smoothing the way. Context involves the environmental and situational factors that trigger a habit. These cues can be physical locations, times of day, emotional states or other specific conditions that prompt the behaviour. By controlling our environment, we can create cues that encourage positive habits and discourage negative ones.

Designing our environment to support our desired habits can significantly enhance our ability to maintain them. This involves reducing friction for good habits – making them easier to perform – and increasing friction for bad habits – making them harder to execute. An affordable jewellery store in my village would have made it much easier to satisfy my fashion cravings. At the same time, the cost and effort to travel to the nearby city curbed the likelihood of me overspending on jewellery.

To reduce friction for a positive habit, make the behaviour as simple and convenient as possible. For example, if you want to develop a habit of drinking more water, keep a filled water bottle at your desk or in your bag. Conversely, increase friction for habits you want to break by creating barriers. If you want to stop mindlessly browsing social media, you might delete the apps from your phone or set up blockers that limit your access.

Habits stem from repetition, plain and simple. Behaviour begets behaviour. The more you do something, the easier it becomes. This principle makes habit formation a powerful tool for achieving our goals. By understanding and leveraging the three pillars of habit formation – reward, repetition and context – we can build and sustain new habits more effectively. Providing immediate rewards, consistently repeating the behaviour and designing our environment to support our goals helps to create a solid foundation for lasting change.

One powerful technique to accelerate habit formation is habit stacking, a strategy already mentioned in Chapter 3. Habit stacking involves building new habits by linking them to existing ones. This creates a chain of behaviours that are easier to remember and consistently perform. For instance, if you already brush your teeth every morning, you can seamlessly add flossing right after, establishing a smooth habit chain. This simple strategy can help you build new routines more effortlessly, creating lasting, positive changes.

Now, let's see what habits we can cultivate to sharpen our cognitive abilities.

Cognitive Workouts

What started as an ordinary lunch turned into an unexpected journey of cognitive enhancement. I'd spent years training my body, but my brain? That was new territory. Yet, here I was, dedicating thirty minutes each day to mental training. Philip's goals were clear: to boost my thinking speed, improve attention, strengthen working memory and unlock creativity. I dove in, hoping the process would sharpen my mind and help chip away at my self-doubt.

The first step was *Human Benchmark*, a very simple, yet

surprisingly addictive platform where each day I would challenge myself with a series of cognitive tests.[7] Each session was a mini-workout for my brain, testing my memory, pattern recognition and reaction speed. Tracking my scores kept me motivated as I had clear evidence of my progress. Over time, tasks that once were tough became much easier. I discovered some strengths, like using images to remember words, and saw my reaction speed, initially a weak spot, improve noticeably with practice.

After about three months, I reached a plateau on each test, a clear signal to step up the challenge. That's when I moved on to *RaiseYourIQ*, a series of seventy levels of progressively harder logic puzzles that required quick, precise decisions.[8] The game's advertised IQ benefits aside, the real value to me was that it forced me to juggle multiple pieces of information, pushing my working memory and mental speed. The higher levels demanded intense focus, which over time helped me concentrate on complex tasks without feeling overwhelmed.

The final phase was *image streaming*, Philip's favourite tool for enhancing creativity, problem-solving and cognitive flexibility.[9] Each day, I'd close my eyes for ten to twenty minutes and quickly recalled the previous day. Then I would describe, in vivid detail, one or two scenes from that day – like lunch with a friend or sitting on a bench in a park. This exercise sharpened my visualisation skills, improved verbal fluency and heightened my ability to observe. It also boosted my episodic memory (our memory for past events and experiences) by actively recalling the information. Though Philip swore by its effectiveness, I found it the most challenging practice to maintain, likely because I couldn't track my progress in any concrete way.

While demanding, my cognitive training undeniably paid off. Over time, I found that learning and absorbing new information became easier. I could just think faster, recall details more easily and apply knowledge on the spot. This journey opened my eyes to the power of training my brain. In my experience, cognitive workouts can lead to real, tangible improvements in everyday life. However, as much as I embraced cognitive training, not everyone shares my enthusiasm.

Despite the widespread popularity of brain games and brain-training programmes and numerous academic studies examining their usefulness, the effectiveness of cognitive training remains a topic of debate. Some research finds positive outcomes, such as enhanced memory, attention and processing speed following a brain training regimen. While other studies provide little to no evidence supporting these claims.[10]

One factor contributing to conflicting results in brain-training studies is the type of cognitive exercises used. Not all brain-training activities are equally effective; some may yield better results than others. The duration and intensity of the training are also crucial. Short-term or sporadic brain training has a much more limited impact compared to consistent, long-term training. We know this from our bodies too. If we do push-ups for a week and then stop, you cannot really expect any long-lasting benefits.

Another important consideration is individual differences among participants. Just like physical exercise, what works for one person may not work for another. Factors such as age, baseline cognitive abilities and motivation can all influence the outcomes of brain training. Additionally, there may be a placebo effect at play – the belief that brain training will lead to improvements can actually result in some level of improvement, even if the training itself is not effective.[11]

When evaluating the effectiveness of cognitive training, it's also important to distinguish between *near transfer* and *far transfer*. Near transfer – improving on a task itself or one very similar to it – is generally considered to be achievable.[12] When we train our working memory, attention or processing speed, we tend to get better at these skills. Sometimes these improvements are the result of discovering more effective strategies, something I experienced myself.

When I first tackled Human Benchmark's Memory Grid task – memorising patterns of lit squares on a grid – I couldn't get past eight squares. Over time, though, I got better, eventually recalling up to fourteen squares. The breakthrough came when I began grouping squares into memorable shapes like 'inverted U', 'rocket' or 'staircase'. By chunking the information this way, my performance rapidly improved. What's encouraging is that once you learn to spot useful strategies for one task, it becomes easier to apply them to other working memory tasks as well.[13]

Far transfer – improvement in tasks different from the training – is much more contentious. Ideally, a well-designed cognitive training programme would not only enhance performance in specific tasks but also bolster skills crucial for everyday functioning, such as problem-solving, reasoning, maths and reading ability. While some research indicates that certain types of brain training can lead to these far transfer effects, other studies contend that improvements are often task-specific and do not generalise to broader cognitive functions.[14]

So, where does this leave us? While commercial brain games can be entertaining, it's important to keep in mind that claims about their cognitive benefits may be overstated. In my experience, two approaches have made a real difference. The first is consistent cognitive training, such as the daily exercises I did through platforms like Human Benchmark. These targeted exercises can strengthen specific areas of cognitive performance over time. The second – just as important – is applying effective learning and memory techniques, which we've explored in depth in Chapters 4 and 5.

A study by researchers at the Donders Institute in Nijmegen, where I spent a few months as a visiting professor, shows that practising the method of loci – visualising information and placing it along a familiar route – for six weeks improves memory in both seasoned 'memory athletes' and beginners. These gains lasted for months. Novices to the technique showed greater connectivity between the hippocampus and the cortex, regions critical for memory. The stronger the connectivity boost, the better participants performed in memory tasks.[15]

As Boris Konrad, one of the authors of the study, explains: using memory techniques is like switching from running to riding a bicycle to reach your destination faster.[16] To that, I'd add: the fitter we are, the faster and further we can go on that bike. In other words, combining consistent cognitive training with powerful learning and memory techniques not only helps us cover more ground but also strengthens the 'muscles' we need to get there. This approach gives us the best of both worlds: the endurance of cognitive training and the efficiency of mnemonics, working together to create meaningful, lasting cognitive improvements. And what about adding physical exercise to the mix?

Brain in Motion

Stepping out of my house, I'm met by the quiet stillness of an early London morning. The cool air sharpens my senses as I make my way towards the park. Inside, the damp grass glistens under the trees, while the soft sunlight filters through the branches. Birdsong fills the air – a sound normally lost in the city's noise.

I keep a steady pace, ensuring my heart rate stays in zone two for optimal fat burning, and immerse myself in the nature around me. Each breath of fresh morning air grounds me, bringing a sense of calm and connection to the present moment. The quietness offers a perfect time for introspection and planning my day ahead. Energised, I head back home, knowing I already bagged a good dose of vitamin D and thirty minutes of exercise.

We all know that regular exercise is good for us. It helps prevent cardiovascular diseases and maintain overall health. But have you ever thought about how it affects your brain? Since the brain is part of the body, it seems logical that what benefits one, benefits the other. Let's have a look at what science says.

While there is still much to discover, existing evidence strongly suggests that regular exercise can lower the risk of cognitive decline and diseases like Alzheimer's and dementia.[17] An interesting recent study, following half a million UK citizens for eleven years, discovered that vigorous activity, like playing sports or workouts, lowered the chance of dementia by 35 per cent. Remarkably, even lower intensity activities like household chores reduced the risk by 21 per cent.[18]

The impact of exercise on general cognitive functioning is still a topic of debate, with some suggesting that the effects may be minimal.[19] However, recent research examining genetic variations related to our inclination for physical activity provides compelling evidence supporting the cognitive benefits of exercise. Interestingly, the study revealed that moderate activities, such as brisk walking and cycling, offer cognitive benefits one-and-a-half times greater than vigorous activities like running or playing basketball. This suggests that extreme exertion is not necessary to enhance cognitive function through exercise.[20]

Doing exercise also seems to enhance cognitive performance immediately after the workout. In particular, executive function – a catch-all term for cognitive processes like working memory, attention, self-control and flexible thinking – shows some improvement post-workout. Additionally, both processing speed and memory seem to strengthen shortly after exercise.[21]

The mechanisms by which exercise enhances cognitive function are complex and not fully understood, but certain factors likely contribute. Exercise amps up blood flow, delivering more oxygen and essential nutrients to the brain, facilitating optimal function and growth of new blood vessels. It also appears to stimulate the production of brain-derived neurotrophic factor (BDNF), a protein vital for neuron survival and growth.[22] Furthermore, it seems to help retain the volume of the hippocampus, the brain region crucial for memory and learning, thus countering age-related decline.[23]

Beyond the direct benefits, exercise also indirectly influences brain function. Regular workouts can improve sleep, which aids memory consolidation and ensures we're better able to focus the next day.[24] It also has a positive effect on stress reduction and our overall mental health.[25] It stimulates the production of endorphins – our body's natural painkiller and mood elevator – and leads to increased levels of serotonin, dopamine and norepinephrine, which are important for mood regulation, motivation and reducing stress. Plus, exercise often involves social interaction and being outdoors, which tends to make us happier.

So how much should we exercise? The World Health Organization recommends at least 150 minutes of moderate activity or 75 minutes of vigorous activity each week for optimal physical and cognitive health.[26] The key is to discover an exercise routine you enjoy, making it easier to keep going. Starting small – like a short morning walk or cycling to work – makes it easier to take the first step. Remember, doing something is always better than doing nothing.

Making exercise a habit will also increase your chances of sticking with it. For instance, I've made it a routine to start my day with a Tabata set while watching the morning news. This workout method, developed by Japanese researcher Izumi Tabata, alternates between 20 seconds of maximum-effort exercise and 10 seconds of rest for a total of eight rounds. You can choose exercises like squats, push-ups, mountain climbers or burpees, and you can alternate between different exercises or stick with the same one for the entire Tabata set. And the best part? It only takes four minutes![27] For me, it's the perfect way to jumpstart my day.

Exercise may energize the body and sharpen the mind, but it's not the only way to nurture our brain. Meditation and mindfulness offer a different kind of training, one that cultivates focus, resilience and inner calm.

Quieting the Brain

Have you ever noticed that you tend to feel happier when you're fully present in the moment? If so, you're not alone. In 2010, psychologists Matthew Killingsworth and Daniel Gilbert set out to explore the connection between mind-wandering and happiness. Using a smartphone app, they pinged 5,000 people across the globe at random times, asking them to report what they were doing, how happy they felt and whether their minds were focused on what they were doing or drifting elsewhere.

Their findings were revealing. Our minds wander nearly 50 per cent of the time, and when they do, it often diminishes our happiness. When our thoughts stray towards neutral or unpleasant topics, we tend to feel less happy. What's more, mind-wandering isn't a consequence of unhappiness – it's often the cause. In fact, what we think about tends to be a stronger predictor of our happiness than the activities we're engaged in. Their conclusion? A wandering mind is often an unhappy mind, which reinforces the age-old wisdom that being present and mindful is key to a fulfilling life.[28]

Still, mind-wandering isn't without its benefits. When our thoughts drift in a constructive direction, they can ignite creativity and help us solve complex problems. Additionally, letting the mind wander can provide a mental break after periods of focused work, helping us recharge. It also plays a role in processing experiences and emotions, allowing for reflection.

Yet, a lot can be gained from learning to quiet our mind and remain present through mindfulness and meditation practices. While the two concepts are closely linked, they are not the same. Mindfulness is the practice of staying fully absorbed in the present, openly acknowledging our thoughts, feelings and sensations without judgement. It can be integrated into everyday activities, like eating, walking or conversations. Meditation, on the other hand, is an umbrella term for practices designed to enhance attention, awareness and mental tranquillity. It includes mindfulness meditation, but also mantra meditation, guided visualisations, yoga, tai chi and chi gong, among others.

Both practices offer a host of benefits by helping us cultivate awareness and presence.[29] One of the most widely recognised benefits is their potent stress-reducing abilities. These practices help cultivate a deep state of relaxation, activating the body's relaxation response and lowering levels of stress hormones like cortisol. Over time, regular practice can ease feelings of stress, reduce anxiety and bolster emotional resilience.

Mindfulness and meditation also help improve our mood and emotional well-being. Being immersed in the moment without judgement puts us in a better position to observe thoughts and emotions with clarity and calmness. This heightened self-awareness leads to improved emotional responses, reduced reactivity and greater emotional strength. With consistent effort, these practices can improve mood, increase feelings of happiness and elevate symptoms of depression.

Finally, these practices can enhance cognitive performance. By training the brain to stay focused on a specific object or focal point, meditation strengthens the neural circuits tied to continuous attention. Even brief daily sessions can lead to noticeable improvements in focus, working memory and overall cognitive function.[30]

While neuroscientists are still deciphering the full impact of mindfulness and meditation on the brain, they seem to lead to changes in brain function and structure. The anterior cingulate cortex and mid-cingulate cortex become more active, enhancing self-control and emotional regulation. The prefrontal cortex shows increased activity, which may sharpen attention and reduce impulsivity, while the insula engages more, fostering greater self-awareness and emotional intelligence. Meanwhile, the amygdala, our emotional centre, seems to react less to negative stimuli, possibly contributing to improved emotional regulation and stress management.[31]

Adding mindfulness or meditation to your life can give your brain and well-being a boost. Although starting might feel intimidating, weaving a meditation practice into your daily routine can be quite easy with the right approach. Here are some tips to kickstart your meditation or mindfulness journey:

- **Start small**: Begin by setting aside just a few minutes each day for meditation. Start with as little as three minutes and gradually increase the duration as you become more comfortable with the practice.

- **Find a quiet space**: Choose a quiet and comfortable space for your meditation practice where you won't be disturbed. It could be a corner of your home, a peaceful outdoor spot or any place where you feel relaxed and at ease.

- **Set an intention**: Before you begin, take a moment to set an intention for your meditation practice. Whether it's to cultivate inner peace, reduce stress or enhance self-awareness, clarifying your intention can provide focus and direction for your meditation session.

- **Focus on the breath**: One of the simplest and most effective meditation techniques is to focus on the breath. Sit comfortably with your eyes closed and bring your attention to the sensation of your breath as it enters and leaves your body. Notice the rise and fall of your chest or the sensation of air passing through your nostrils. Whenever your mind wanders, gently bring your focus back to the breath without judgement.

- **Embrace guided meditations**: If you're new to meditation, guided meditations can be a helpful way to get started. There are countless guided meditation apps, videos and podcasts available that offer step-by-step instructions and guidance to support your practice. Experiment with different styles and teachers to find what resonates with you.

- **Be patient and gentle with yourself**: Remember that meditation is a practice and, like any skill, it takes time and patience to develop. Be gentle with yourself and let go of any expectations or judgments. It's natural for the mind to wander during meditation – simply acknowledge any distractions and gently guide your focus back to the present moment.

- **Make it a habit**: Consistency is key to establishing a meditation practice. Try to meditate at the same time each day to build momentum and make it a habit. Whether it's first thing in the morning, during your lunch break or before bed, find a time that works for you and commit to showing up for yourself each day.

If you're looking for a simple way to get started with mindfulness, I found the 3-Minute Breathing Space effective and easy to implement. It is a brief practice developed as part of Mindfulness-Based Stress Reduction (MBSR), a programme created by Jon Kabat-Zinn, who introduced mindfulness into mainstream medicine.[32] Here is how you practise it:

Step 1 – Awareness: Begin by bringing your attention to your present experience, whatever it may be. Close your eyes if it feels comfortable and take a few deep breaths to centre yourself. Notice any thoughts, feelings or sensations that are present in your mind and body without trying to change them or judge them in any way. Simply observe what is happening within you with an attitude of curiosity and acceptance.

Step 2 – Gathering: Next, direct your attention to your breath. Feel the sensation of your breath as it moves in and out of your body. Notice the rise and fall of your chest or the movement of air through your nostrils. Use the breath as an anchor to keep you grounded in the present moment, allowing it to serve as a focal point for your awareness.

Step 3 – Expanding: Finally, expand your awareness to include your entire body and surroundings. Notice any physical sensations, such as tension or relaxation, as well as any sounds, smells or sights that are present in your environment. Allow yourself to be fully present with whatever is happening in this moment, without trying to change or fix anything. Embrace a sense of spacious awareness that encompasses all aspects of your experience.

Closing: After three minutes, gently bring your attention back to your breath for a few moments before slowly opening your eyes and returning to your daily activities. Take a moment to reflect on your experience and notice any shifts in your thoughts, emotions or bodily sensations that may have occurred during the practice.

The 3-Minute Breathing Space can be practised anytime, anywhere, making it a versatile tool for managing stress and promoting mindfulness in daily life. Incorporating this brief practice helps to lay the foundation for a lasting meditation habit. Carving out a few moments of stillness can work wonders for our brain, but nothing rivals the rejuvenating power of a full night's sleep.

The Need for Sleep

Imagine this: you're about to run a marathon. You've trained for months, pushing your body to its limits. You know you have the strength, the speed, the endurance. But here's the catch – you're starting the race after several consecutive nights of minimal sleep. It seems absurd, doesn't it? No athlete would intentionally deprive themselves of rest before a big event. Yet many of us do exactly that, tackling our daily marathons – busy work days, social obligations, personal projects – without the rest we really need.

Curious about why lack of sleep is so problematic, I turned to Martin Dresler, head of the Sleep & Memory Lab at the Donders Institute in Nijmegen. His perspective completely shifted how I view sleep. He pointed out something which I hadn't considered before: sleep leaves us uniquely vulnerable. Our senses and reflexes shut down, leaving us unable to react quickly to potential dangers. That we willingly enter this risky state nightly proves just how vital sleep is for our survival and well-being.

As Martin explained, one of the most fundamental roles of sleep is its role in brain clearance. During sleep the brain's glymphatic system flushes out waste products, such as beta-amyloid, that accumulate throughout the day. While this cleaning process doesn't provide immediate benefits, it's essential for preserving brain health over the long term. Without it, these toxins can build up, contributing to conditions like Alzheimer's.

But the brain isn't the only part of us recharging during sleep. Our immune system also receives a boost. Studies show that a full night's sleep following vaccination enhances the body's immune response, and this effect can last for up to a year.[33]

Sleep also plays a vital role in physical restoration. During deep sleep, the body produces growth hormones essential for maintaining muscle mass, bone health and tissue repair. The importance of this process is highlighted by a study on polyphasic sleep schedules, where participants took only twenty-minute naps every four hours. Within just five weeks, their growth hormone production plummeted by a staggering 95 per cent.[34]

Metabolism is yet another area where sleep exerts its influence. Sleep deprivation disrupts insulin regulation, impairing glucose metabolism and fuelling cravings that lead to overeating, even at breakfast. Over time, these disruptions make it harder to maintain a healthy diet and weight.

And let's not overlook sleep's impact on our emotional regulation. Without enough rest, we become more irritable, anxious and emotionally fragile. Prolonged lack of sleep, especially when paired with a heavy workload, is a fast track to burnout.

Lastly, as we already saw in Chapter 4, sleep is a powerhouse for memory and learning. It helps our brain sort, process and store information from the day, solidifying our memories and enhancing our ability to learn. While some researchers debate whether resting quietly might offer similar results, there's no denying that sleep deprivation makes us unfocused and less alert the next day.

After learning about the critical functions of sleep, I realised just how counterproductive it is to prioritise work, social activities and personal responsibilities over sleep. The many processes going on during sleep underscore its role in preserving both mental and physical health. Sleep isn't a luxury, but a necessity. Thus, I made the decision to prioritise sleep in my life – a change that I knew would boost my performance and resilience.

While the ideal amount of sleep can differ from person to person, adults aged 18 to 60 are generally advised to get at least seven hours of sleep each night.[35] Falling short of this minimum creates a sleep deficit, a growing gap between the rest we need and the rest we actually get. Each night of inadequate sleep adds to this deficit, accumulating a debt that can affect our health and well-being. But it's not just about hitting that seven-hour mark; the quality of our sleep matters just as much.

The good news? There are a number of things you can do to improve your sleep quality and quantity:[36]

- **Stick to the same wake-up and bedtime hours.** This helps your body anticipate when it's time to sleep and wake up, supporting your natural sleep cycle. Matching your sleep routine with your chronotype enhances sleep quality. Night owls might face some challenges as work and school schedules tend to favour early risers.

- **Avoid bright light exposure at least thirty minutes before bed**. Bright light – not just blue light emitted by electronic screens – can disrupt your sleep. It hinders the production of melatonin, a hormone that regulates sleep, making it harder to fall and stay asleep.[37]

- **Keep work out of your bedroom.** By using your bed only for sleep and sex, you create a mental association between your bedroom and sleep. In smaller living spaces, consider setting distinct spaces for work, entertainment and sleep to create clear boundaries.

- **Create a sleep environment that is quiet, dark, cool and comfortable.** This helps minimise disruptions that could wake you up. For a better rest, you can also put your phone in aeroplane mode to avoid disturbances that might wake you up.

- **Avoid caffeine later in the day.** Coffee, tea, maté, some soft drinks and chocolate all contain caffeine. This stimulant works by blocking adenosine, a neurotransmitter that makes you feel drowsy, which is why it boosts alertness. Caffeine not only hinders falling asleep but also affects sleep quality. The time from which to avoid caffeine varies per person as it depends on your bedtime and how quickly your body metabolises caffeine.[38]

- **Avoid alcohol at least 4 hours before sleep.** Drinking alcohol before bed disrupts your sleep. While it may make you drowsy initially, it leads to fragmented and shallow sleep as it metabolises during the night. Moreover, it diminishes the duration of REM sleep – a crucial phase for memory consolidation and mood regulation. If you do drink alcohol, drink plenty of water as well.[39]

All these tips can boost both the quantity and quality of your sleep, but if you're looking for the most impactful change, Matthew Walker, author of *Why We Sleep*, says the first one is the real game-changer. So, if better sleep is what you're after, try going to bed and waking up at the same time every day – even on weekends. It might feel a bit rigid at first, and you might need to rely on an alarm clock, but once your body adjusts, you'll likely see the benefits of consistent, restorative sleep.[40]

That said, if you struggle to fall asleep, it's just as important not to force it. Trying to sleep when you're not tired often backfires. This is why sticking to regular wake-up times is more critical than rigid bedtimes. If you're lying awake for an extended period, get up and do something relaxing (that won't stimulate your brain) until you feel sleepy. And yes, get up at your usual time the next morning – even if you're a little sleep-deprived – this will help with going to sleep the next evening. If you can't sleep because something is bothering you, it can help to remind yourself that this isn't the right moment to find a brilliant solution or tackle the issue. Give yourself permission to let it rest until the morning when you're refreshed and able to think clearly.

Also keep in mind that everyone's sleep needs are different. Some people can drink coffee late or scroll through their phones before bed with no issue, while others find that even the slightest bit of caffeine or light exposure ruins their night. Some do perfectly well on six hours, while others need eight. This is where a little self-experimentation comes in. Try not drinking caffeine after a certain time or minimising screen time before bed and note down your sleep quality and quantity. The key is how you feel during the day: if you're alert and energised – even during boring meetings or lectures – you're likely getting the rest you need, even if your sleep habits don't line up perfectly with the usual advice.

There will be nights when your sleep gets disrupted by stress, a sick child or a mischievous pet. Such restless nights can leave you feeling groggy and unfocused the next day. On those days be sure to take regular breaks and stay active. Breaks allow your mind to recharge, while activities like a brisk walk or some push-ups get your blood pumping and enhance alertness and well-being. If possible, opt for outdoor exercise, preferably in the morning, for an added energy boost from natural light. A cold shower can also work wonders for those unfazed by the chill.

If you're really struggling, a short power nap can help you stay alert. But keep it under thirty minutes and avoid late-afternoon naps to prevent disrupting your sleep routine.[41] And here's a powerful tip: take a shot of espresso right before your nap. By the time you wake up the caffeine has kicked in, giving you a double boost of alertness.

Think of sleep as the fuel that drives your brain's performance. By prioritising quality sleep, you enhance your mental sharpness, sustain your energy and protect your long-term health. While sleep is essential, fixating on its importance can ironically disrupt it. It's normal to experience occasional awakenings or restless nights and there is no need to fret about it. In fact, after a particularly rough night, you may find it easier to fall asleep the next evening as you're sleep deprived. While the tips above can improve sleep, persistent difficulties may signal the need for advice from a healthcare professional.

Now that we've seen how sleep powers our brain, let's look at how the right foods can further boost our mental performance.

Brain Diet

Our brain is a very energy-hungry organ. Despite accounting for just 2 per cent of our body's mass, it consumes about a fifth of the oxygen we breathe and burns a quarter of all glucose. It thus requires proper nourishment to function at its best. So, how do we fuel our brain effectively? The answer lies in simple, well-known principles of a healthy diet.

The brain needs a steady supply of oxygen, delivered through our bloodstream. To keep the blood flow smooth, we need to stay hydrated by drinking plenty of fluid, preferably flat water or unsweetened herbal tea. The exact quantity our body needs depends on factors like body size, gender, activity level and environment, making it difficult to provide a guideline, but the common one of 2 litres per day seems on the high side.[42] It's better to hydrate at regular intervals rather than waiting until we're thirsty, as that's a sign that we're already dehydrated. A good trick is to keep a glass or bottle of water handy as you go about your business and start the day with a glass of water to compensate for the hydration lost during sleep.

Our brain uses glucose as fuel and it needs it throughout the day to remain energised. Glucose has been found to improve attention, response speed, working memory and memory function.[43] Now this doesn't justify devouring a bag of M&Ms at work. Our normal food intake provides ample glucose, as our body converts carbohydrates into glucose. However, not all carbohydrates are created equal. Those with a high glycaemic index (GI) create a quick glucose spike followed by a fast drop, whereas low GI, or complex carbohydrates, keep you energised for longer. Thus, carbs like quinoa, sweet potatoes and lentils are better choices than high GI foods like white pasta or potatoes.

Just as crucial for the brain are healthy fats, particularly omega-3 fatty acids.[44] They are abundant in oily fish, like salmon and mackerel, in nuts, particularly walnuts, and seeds, such as chia seeds, flaxseeds and hemp seeds. Try to reduce saturated fats found in butter and full-fat dairy products, and replace them with healthier fats such as olive oil, avocado and nuts.

Finally, the brain needs proteins, especially amino acids. Fish, lean meat, beans and nuts are all excellent protein sources. If you're struggling to take in enough protein, you can try supplementing with protein powders but opt for sugar-free options, for example, hemp or pea protein. To determine the right amount for your needs, it's best to consult a nutritionist who can tailor recommendations based on your specific requirements and lifestyle.

In essence, and unsurprisingly, a healthy, balanced diet is the recipe for a well-nourished brain. Just like a high-performance car needs quality fuel to run efficiently, your brain needs nutrient-rich foods. And, for the coffee and chocolate lovers, caffeine (in moderation, and for most of us, early in the day) and dark chocolate also boost our brain function.[45] So you don't have to feel guilty treating yourself to a piece of dark chocolate now and then!

> ### *The Key Takeaways*
>
> When it comes to boosting your cognitive abilities, there are several practical options to explore. You can engage in cognitive workouts and apply proven memory techniques to increase cognitive functioning. By incorporating regular physical exercise, you help both your body and brain function at their best. Meditation can help you find focus and calm amidst the chaos of daily life, while a healthy diet and sufficient, high-quality sleep provides your brain with the energy it needs. By integrating some or all of these practices in your daily routine, you will create a strong foundation for a sharper, more resilient brain.
>
> - To build and maintain new habits, it helps to focus on three key pillars: reward, repetition and context. Immediate rewards incentivise behaviour, while repeating actions in response to consistent cues solidifies the habit. Designing your environment to support desired behaviours makes positive habits easier to adopt and negative ones harder to sustain. Using these strategies, along with habit stacking, can help implement habits that strengthen your cognitive performance.
>
> - While commercial brain games can be fun and might offer some improvement in task-specific abilities, their impact on general cognitive functioning remains uncertain. For broader, lasting gains combine cognitive

training with proven memory and learning techniques such as the method of loci and active recall.

- Establishing a regular exercise routine not only enhances physical well-being but also provides significant cognitive benefits, from reducing the risk of cognitive decline, to improving executive function right after a workout. Incorporating enjoyable and manageable exercise routines into your daily life is beneficial for both body and mind.

- Introducing a mindfulness or meditation practice into your life can significantly enhance brain function and overall well-being by promoting emotional regulation, self-awareness and stress management. Begin with small, consistent steps – for example the 3-Minute Breathing Space – to integrate such a practice into your daily routine.

- Sleep isn't just downtime – it's a crucial investment in your cognitive health and daily performance. Prioritising quality rest helps sharpen your mental clarity and sustain your energy levels. To enhance your sleep quality, establish a consistent bedtime routine, limit caffeine intake in the afternoon and alcohol at night, and create a calming sleep environment

- Maintaining optimal brain health doesn't require complex strategies; it's about integrating simple, nutritious choices into your daily diet. Regular hydration, balanced intake of healthy fats, proteins and low GI carbohydrates helps your brain perform optimally. And yes, you can still enjoy your coffee and dark chocolate in moderation.

PART 3

Elevate Your Mindset: Freeing Yourself from Limiting Beliefs

In Part 1 we focused on reclaiming and optimising our time and mental energy while maintaining motivation. Then, in Part 2, we explored ways to enhance cognitive performance by boosting memory, optimising learning and sparking creativity – all while helping our brain perform at its best. With these strategies in hand, you have a variety of options at your disposal to harness your brain's capabilities more effectively.

As we embark on the final part of our journey, we confront one of the most challenging aspects of unlocking our brain's true potential: transforming unhelpful beliefs and behaviours. Such beliefs – mostly shaped by our upbringing, culture and personal experiences – tend to be deeply engrained and can be difficult to change.

You might believe – like I used to – that you're not good enough despite numerous achievements. Or maybe you think you always mess things up, despite evidence that you've successfully navigated challenges before. Perhaps you think that you're not worthy of love, even though you have several close friends. We often hold onto such beliefs as they provide comfort in their predictability, even when they hinder our happiness and growth. Transforming these deeply ingrained notions isn't a simple task; it requires patience and persistence. Yet, with dedication and effort, change is possible.

In this final part, we will first explore how beliefs form and why they are so persistent (Chapter 8). From there, we'll move to practical strategies designed to help us break free from self-defeating beliefs and unhelpful behaviours (Chapter 9). Finally, in the concluding chapter, we'll turn our attention to what we all ultimately seek – a fulfilling, happy life – and explore tools to help us reach that goal (Chapter 10).

By the end of this final part, you'll have all the insights, tools and techniques I've discovered on my journey. These should give you the power to unlock your brain's true potential and pave the way towards a more fulfilling and joyful life.

8
Inner Truths

In the relentless downpour, he stands motionless, watching as the bus retreats into the distance. His eyes, unlike hers, are devoid of tears. His face betrays no emotion. He has made his decision. He will return to Darlington Hall, back to his solitary existence, back to the only life he knows. It was never truly a choice. Not for him.

His entire life has centred around a single goal: to become the best butler a man can be. And, according to Stevens, great butlers have one thing in common: dignity. The cornerstone of which, he believes, is emotional restraint. A lesson his father taught him well.

Years of dedicated service have honed his emotional armour to perfection. And he takes immense pride in it. Even when his father passed away, he didn't falter; his duties weren't neglected. He doesn't look back with regret. Quite the contrary. He brandishes this episode as tangible evidence of his standing as one of Britain's greatest butlers.

He would never admit his feelings for Miss Kenton. The thought of such vulnerability, such candour, is unfathomable to him. The closest he ever came was a muttered admission, 'I'd be lost without her', when a visitor praised her housekeeping. Somewhere deep inside, he knows that her departure from Darlington Hall and her choice to marry another man were borne out of his inability to confess his love.

Now twenty years later, fate offers him a second chance. Her letter revealed the unravelling of her marriage. He drives all the way to Cornwall to see her. But he soon realises that his commitment to being a great butler and his steadfast beliefs about what that entails haven't changed. Intimacy, love – they find no room in his carefully ordered life. Everything remains as it was, and always will.

I've lost count of the number of times I've watched *Remains of the Day*. Yet, this time, it wasn't the agonising tale of unrequited love that lingered in my thoughts, but rather the forces that fuelled it. Stevens painstakingly crafted his life around two core principles. His raison d'être, his relentless pursuit, was to achieve greatness as a butler. And emotional restraint, in his mind, was what makes a butler exceptional. This was the prism through which he viewed his world, moulding his perceptions, guiding his choices and dictating his actions. Unfortunately, this mental model, so rigidly followed, left Stevens with nothing more than a life of solitude and the poignant memory of Miss Kenton and the life they could have shared.

I find myself thinking about my own life. How different am I from Stevens? Truly. Obviously, I harbour no ambition to become the world's greatest butler. Nor do I place much value in emotional restraint, except in certain circumstances. However, like Stevens, I view my life through a specific lens and it affects my perceptions, my choices and my actions.

For me, the lens is that of an academic who believes she's an imposter. The constant questioning of my own abilities, my own worthiness, is a dissonant backdrop of my existence. Praise or accomplishments I tend to see as a product of luck or timing rather than a result of my skill or intellect. Failures and setbacks, on the other hand, I magnify in an attempt to validate my perceived incompetence. My constant fear of exposure stokes my anxiety and fuels an obsessive pursuit of perfection.

Just as Stevens found solace in his emotional restraint, I find a strange sense of comfort in my perpetual self-doubt. Not because it's pleasant, but because it's familiar – it's the world as I know it. In many ways, this familiarity provides a kind of stability, a constant amid the chaos of life. But it's clearly not helping me; it's creating a lot of stress and chips away at my happiness. It makes me wonder. Why do I cling to such harmful beliefs about myself? I needed to understand more.

Who Am I?

This is one of the most fundamental questions we ask ourselves throughout our lives, and also one of the hardest to answer. The difficulty lies in the fact that our identity isn't just one thing – it's a complex and ever-changing construct. In simple terms, our identity is a mix of physical and behavioural traits that make us who we are. It includes our personality, beliefs, values, abilities, motivations and the roles we take on in different parts of our life. Together they determine how we perceive ourselves, how we interact with the world around us and react to events in our lives.

Our identity shapes our sense of self, acting like a unique fingerprint of traits that distinguishes us from everyone else. While we might share some traits with others, no one has the exact same combination. This distinct blend of characteristics not only makes us unique but also gives us a sense of continuity – the reassuring feeling that we are the same person today as we were a few years ago and will be in the future.

Forming our identity is a complex process that starts early in life and continues throughout our lifetime. It's shaped by a blend of genetic factors, early life experiences, social influences and personal choices. While some aspects of our identity – like our personality and values – are more fixed, others – such as our beliefs, aspirations and social roles – are more fluid. These parts evolve as we encounter new experiences and ideas, implying that our identity isn't set in stone but can adapt over time.

One of the foundational elements of our identity is our genetic makeup. Genetics influence a wide array of physical traits, including eye colour, height and facial features, which contribute to our physical identity. Beyond the surface, genetics also play a significant role in shaping our personality traits, such as our temperament and behavioural tendencies, as well as our natural aptitudes and talents, like musical ability or athletic prowess. Additionally, our intelligence and predisposition to certain mental health conditions are influenced by our genetic code.[1]

However, genetics are only part of the equation. Our environment plays a critical role as well. Early relationships, particularly with caregivers, are vital. Psychologists like John Bowlby have shown that the nature of attachment formed in early childhood can profoundly affect a person's self-concept and interpersonal relationships. Secure attachment tends to lead to a stable sense of self, while insecure attachment may result in difficulties with self-esteem and identity formation.[2]

In addition, parents pass down more than just their genes to their children; they also shape the home environment, which is influenced by their own genetic makeup. Take intelligence, for instance. Since it's heritable, parents with high intelligence often have children who are similarly gifted.[3] But these parents also tend to create an intellectually enriching environment for their kids, filled with books, music lessons, museum visits and other stimulating experiences that nurture learning.

As we grow, cultural and social influences become increasingly important. Socialisation processes – how we learn the norms, values and behaviours appropriate in our society – are pivotal in shaping our identity. Cultural background provides a framework for understanding the world, influencing everything from our worldview to the roles we adopt in society. Social roles, such as being a student, professional or parent, also contribute to our identity by providing structure and a sense of belonging.

Personal experiences further refine our identity, particularly through what's called our *narrative identity*. This concept, developed by psychologist Dan McAdams, suggests that we create a personal narrative or life story that combines our past, present and future, to understand our lives better and find meaning. These stories help us know who we are, where we've been and where we're going. As we go through new experiences and learn new things, our story changes, helping us to see things differently and refine who we are.[4]

The question, 'Who am I?', is therefore far from simple. To explore this further, let's focus on three key parts of our identity, our personality traits, values and core beliefs. Understanding these parts of ourselves better, can be a powerful first step in letting go of what no longer serves us.

Core Pillars

As I stood at the kitchen counter, the sunlight streaming through the windows, I carefully measured out the flour. The digital scale blinked up at me, the numbers shifting as I added a little more, then took a pinch away. Finally, it settled at exactly 200 grams. Perfect. I smiled to myself, pleased with the precision. There was something deeply satisfying about getting it just right.

As I moved to the sugar, my partner Graeme walked in, chuckling at the familiar scene. 'You know, it still tastes good if it's 201 grams,' he teased, his eyes bright with amusement. I couldn't help but smile back. 'Maybe,' I replied, 'but why leave it to chance when I can make sure it's just right?' He grinned, watching me measure the sugar with the same care. 'You and your precision,' he said. 'Like the cake's going to explode if it's off by a gram.' I shrugged, unfazed. 'Every gram just counts in my world.'

Graeme's words were light-hearted, but they touched on something deeper. My focus on accuracy and attention to detail goes far beyond baking – it's woven into every aspect of my life. This isn't just a quirk or a habit, but a reflection of how I live. Whether in my work, relationships or something as simple as baking a cake, I approach everything with the same thoughtfulness and care. Conscientiousness defines me; it's an essential part of who I am.

Personality traits, like my conscientiousness, are among the most stable elements of our identity. Whether inherited, learned or shaped by our experiences, these traits form the foundation of our character. They define the unique ways we think, feel and behave. They guide our interactions with the world, offering a reassuring continuity amid the inevitable ebbs and flows of life. By understanding and embracing our inherent qualities, we can live a more authentic life.

To better understand our personality, the HEXACO framework offers a powerful tool. It builds on the traditional Big Five framework by introducing a sixth personality trait – Honesty-Humility – and offers a comprehensive view of the factors that shape our distinct personalities:[5]

- **Honesty-Humility (H):** Reflects sincerity, fairness and modesty. Individuals high in this trait avoid manipulating others for personal gain and are not driven by material wealth.

- **Emotionality (E):** Captures emotional sensitivity, anxiety and dependence. People high in this trait are more likely to experience fear, sadness and emotional attachment.

- **Extraversion (X):** Indicates sociability, enthusiasm and assertiveness. Extraverted individuals are energised by social interactions and often seek out companionship.

- **Agreeableness (A):** Encompasses compassion, forgiveness and trust. Those high in agreeableness are generally kind, cooperative and sympathetic towards others.

- **Conscientiousness (C):** Reflects organisation, diligence and reliability. Conscientious individuals are goal-oriented, responsible and dependable.

- **Openness to Experience (O):** Includes creativity, curiosity and intellectual exploration. People high in openness are open-minded and drawn to new experiences and ideas.

If you're curious about your own personality traits, you might want to complete a self-report questionnaire. The HEXACO-PI-R is a popular choice; it is available on hexaco.org, a website developed by Michael Ashton and Kibeom Lee, the researchers behind the HEXACO model. Knowing your personality traits is like having a personalised guide to help you understand yourself. It highlights your strengths and warns you of potential pitfalls. With this knowledge you can make more informed decisions that play to your strengths and circumvent your weaknesses.

I completed the questionnaire and found the results quite enlightening. I had always known that I was conscientious, but seeing my exceptionally high score on this scale was eye-opening. Being highly conscientious is a double-edged sword. On the one hand, it means I'm adept at organising my time and diligently working towards my goals — traits that were indispensable in completing this book. On the other hand, it makes me susceptible to perfectionism, often getting lost in the details, as I meticulously check for mistakes or measure the exact amount of flour, which can be highly time-consuming.

But as much as our personality traits shape how we generally respond to situations, it's our values that influence how we prioritise our time, energy and resources. They are another mostly stable part of our identity. Values are the principles we hold that guide our behaviour and decision-making. They represent what is important to us and serve as a standard for evaluating our actions, choices and goals.

The Schwartz theory of basic values identifies ten basic values: self-direction, stimulation, hedonism, achievement, power, security, conformity, tradition, benevolence and universalism. These values are organised along two primary dimensions:

- **Openness to change vs Conservation:** This dimension reflects a tension between values that emphasise independence, novelty and personal freedom (Openness to change), and those that prioritise tradition, security and conformity (Conservation).

- **Self-enhancement vs Self-transcendence:** This dimension captures the contrast between values that focus on personal success, power and hedonism (Self-enhancement), and those that emphasise concern for the welfare of others, equality and altruism (Self-transcendence).

This core set of values is recognised and relevant in virtually all human societies, but the emphasis placed on each value can differ depending on cultural, social and individual contexts.[6] While our values are relatively stable, they can evolve, especially during major life transitions like entering adulthood, changing careers or after experiencing significant personal events.[7] Values also adapt in response to societal changes and cultural shifts, making them more dynamic than our personality traits.[8] So, even though we have a foundational set of values, they're not set in stone and can grow with us as we navigate our life.

Most people gravitate towards one end of each value spectrum, and you might already have a good sense of where you stand on this scale. But if you don't and you're curious, two popular tools can help: the Schwartz Value Survey (SVS) and the Portrait Values Questionnaire (PVQ), designed by Schwartz and his colleagues. These tools can offer a deeper understanding of what values you adhere to.[9]

Our personality traits provide the foundational structure of our identity. They determine how we generally respond to situations. Our values are the principles or standards that guide our decisions and actions. They represent what we consider important in life. But there's another important layer: our core beliefs. This part of our identity fundamentally influences how we perceive reality and navigate our lives.

The Lens Through Which We See

Core beliefs, also known as cognitive schemas, are deeply rooted convictions that we hold about ourselves, others and the world. They act like a lens, framing every situation and life experience we encounter. These beliefs are firmly embedded in our thought processes, greatly shaping our reality and behaviours. While our core beliefs can be very helpful, they can also be a tremendous force holding us back.

Take Stevens from *Remains of the Day*. His core belief is that his primary worth stems from his role as a butler, and that personal emotions and desires should be subordinated to his professional responsibilities. This deeply held conviction compels him to uphold an unwavering sense of duty and professionalism, regardless of the toll it takes on his personal life. By highlighting Steven's regrets and missed opportunities, the movie poignantly illustrates the potential high cost of adhering to our core beliefs without questioning their validity.

Core beliefs, such as Stevens', tend to be rigid and inflexible. They're also not necessarily reasonable, accurate or based on evidence. For example, a person might have close friends yet still believe they are fundamentally unlikable or, despite having a PhD, someone may feel they're not very smart. Core beliefs can also be inconsistent with one another. A person might consider themselves unworthy of success, yet also feel they must achieve greatness to be appreciated. This can create *cognitive dissonance*, which is the discomfort we feel when we believe in two conflicting ideas or when our actions don't fit with our beliefs or attitudes.[10]

Core beliefs don't have to be negative; they can also be positive or neutral. Their connotation depends on how they make us and the people around us feel, and how they influence our ability to function in society. A person who holds the core belief, 'I am capable and competent', is likely to approach challenges with confidence, often inspiring those around them with their proactive approach. Someone who believes 'I am inadequate', instead may struggle with self-doubt, leading to avoidance and missed opportunities.

Aaron Beck, an American psychiatrist, introduced the concept of core beliefs in the 1960s as part of his cognitive theory, which later evolved into cognitive behavioural therapy (CBT).[11] Beck recognised that a key factor in depression and other psychological disturbances is a pattern of distorted or dysfunctional thinking, which significantly impacts mood and behaviour. He observed that individuals with depression often interpret events through a negative lens, leading them to perceive the same situation differently than someone without depression. While this might seem obvious, it highlights a crucial insight: our mental frameworks can cause us to experience the same world in fundamentally different ways.

According to Beck, core beliefs are not innate but develop early in life as we interpret and internalise the meanings of significant experiences, particularly those involving our caregivers, family and social environment. These beliefs often emerge from repeated interactions and observations during childhood, when we are highly impressionable and our understanding of the world is still forming. For example, repeated experiences of criticism or neglect might lead a child to form a core belief, such as 'I am unworthy' or 'I am not good enough'.

Because these beliefs are formed during our formative years when our cognitive and emotional capacities are still developing, they are often simplistic, all-or-nothing statements, like 'I am good' or 'I am bad'. Over time, these beliefs become deeply embedded in our cognitive framework, without us being fully aware of their presence or impact. We often perceive them as undeniable truths – simply 'the way things are'.

As we navigate through life, our core beliefs are further solidified by confirmation bias, our brain's tendency to favour information that aligns with our existing views while conveniently dismissing anything that challenges them. This mental shortcut acts like a filter, selectively steering our attention towards evidence that bolsters our deeply held beliefs and away from anything that might unsettle them. If we believe we are 'unlovable', we are more likely to notice and dwell on instances of rejection and criticism, while overlooking or dismissing signs of affection and attention. This selective processing of information strengthens the core belief, making it increasingly difficult to challenge or change it.

Effectively, we gradually shape a reality that, though comforting in its familiarity, may not align with the truth. This carefully constructed illusion can act as a barrier, holding us back from realising our potential and diminishing our happiness. While cognitive scientists don't yet fully understand why it's so hard for us to change our deeply held beliefs, our brain's predictive nature and dislike of uncertainty could play an important role.

The Predictive Brain

It's a warm, sunny spring day in London. For the last hour, I've been working in the garden, planting new shrubs and pulling up stubborn weeds. The sun is high and my throat feels parched. I head to the kitchen, eager for a glass of water. I pour the cool liquid and drink deeply. As soon as the last drop slides down my throat, a sense of relief washes over me – my thirst vanishes instantly. Feeling fully rehydrated, I return to the garden, ready to tackle the remaining weeds.

But here's the curious thing: it takes about twenty minutes for that water to reach my bloodstream and truly hydrate my body. So, what quenched my thirst in mere seconds? The answer is prediction. One of the most groundbreaking insights in modern cognitive science is the understanding that our brain functions as a predictive machine. It might sound counterintuitive, but the world we experience – its colours, sounds, smells and textures – is a reconstruction of reality inside our heads.[12]

You might be puzzled by this idea. I certainly was when I first learned that what we perceive is actually an act of creation by our predicting brain. Looking to improve my understanding, I turned to cognitive neuroscientist Floris de Lange, who is one of the world's leading experts on perception and leads the Predictive Brain Lab at the Donders Institute in Nijmegen. He quickly captivated me with his explanation of our brain's remarkable ability to shape our reality through predictions.

'Your brain constantly predicts what you will see, hear, taste and feel,' Floris started. 'It uses past experiences and contextual cues to predict the meaning of sensory input. This predictive process begins with your brain creating models – or beliefs – about the world based on previous encounters and expectations. Using these models it predicts what should be experienced in a given situation. It then compares its prediction with the actual sensory information it receives.

'For example, if you're about to bite into a chocolate chip cookie, your brain predicts its taste, smell and texture, based on its internal model for chocolate chip cookies. Once you do, your senses send information to your brain. Your brain then compares what it predicted with the actual sensory information it receives. If there's a match, the experience feels smooth and familiar. You'll enjoy your cookie just as you expected.

'But if it turns out to be an oatmeal raisin cookie, your brain encounters a mismatch. In the short run, this mismatch creates a sense of surprise. In the longer run, the experience prompts your brain to adjust its internal model for cookies, acknowledging that not every cookie that looks like a chocolate chip cookie will taste like one. This way it improves future predictions, allowing you to better anticipate what you might actually be biting into next time. This adjustment process – adapting based on new experiences – is what we call learning.'

Floris continued, 'Perception – how we understand and make sense of what we see, hear and feel – happens through a continual process of so-called "prediction error minimization". It's a continuous cycle: predicting, integrating information, tweaking those predictions and then predicting all over again.

By continuously fine-tuning your predictions based on real-time feedback, your brain helps you respond quickly and appropriately to your surroundings.'

'Let me give you another example,' he said, picking up a glass of water from the table. 'When I lift this glass, your brain predicts that I'll bring it to my mouth to take a sip. However, if instead I empty the glass over my shoulder, you would be very surprised. Your brain would have to adjust its understanding of my intentions, and the typical behaviour associated with picking up a glass. There is a clear link between how accurate your predictive model is and how surprised you are.

'This predictive processing isn't just about interpreting the present; it's also about preparing for the future. Your brain uses predictions to guide your actions and decisions. This way you can navigate your world with minimal cognitive effort, making life a seamless experience most of the time.'

As Floris spoke, the pieces of the puzzle started to come together. My experience with the glass of water suddenly made sense. The moment I drank it, my brain predicted the imminent relief based on past experiences of hydration. It wasn't the immediate physical effect of the water quenching my thirst, but my brain's expectation of that relief, constructed from countless prior experiences.

Leaving Floris' office, I marvelled at how deeply our brains rely on prediction to navigate the world. Everything we see, hear, taste, smell and feel is a combination of incoming sensory information and our brain's best guess of what's happening. This predictive capability allows us to interact with our environment swiftly and efficiently, often without conscious thought. Our brain is not merely reactive but possesses the extraordinary ability to predict and prepare for future events based on past associations.

You can try this out yourself right now. Close your eyes and picture biting into a bright yellow lemon. Imagine smelling the zesty citrus and tasting the sharp sourness. Are you starting to salivate? That's your predictive brain at work. It predicts the sensory experience based on your past encounters with lemons. It links the thought of a lemon with its tangy flavour, preparing your mouth to handle the expected sourness. This anticipation helps you respond more effectively when you actually encounter the lemon.

While our predictive brain is immensely helpful, it can also lead us astray. The world as we perceive it is a construction of our brain that's so fluid and so convincing that it appears to be accurate. But sometimes it's not. We sometimes 'see' or 'hear' things that aren't there. You've likely experienced it: you're sure to see a friend among a crowd, but it soon turns out that it was a perfect stranger. It was your brain generating the expectation of seeing a familiar face, causing you to momentarily perceive a friend who isn't actually there. Or perhaps you've felt your phone vibrating in your pocket, but when you checked for a message, none had arrived.

Similarly, our brain sometimes fails to see things that are there. An incredible demonstration of this is the basketball demo conducted by psychologists Christopher Chabris and Daniel Simons. In this study, participants are asked to count the number of times players in white shirts pass the ball in a video. Halfway through, a person dressed in a gorilla suit walks through the game, bangs his chest and leaves after nine seconds. Remarkably, many participants fail to notice the gorilla.[13]

This phenomenon is known as *inattentional blindness*. While you're focused on counting basketball passes, your brain is deeply engaged in filtering and processing information that's directly relevant to the task. It forms predictions about what you expect to see in the video when zeroing in on the specific goal of counting basketball passes. This intense concentration narrows your attention, making it harder for your brain to process anything outside of your immediate focus. As a result, the gorilla, despite being right in front of you, effectively becomes invisible – your brain simply doesn't register it, prioritizing the task at hand over everything else.

At its core, our brain is a prediction machine, using past experiences and context to inform expectations about the future. From the signals it receives, it extracts patterns, assigns meaning to them and creates our subjective experience of the outside world. Neuroscientist Anil Seth, author of *Being You*, refers to it as 'controlled hallucinations'. What we perceive is our brain's best guess of what's out there in the world – a carefully controlled hallucination, constrained by the world and our body but ultimately constructed by our brain.[14]

Our brain's predictions about the world are thus shaped by our past experiences and learning. This made me wonder if the same process can explain why I still hold on to the belief that 'I'm an inadequate researcher'. If my earlier experiences – whether justified or not – instilled this belief in me, could it be that my negative self-view is shaped by my brain's predictions based on these old beliefs rather than my current reality?

Holding on to Beliefs

With this question in mind, I decided to visit Harold Bekkering, Professor of Cognitive Psychology and former chair of the Donders Institute. Harold is renowned for his pioneering work on human learning, and I hoped he could help me gain some further insight. When I arrived at his office, it was immediately clear why he's an expert in how we learn – he radiated a genuine curiosity and openness that instantly put me at ease.

I asked Harold whether our predictive brain could perhaps also explain why we perpetuate our core beliefs. 'It's a compelling idea,' he said, 'but it hasn't been proven yet.' It would imply that we need to view the predictive coding theory to also predict our sense of self and not only the world.' 'Let me explain,' he said, ready to delve deeper into the topic.

'The predictive coding theory, developed by Karl Friston, suggests that our brains constantly make predictions to avoid being surprised. When something doesn't match our expectations, known as a "prediction error", the brain updates to make its mental model align with what we perceive.' His words sounded familiar. It was the same process Floris had explained earlier.

'Friston then expands on this idea by proposing that we don't just update our predictions; we also take proactive steps to ensure they come true. He refers to this process as "minimising surprise" or "reducing free energy". Essentially, the goal is to align our reality with our mental models of how things should work. We can achieve this alignment by either altering ourselves or modifying our environment. This process of minimising prediction error through action is what Friston calls "active inference".[15]

'For example, when you flip a light switch, your brain predicts that the light will turn on, based on past experiences. If the light turns on as expected, your brain's prediction is confirmed. However, if the light doesn't turn on, your brain notices this discrepancy – a prediction error – and needs to update its model. It might adjust its expectations, like "The light doesn't always turn on when I flip the switch." Alternatively, you could take action, such as checking the bulb or wiring, to fix the issue and restore the expected outcome. Either way, you're reducing the surprise by aligning your predictions with reality, through either updating your beliefs or changing the world around you.'

Harold further explained, 'When we as cognitive scientists think about active inference, i.e. how we behave, we focus on the world around us. How do we adjust so our world aligns with our mental model of it? However, in principle, Friston's ideas can be expanded to include our identity, our sense of self. You can think of it this way: just as we adjust our actions to make sure our predictions about the external world are accurate, it's very well possible that we continuously adjust our behaviour and our interpretation of experiences to fit our internal model of who we are, trying to minimise surprise.'

This explanation felt logical to me. Viewed this way, my brain works to ensure that not only my external environment but also how I view myself fits the mental models it holds. If I believe that 'I am inadequate' and I win a prize for my research, I'm likely to dismiss the accolade as a fluke or attribute it to factors unrelated to my own abilities, such as luck or the judgement of others. This way, I continue to align my (perceived) reality with the belief of inadequacy, minimising surprise.

It can explain why we have such a strong confirmation bias. One would think our brain should consciously search for errors in our beliefs and correct them to create the most accurate model of ourselves. That's what an optimised system would do. But, in reality, we mostly do the opposite – we constantly look for evidence that confirms our current beliefs, while discarding anything that contradicts them. If our brain wants to minimise surprises about ourselves, it should naturally gravitate towards evidence that reinforces our existing beliefs, regardless of whether they are accurate or not.

Still, I wondered why, even when faced with evidence that so blatantly contradicts my existing belief – like winning a prize for my research – I struggle to change my identity to fit this new reality. The most compelling explanation I found relates to our strong aversion to uncertainty. We tend to shy away from situations we perceive as uncertain, particularly when they can result in a loss, despite the potential for significant benefits.

Uncertainty is deeply unsettling for us, which makes sense from an evolutionary perspective. Our ancestors lived in environments where the unknown often meant danger – such as the presence of predators, scarcity of resources or unfamiliar terrain. For instance, imagine encountering a strange fruit in the wild. It could be nourishing or toxic and the instinct would be to avoid it. The potential risk of harm outweigh the possible benefit of nourishment. This natural tendency to stay clear of uncertainty helped our ancestors stay safe, even if it meant missing out on a valuable resource. The brain's primary role is to keep us alive, which it does by continually predicting what will happen next, based on past experiences and the current situation, in order to prepare for the most effective responses.[16] Uncertainty complicates this predictive process, making planning and decision-making more challenging. Consequently, our brains have evolved to err on the side of caution, avoiding uncertain situations wherever possible.

Our dislike for uncertainty is very strong. Participants in a study who knew they would definitely receive a slightly painful electric shock felt calmer and less agitated than those who faced a 50 per cent chance of the shock.[17] This suggests that the uncertainty surrounding the potential shock is more stressful than the certainty of experiencing pain. If our primary concern were merely the threat itself, we would experience greater stress from knowing we would definitely receive a shock. Instead, it appears that the ongoing 'what ifs' of uncertainty are more burdensome than the certainty of enduring something painful.

This preference for certainty extends beyond negative outcomes. Also, when a situation is potentially beneficial, we're reluctant to engage if the outcome is uncertain. For instance, imagine you're presented with a choice between a guaranteed gain of £50 and a gamble that has a 50 per cent chance of winning £100 and a 50 per cent chance of winning nothing. Despite the higher potential reward of the gamble, many of us would opt for the guaranteed £50.[18] This highlights our preference for certainty over uncertainty, even when the uncertain option has a potential benefit.

In the brain, uncertainty is associated with heightened activity in the amygdala. This activation can lead to stress and discomfort, driving us to seek out familiar patterns and stable environments where we feel in control. It's also associated with an activation of the anterior insula, a region responsible for assessing the outcomes of events, which might lead the brain to overestimate the possible negative consequences of venturing into the unknown.[19]

Given that we really dislike uncertainty, it's understandable that we're not very keen to change our beliefs as this would force us into a state of ambiguity. Our core beliefs are deeply intertwined with our sense of identity, providing stability and predictability. Altering them requires stepping into unfamiliar territory and confronting the possibility that our previous understanding of ourselves might be flawed.

Furthermore, changing our beliefs requires us to take a risk that we might fail, so there is a potential for loss. Another thing our brain doesn't like. It's loss averse, meaning that from our brain's point of view losses loom larger than gains. Losing £100 tends to feel far more distressing than gaining £100 feels satisfying.[20] If you're a parent, you've likely seen this firsthand. Take away an hour of screen time from your child, after having promised it, and you'll have an extremely disappointed child on your hand.

To change beliefs we need to leap into the unknown and thus face a double whammy of uncertainty and potential loss. This prospect can be frightening and is something most people naturally resist. The fear of what we might lose – whether it's our identity, relationships or sense of security – creates a significant barrier to embracing a new view about ourselves.

Moreover, changing a belief is not simply about accepting new evidence. It involves a more complex process of first identifying unhelpful beliefs and then overcoming ingrained thought patterns and emotional responses. This process demands considerable effort and self-reflection, which can feel overwhelming and discouraging.

Finally, our brain is wired to prefer consistency. It seeks to minimise the mental discomfort that arises from holding conflicting beliefs or ideas (cognitive dissonance). As a result, sticking with familiar beliefs, even if harmful, often feels like the better option, rather than disrupting the situation in search of greener pastures.

The idea that our brain is constantly making predictions and updating them based on what actually happens is well-established. However, whether this predictive process applies to all aspects of cognition – especially the beliefs we hold about ourselves – remains uncertain. This uncertainty exists, in part, because studying beliefs is far more complex than studying basic cognitive processes like sensory perception.

Yet, I've found that viewing my brain as a predictive machine offers a useful framework for understanding my struggles. From this perspective, my deeply ingrained core beliefs function as mental models that my brain uses to predict and guide my behaviour. In its drive to minimise surprises, it constantly seeks evidence to validate these beliefs, whether they are true or not, keeping me perpetually locked in. These predictions don't just shape my behaviour – they also shape my perception of reality, leading me to mistake subjective interpretations for objective truths.

The Mirage of Objectivity

In September 2001, the unexplained death of a baby in a Dutch hospital sparked a review of other deaths that had occurred over the past year. Alarmingly, the hospital soon discovered that several of these deaths and near-fatal accidents were suspicious. Amid the growing fear and confusion, attention quickly turned to Lucia de Berk, a quiet and unassuming nurse who had been on duty at the time of the baby's death.

Hospital administrators, desperate for answers, turned to a statistical expert to uncover a pattern. He found what seemed like irrefutable evidence of Lucia's guilt: a disproportionate number of the suspicious deaths and resuscitations had occurred during Lucia's shifts. The odds, he argued, of this happening by chance were 1 in 342 million. The media quickly dubbed Lucia de Berk the 'Angel of Death' and the statistical analysis became the cornerstone of the case against her.

The prosecutors, armed with the statistics, painted a chilling picture of a nurse who, behind her calm demeanour, was a cold-blooded killer. They interpreted her private diary entries, which contained ambiguous phrases, such as 'I've given in to my compulsion', as confessions of guilt. To them, the numbers spoke clearly: Lucia de Berk was a murderer. Despite the lack of direct evidence, she was sentenced to life imprisonment without parole.

But the numbers, as it turned out, were misleading. The statistical analysis that condemned Lucia de Berk was fundamentally flawed. It overlooked that she often worked in high-risk wards where patients were already critically ill and failed to take into consideration the probability that the deaths had occurred naturally. Furthermore, it ignored incidents that happened before Lucia de Berk worked in those wards, leaving it unclear whether there actually was a higher number of suspicious deaths during her shifts.

It wasn't until 2010, after relentless efforts by a few who questioned the certainty of her guilt, that Lucia de Berk was exonerated. A re-examination of the evidence showed that the deaths attributed to her were natural, the product of a flawed understanding of probability and a rush to judgement. The real tragedy was not the deaths in the hospital but the life nearly destroyed by our human tendency to look for patterns, even when there are none.

Lucia de Berk's ordeal serves as a sobering reminder that the world is often more complex and less predictable than our predictive brain leads us to believe. As our brain constantly searches for familiar patterns, we have a tendency to 'see' what we expect rather than what's objectively there. In Lucia's case, investigators and prosecutors began with a conclusion – she was guilty – and then selectively sought evidence to support it, overlooking evidence that could suggest otherwise.

While Lucia de Berk's story is an extreme case of how we can mistake subjective interpretations for objective truths, this same cognitive trap often plays out in our daily lives. Just as investigators and prosecutors selectively interpreted evidence to support their belief in her guilt, we often do the same with the people and events around us. When a friend cancels plans twice in a row, we might immediately assume they're upset with us or no longer value the friendship. This assumption feels undeniable – we 'know' they're avoiding us. But in reality, this interpretation is shaped more by our own insecurities or past experiences than by the actual facts. The friend may be dealing with an entirely unrelated issue, but our subjective lens distorts our perception, leading us to the wrong conclusion.

Similarly, if someone folds their arms during a conversation, we might interpret it as a sign of disinterest or defensiveness. Yet, they could simply be cold or find that stance comfortable, with no intention of being defensive. Similarly, when a colleague appears quiet in meetings, we might assume they're disengaged or uninterested. But perhaps they are deeply focused or simply introverted. These quick judgments, based on limited information, often miss the mark because they stem from our own biases and expectations.

This tendency extends to how we consume information, too. When we read an article or watch a news segment, we often believe our interpretation of the events is objective. However, our prior beliefs, political leanings and the way information is presented all shape how we understand what's happening. Two people can read the same news story and come away with completely different interpretations, each convinced they've grasped the 'truth' of the matter.[21] In reality, both interpretations are shaped by subjective factors.

Just as we subjectively interpret the behaviour of others or the information we encounter, we also apply this same subjectivity to ourselves. When we fail at a task or face a setback, it's easy to conclude that we're simply not good enough or that success is out of reach. These self-judgments often feel as irrefutable as any assumption we make about the world. Much like the investigators in Lucia de Berk's case who began with a conclusion and then sought evidence to support it, we do the same with our self-beliefs. We start with a narrative – we're not good enough, we don't deserve success – and then selectively focus on evidence that reinforces it. We zero in on mistakes, ignoring the context or external factors that may have contributed to things not going as planned. We trap ourselves in limiting beliefs, mistaking them for objective truths.

Just as the re-examination of Lucia de Berk's case ultimately revealed her innocence, we too can challenge the narratives we hold about ourselves and others. When we recognise that our interpretations are often based on selective evidence – shaped by personal experiences, expectations and assumptions – we open ourselves to a more nuanced understanding. By pausing to question these beliefs and consider alternative perspectives, we can step back and view ourselves and others through a more balanced lens. By realising that much of what we perceive as objective truth is, in fact, shaped by subjective interpretation, we can begin to unravel the limiting beliefs that hold us back. This shift not only improves our relationships with others but also deepens the relationship with the most important person in our life: ourselves.

Your Life, Your Call

With my newfound understanding of the predictive brain and how our perceptions shape reality, I began to see my own mental landscape more clearly. For so long, I had felt trapped by the suffocating grip of imposter syndrome, allowing my self-doubts to dictate my actions and decisions. Now I could finally see that my beliefs were not immutable truths; they were merely mental models I'd constructed from past experiences and were perpetuated by my predictive brain.

I understood that the key to breaking free lay in taking responsibility for my own narrative. I alone had the power to reshape my story. Rather than letting my past define me, I could consciously challenge my ingrained beliefs and actively reshape my future. I knew the process wouldn't be easy, but I was ready to embark on this journey.

Determined, I began to actively question my thoughts. When my inner voice insisted I wasn't qualified, I pushed back, asking myself, 'What evidence supports this? Have I truly failed, or am I letting fear cloud my judgment?' I started to take stock of my accomplishments, no matter how small, reminding myself that each one was a testament to my capabilities. This process of reflection and questioning was the first step towards reshaping my future.

Our brain is an extraordinary prediction machine, constantly forecasting the future based on past experiences. This means we have far more influence over our future lives than we might realise – or want to acknowledge. Every new experience and piece of knowledge reshapes our mental models, adjusting how our brains anticipate what's to come.

While we can't rewrite the past, we all possess the ability to shape our future and with that comes its own kind of responsibility. This doesn't mean we're to blame for everything that befalls us. We don't get to choose every experience we encounter, tragedies we have to endure or challenges life throws our way. We aren't responsible for the core beliefs instilled in us by our caregivers or the limitations imposed by our circumstances.

However, we are responsible for how we respond to these influences and how we choose to grow from them. Not because they're our fault, but because we alone hold the power to change them. It's up to us to take control of our journey, recognising that while we didn't choose our starting point, we can determine the future direction of our path.

Not everyone has the same resources or opportunities, but everyone has some degree of choice. Even the smallest step can spark a shift in our mental patterns. When we recognise and harness the predictive nature of our brains, we seize the power to shape our future. Although this responsibility may feel daunting, it opens the door to incredible possibilities. Each choice we make today and every new experience we embrace helps to dismantle old patterns, paving the way for more positive and hopeful projections. By embracing our responsibility in this process, we unlock a future shaped by our intentional choices rather than one dictated by our past. The power to change lies within each of us, one small step at the time.

The Key Takeaways

You never really see the world as it is; you see it through the lens of who you are. Your personal truths – shaped by your personality traits, values and past experiences – tint your perception of reality. Your brain, acting like a prediction machine, relies on these internal stories to interpret and anticipate the world around you. When you understand that your experience of the world and yourself is filtered through your own mental frameworks, you open the door to challenging and reframing your inner truths. It hands you the keys to breaking free from your limiting beliefs and associated behaviours and cultivate more helpful ones.

- Identity is your unique fingerprint, setting you apart from everyone else. It's not a static, predetermined aspect of who you are; it's continually shaped and reshaped by your experiences, interactions and self-reflections. While some parts of your identity, such as your personality traits and values, are mostly stable, other aspects, like your beliefs, aspirations and social roles, are more malleable and able to adapt to new circumstances and insights.

- Personality traits and values play a pivotal role in defining your identity. The former provide the foundational structure of your identity, determining how you generally respond to situations. The latter are the principles or standards that guide your decisions and actions. They represent what you consider important in life. By getting to know them, you gain a deeper understanding of who you are.

- Core beliefs are also foundational to your identity, deeply influencing how you perceive yourself and the world around you. These fundamental convictions develop from early childhood experiences, cultural influences and significant life events. They guide your thoughts, actions and reactions, often operating without you even noticing.

- Your brain is a powerful prediction machine, constantly forecasting future events based on past experiences and patterns. While this helps you navigate the world efficiently, it can also shape your perceptions with biases and expectations. Recognising this tendency allows you to challenge assumptions and see situations in a different light.

- We tend to cling to our core beliefs, even when they are harmful or outdated. Your brain has a bias to seek out evidence that confirms what you already believe, probably to minimise surprises and maintain a sense of consistency. Your brain's evolutionary tendency to avoid uncertainty and loss makes it challenging to let go of entrenched beliefs and embrace new possibilities.

- What we consider facts are often subjective interpretations of reality. Your brain naturally prioritises information that aligns with your existing views, which can distort your sense of reality. By recognising the subjectivity of your perceptions, you can stay open to alternative interpretations and critically evaluate the information you encounter.

- Your brain, as a prediction machine, gives you more control over your future than you might realise. While you can't change the past or control all external factors, you can influence how your brain forecasts what's ahead. By recognising this responsibility, you can change your behaviour today, so your brain predicts differently tomorrow.

9
Letting Go

In 1665, the Dutch mathematician and physicist Christiaan Huygens made a remarkable discovery while recovering from an illness. Confined to bed, Huygens spent his time observing two pendulum clocks he had suspended side by side from the same beam. Initially, the pendulums swung at different rates, seemingly independent of each other. But as he watched, something unexpected caught his eye.

Slowly and almost imperceptibly, the pendulums began to align their movements. Over time, they started to swing in perfect harmony, though in opposite directions, as if guided by an invisible force. It was as if they had discovered a shared rhythm, a common frequency that brought them into sync.[1]

Although Huygens didn't call it *resonance*, his observations laid the groundwork for this concept – a phenomenon where interconnected systems naturally begin to synchronise their rhythms. The principle can be easily demonstrated with tuning forks: if you strike a tuning fork vibrating at 440 Hz and place it near a second, silent tuning fork of the same frequency, the second fork will soon start to vibrate as well, picking up the same frequency and resonating in harmony.[2]

Huygens' discovery and the example of the tuning forks offers more than just scientific insight; it reveals a deeper truth about life. Just as two pendulums find their rhythm and the tuning forks vibrate in harmony, our inner world – our thoughts, beliefs and emotions – and outer world move in tandem as well. When we change what's within us, when we let go of limiting beliefs and embrace more empowering ones, our external world begins to respond in kind.

If we carry the weight of negative beliefs, those vibrations will echo out into our lives, influencing everything we do. But if we shift our internal frequencies, aligning them with positivity and possibility, we'll find that the world around us begins to change as well. The people we meet, the opportunities that come our way and the experiences we have will start to resonate with our new, more positive frequency. How can we make that happen? Let's have a look.

Unravelling Old Beliefs

It wasn't an instant revelation or a single breakthrough that sparked the change within me. Instead, the shift unfolded gradually, like the breaking of dawn – subtle and almost imperceptible. An inner process had begun, but the transformation would take time to unfold.

The first real sign of change emerged when I began to catch my automatic negative thoughts. They had always been there, like a background noise you don't notice until it gets louder: 'I should do this much faster', 'I don't know enough to comment on this paper', 'I don't get this equation; I'm just not smart enough'. But now, I could hear them clearly and it struck me how often they appeared.

In the past, I would have accepted these thoughts without question, allowing the familiar weight of inadequacy to settle in. Now, I paused and asked myself, 'Why am I thinking this?' 'Is this really true?', 'Do I have evidence to support this?' I began to recognise them for what they were: just beliefs; not truths.

After a while, I began to dig deeper, recognising that these automatic thoughts were tied to ingrained assumptions rooted in fear. Fear that I wasn't good enough. Fear that any lack of excellence would reveal my shortcomings. Fear that others would lose respect if I made a mistake.

Gradually, I pieced together the core of my self-doubt. Beneath the layers of insecurity and imposter syndrome lay a singular belief: I am incompetent. This belief shaped many of my actions and decisions, influencing everything from how I approached my work to how I responded to failure and praise. When something went well, I brushed it off as a fluke; when things went wrong, it confirmed my worst fears – that I wasn't good enough.

Uncovering this core belief was like shining a light on a hidden corner of my mind. It revealed so much that had been lurking in the shadows. Recognising it gave me the clarity I needed to move forward. Transforming it? That was the next challenge ahead.

Letting go of unhelpful beliefs is a journey that can be challenging and is deeply personal. It's not a straightforward process and, for many, it may require the guidance and support of a mental health professional. I want to be clear that I am not a mental health professional, nor do I claim to offer expert advice. Instead, I share with you the insights and experiences that have helped me understand and gradually release some of my own limiting beliefs. My hope is that by sharing these insights, you might find inspiration or a new perspective that can help you navigate your own path.

Core beliefs, as we saw in Chapter 8, are the fundamental convictions we carry about ourselves, others and the world around us. They function like a lens, shaping our perceptions and colouring every situation and experience we face. Core beliefs can be positive, negative or neutral, depending on how they make us and the people around us feel, and how they influence our ability to function in society.

To help us start recognising unhelpful core beliefs and understand how they influence our thoughts and behaviours, we can again look to Aaron Beck. As part of his cognitive theory, he outlined three levels of cognition that work together to shape how we perceive and respond to the world:

- **Core beliefs**: The deepest level of cognition, representing our fundamental, often unconscious, beliefs about ourselves, others and the world
- **Dysfunctional assumptions**: The intermediate rules or 'if-then' statements that stem from unhelpful core beliefs, guiding our behaviour and expectations about how the world operates and how we should behave.
- **Automatic negative thoughts (ANTs)**: The spontaneous, surface-level thoughts that arise in response to daily situations. They are often negative and distorted, reflecting underlying core beliefs and dysfunctional assumptions.

For example, if someone holds the core belief, 'I am not good enough', they may develop the dysfunctional assumption, 'If I don't perform perfectly, I will fail and be worthless'. When confronted with a challenging task, this assumption might trigger ANTs such as, 'I'm going to mess this up' or 'Everyone will see how incompetent I am'. These thoughts are directly tied to the dysfunctional assumption, which, in turn, stems from the deeper core belief.

Detecting our core beliefs and dysfunctional assumptions can be challenging and takes time. These deeper levels of cognition are often unconscious and deeply ingrained, making them difficult to uncover through casual self-reflection. Identifying them typically requires more structured approaches, such as cognitive behavioural therapy (CBT).

Recognising ANTs through self-reflection is easier. Because they are fleeting and automatic, they can be difficult to catch at first, but mindfulness and reflection can help us become more attuned to these thoughts as they arise. Here are a few techniques that I found particularly helpful in gaining a better understanding of my ANTs:

LETTING GO

- **Mindfulness practice**: Mindfulness involves paying close attention to your thoughts, feelings and bodily sensations in the present moment without judgement. Regular mindfulness meditation can help you become more aware of ANTs as they arise.
- **Journaling**: Keeping a thought diary or journal can help you track your thoughts throughout the day. Write down situations that triggered strong emotions, and then note the thoughts that accompanied those feelings. Over time, patterns will emerge, making it easier to identify ANTs.
- **Mood monitoring**: Track your mood at various points during the day and note what thoughts were present when your mood shifted. This can help you connect specific thoughts with changes in your emotional state.

The goal is to start noticing patterns in your thinking that cause emotional pain. Once a pattern is identified, you can start questioning those recurring automatic thoughts. When you notice a negative thought, pause and ask yourself: 'Is this thought realistic?'; 'What's the worst that could happen if this thought were true?'; 'Is there any evidence that supports or contradicts this thought?'; 'Has the negative outcome I fear actually happened, or is it likely to happen?' This evaluative process helps you to view the thought more objectively, providing a helpful starting point for replacing it with one that is more balanced and accurate.

After identifying and questioning a thought pattern, you can go a step further and start exploring the dysfunctional assumptions and core beliefs that might underlie these thoughts. For example, if you worry excessively about being late, ask yourself why. What do you fear will happen if you're late? What does being late say about you, and why does it matter? You might discover an underlying belief that you must be perfect to be likeable. If you find that you cannot change a belief despite having strong evidence that contradicts it or feel a strong emotional need to defend it, it's likely a core belief.

From my own experience, it's entirely possible to transform negative core beliefs into more positive ones. Even though they might feel like they're absolute truths, they're nothing more than mental models we've developed over time. They're not fixed or unchangeable. Undertaking the emotional work to shift these beliefs can take time and might require professional support, but I can personally attest that the reward is immense and lasting.

In the end, our beliefs shape our reality; by redefining them we open the door to a new reality, a new world of possibilities. This journey will require time and patience, but we can smooth the way by transforming our inner critic into a compassionate ally.

Mental Chatter

In my high school, gym class was the highlight of the week for many kids. The excitement of playing games, the thrill of competition and the camaraderie of teammates made it a break from the routine of the classroom. But for me, gym class held a different kind of anticipation – one tinged with dread.

Every week, two students were called to the front to pick their teams for the game we were about to play. As they scanned the field, sizing up their classmates, I could feel my palms grow sweaty and my heart beat faster. The captains, in turn, called out a name, thus forming their teams. I stood there waiting, staring at the floor and willing my name to be called, but knowing deep down it would be one of the last.

Watching as friends and classmates were chosen, I felt like an outsider, unwanted and unnoticed. My cheeks would flush with a mix of shame and frustration, and a knot of anxiety would tighten in my stomach. Being one of the last picks wasn't just about being less athletic or less popular – it felt like a reflection of my worth.

What made it worse was the mental chatter that followed me long after gym class ended. 'Why am I always the last one? Am

I really that bad? Maybe they don't like me. Maybe I'm not good enough.' These thoughts replayed in my mind, amplifying the sting of rejection. It wasn't just the physical act of being picked last that hurt; it was the relentless mental chatter that followed.

Our mental chatter is a constant companion – sometimes helpful, other times not so much. It's the voice that cheers you on with a triumphant, 'You nailed it', after a job well done, yet also the critic that murmurs, 'How could you mess that up?', when things don't go as planned. This internal dialogue shapes our perceptions, influences our choices and ultimately affects how we feel about ourselves and the world around us.

The power of mental chatter lies in its ability to both uplift and undermine, depending on the nature of the conversation we're having with ourselves. When positive, it acts as a supportive inner dialogue that spurs us forward, boosting our self-confidence and enhancing our performance. This constructive self-talk turns obstacles into stepping stones and setbacks into valuable lessons, allowing us to draw on past experiences as we plan for our future goals.

But when it turns negative, it can become a relentless critic, eroding our self-esteem and planting seeds of doubt. This critical voice amplifies our fears and magnifies our shortcomings, often making mountains out of molehills. By fixating on past mistakes or excessively worrying about future failures, it can paralyse us, stifle growth and hinder our ability to seize new opportunities. Moreover, such rumination narrows our attention to the source of distress, making it difficult to concentrate on anything else.

Of course, there's nothing wrong with a critical evaluation of ourselves occasionally. It's even necessary as it serves as a valuable tool to identify areas for personal growth or to strengthen our relationships. However, when this inner critique becomes excessively harsh or persistent and repeatedly pops up uninvited, it shifts from being constructive to destructive.

When our inner dialogue becomes overly focused and emotionally charged, it activates brain regions involved in self-reflection and emotional responses, pushing our stress response system into overdrive. This leads to the release of stress hormones like adrenaline and cortisol, heightening our distress and intensifying negative thought patterns. As a result, we become trapped in a self-perpetuating cycle of anxiety, where heightened emotional responses further fixate our worries, making it increasingly challenging to gain a broader perspective.[3]

Repetitive negative thinking also impairs effective problem-solving. While we may believe we're 'working through' a problem by ruminating, this process clouds our judgment, preventing us from finding solutions. Instead of actively trying to solve the problem, those who ruminate tend to remain fixated on the issue and their feelings, keeping them stuck in a negative cycle and increasing feelings of helplessness.[4]

Additionally, negative mental chatter can act as a social repellent. We all tend to share the things that affect us most, but excessive sharing of negative inner thoughts can alienate the very people we need most. Many of us have a threshold for how much venting we can tolerate, especially when the conversation is one-sided. Furthermore, rumination is associated with personality traits such as dependence, clinginess and aggressiveness – qualities that can lead to a loss of social support.[5]

Given these factors, it's not surprising that rumination is a robust predictor of depressive symptoms and depression. It's also linked to other mental health issues, including anxiety, binge eating and drinking, and self-harm. While rumination isn't synonymous with these conditions, it is a common feature.[6]

Negative inner chatter often stems from our ANTs. A situation triggers an ANT – an immediate, negative reaction to what's happening – but the negativity rarely stops there. That initial thought can set off a cascade of inner dialogue, continuing the negative narrative and amplifying the impact of the original thought.

For instance, imagine you've had a minor argument with a friend. Your initial thought might be, 'I shouldn't have said that.' However, your inner voice escalates the situation: 'This is typical of me; I always ruin my friendships. What if they don't want to be friends anymore? I'll be alone.' This snowball effect transforms a single negative thought into a broad, negative self-assessment that undermines your confidence and fuels anxiety.

While ANTs may trigger an initial wave of negativity, it's the ongoing mental chatter that sustains and deepens their impact. Recognising this pattern is the first step in breaking free from it. Earlier, we explored strategies for becoming more aware of our ANTs. Now, let's delve into the tools we can use to halt the negative mental chatter that often follows in their wake.

Psychologist and neuroscientist Ethan Kross explains in his book *Chatter* that it all boils down to creating distance between ourselves and our inner dialogue. As he clarifies, 'chatter is what happens when we zoom in close on something, inflaming our emotions to the exclusion of all the alternative ways of thinking about the issue ... In other words, we lose perspective.'[7]

The antidote to this is to intentionally create distance by zooming out. While this may not solve our problems directly, it significantly increases the likelihood that we can. By zooming out, we give ourselves the opportunity to see the bigger picture and explore different perspectives. This wider lens helps us detach from our immediate emotional reactions and allows us to approach our problems with greater clarity.

As Kross explains, the ability to distance ourselves from our mental chatter is more than just a theoretical idea; it's a practical skill we can cultivate. In his book, he offers various science-based techniques, and I found a few particularly useful:

- **Distanced self-talk**: When working through an emotional experience, shift from the first-person 'I' to the second-person 'you' or the third-person 'he/she/they'. You can even use your own name. For instance, instead of thinking, 'I'm overwhelmed and can't handle this', frame it as, 'She's feeling overwhelmed right now'. This shift in perspective enables you to approach your problems with greater objectivity. It's remarkably quick and helps you step back from your emotions almost instantly.[8]

- **Imagine advising a friend**: Envisage offering advice to a close friend facing the same situation. What would you tell them? What guidance would you give them? Putting yourself in the role of a supportive advisor helps you detach from your emotions and consider the situation more rationally. It also taps into your natural empathy and kindness, helping you move away from self-criticism to self-support.

- **Engage in mental time-travelling**: Imagine yourself a few months or years down the road, looking back on this moment. Ask yourself, 'How will I view this situation in the future? Will it seem as pressing or significant then as it does now?' Alternatively, think about how you might have handled a similar situation in the past and what you've learned from it. By placing the situation in a longer timeline, you can better appreciate its relative importance.

In addition to these techniques, I developed my own visualisation exercise, which halts my mental chatter almost instantly. I imagine my inner dialogue unfolding in a vast garden enclosed by a high wall with a gate. All thoughts must pass through this gate, guarded by a vigilant sentinel named Ronnie. When I notice my thoughts beginning to spiral, I call on Ronnie to close the gate. I picture him stepping in front of it, his chest puffed out in a firm stance, signalling that 'no thought shall pass'. This vivid imagery swiftly interrupts my inner narrative and helps me redirect my thoughts to something more constructive.

Another powerful tool is to create a separate persona for your inner critic. This also creates distance between yourself and your critical thoughts and view them more objectively. I imagine my inner critic as a nasty head teacher at a strict boarding school. She's a tall and imposing older female with piercing eyes and a stern expression. She's dressed in a black suit and always has her hands crossed in front of her body. Her voice is strong and unwavering with an air of authority. Nowadays, when she makes an appearance, I picture her tripping and falling over in the mud. Doing this immediately makes me feel much better.

Being able to interrupt our mental chatter is a powerful skill that can greatly enhance our mood. It enables us to reclaim our focus, reduce stress and approach challenges with a clearer, more balanced perspective. This ability not only helps us manage our ANTs but also proves invaluable when we face adversity in our lives.

Life will inevitably present us with some form of pain or hardship. Whether it's losing a job that shifts our financial stability from secure to precarious, experiencing the death of a family member or close friend that leaves an irreplaceable void, dealing with health issues that require us to alter our way of living or navigating relationships that sometimes unravel, these events are unavoidable – and when they occur, they can hurt deeply.

While pain is inevitable, we do have a choice in how we respond to it. When a loved one dies, we can feel grateful for the time we've shared together. We can also beat ourselves up for not spending more time with them. The choice is ours. There's a critical difference between pain and suffering. Pain is an inevitable part of life; while suffering arises from how we respond to that pain. When we dwell on our misfortunes, replaying painful moments in our minds, we can inadvertently prolong our suffering and let it consume us. Yet, if we take a step back – pausing to breathe and reflect – we can gain a fresh perspective and possibly opt for a more balanced response. One reason why older adults experience fewer stressors is that they tend to focus on the positive, whereas younger adults are more prone to ruminate about the negative.[9]

The moment you notice your thoughts starting to spiral, remember that you hold the power to shift your response. Instead of getting swept away, you can hit the mental pause button using the distancing tools just discussed. Acknowledge the hurt but choose not to let negative thoughts dictate your reaction. This practice not only alleviates suffering but also empowers you to navigate life's challenges with greater resilience. For some, this may come naturally, while others might find it more challenging at first. However, as you commit to this practice, you likely find it becomes easier over time.

Victor Frankl, the Austrian philosopher and Holocaust survivor, famously said, 'The one thing you can't take away from me is the way I choose to respond to what you do to me. The last of one's freedoms is to choose one's attitude in any given circumstance.'[10] While pain may be unavoidable, suffering is a choice. It's a simple saying, but incredibly powerful when truly embraced. That being said, we also need to give ourselves time and space to heal, to reflect and to make sense of what we've been through. Writing can be a powerful tool in this healing process.

Writing That Heals

As the sun sets over the sea around Koh Samui, the sky lights up with warm shades of pink and orange. Seated at a wooden desk by the window, I gaze out over the palm trees and the turquoise ocean beyond. The rhythmic chirping of the geckos creates a soothing background to my thoughts.

This morning, during our session, the wise monk gave me a task. His eyes, filled with compassion, held mine as he spoke. 'Expressive writing,' he said, 'is a way to confront and process your pain. Write about what happened to you. Let your emotions flow freely. Don't hold back. Do this for fifteen to thirty minutes without stopping. Afterwards, take some time for yourself, a walk down the beach perhaps, to process the emotions that surfaced.'

As the scent of frangipani drifts in, I pick up my pen. At first, the words come slowly, hesitantly, as if afraid to emerge. But soon, they begin to flow, a torrent of memories and emotions surging onto the page. I write about the loss, the piercing pain in my heart, the chilling numbness that gripped me. About the day it happened. The shock, the disbelief, the agony of knowing that it was my father's choice.

My chest tightens, and I have to force myself to keep writing. The monk's words echo in my mind: 'Let it out. It's a healing process.' I take a deep breath, steadying myself. I write about the guilt, about understanding his reasons, about the anger that he abandoned us and, in doing so, shattered our world. As tears blur my vision, I write about the loneliness, the isolation, the feeling that no one truly understood what I was going through. I write about my relationship that fell apart as a result.

Then somehow the darkness subsides and a ray of light enters. Thoughts resurface of the small acts of kindness that had helped me hold on, the friends who stood by me, the familial bonds that grew stronger. Gradually, my writing shifts from the painful event that shaped me to the personal growth that followed. I write about the unexpected strength I discovered within me; the resilience that saw me through the darkest days. I recall the long conversations with my sister and how our relationship deepened because of our shared loss.

After thirty minutes, I put down my pen and a strange sense of relief washes over me. The pain is still there, raw and aching, but it feels somewhat lighter, less suffocating. I sit quietly in my room, now bathed in the soft glow of twilight, grateful for the monk's wisdom and the therapeutic power of expressive writing.

The writing exercise I did on the retreat was immensely powerful and profoundly aided my healing process. I don't need any scientific proof to convince me of its effectiveness. However, as it turns out, the technique, or at least a form of it, has been the subject of extensive research. James Pennebaker, a psychologist who laid the groundwork for the method, discovered that writing about traumatic experiences not only facilitates emotional healing but also improves physical health – something I can personally attest to.

In 1986, Pennebaker conducted a seminal study on expressive writing. Over four days, participants wrote continuously for fifteen minutes each day. The control group was instructed to write objectively about superficial topics, while the experimental group was asked to write about their most traumatic experience. Despite increased emotional distress immediately after writing, participants who wrote about their deepest thoughts and feelings showed significant improvements in mental well-being and physical health in the following months.[11]

Pennebaker's findings sparked hundreds of follow-up studies by his team and others. These studies found that expressive writing not only helps us process past experiences and envision a path forward but also lowers blood pressure, strengthens the immune system and improves sleep quality. Writing about trauma can reduce stress, anxiety and depression. It can also enhance cognitive performance by bringing greater focus and clarity.[12]

Why can pouring our heart onto the page lead to reduced stress and enhanced overall well-being? Through writing, we externalise our thoughts and experiences, giving them tangible form. This process helps us make sense of them in a way that thinking alone cannot. Expressing our emotions and experiences through words releases the pent-up energy associated with those emotions, enabling emotional catharsis and reducing stress.

Moreover, writing about our experiences gives us perspective. We can see things from multiple angles and reflect on how they've shaped us, leading to improved self-understanding. Perhaps one of the most significant benefits of expressive writing is its ability to provide a safe space to express our emotions without judgement. In a world where we may feel pressured to hide or suppress our feelings, expressive writing allows us to be honest and vulnerable with ourselves.

Expressive writing not only provides emotional relief but can also help us manage emotions better and make us less reactive to stress. It helps lower stress markers like cortisol levels. Furthermore, brain scans reveal that when we write about our emotions activity in the amygdala decreases. At the same time, there's more activity in the right ventrolateral prefrontal cortex, which helps us regulate our emotions.[13]

Expressive writing in the style of Pennebaker involves setting time aside to write freely about something that profoundly affected you. It could be a loss, a failure, a conflict or any other personal challenge. It's a highly adaptable, low-cost intervention, but here are a few key elements that are good to keep in mind:[14]

- Find a location where you cannot be disturbed and ensure you have some time after your writing session to compose yourself.

- Write continuously for 15–30 minutes. In general, this writing session is repeated three to four times, but there is no magical number as it depends on the person. The sessions can take place on consecutive days or spread out over several weeks. You can write about the same thing each day or about different issues.

- During each writing session, explore your deepest thoughts and feelings about the experience. You can explore how it might be related to your childhood, relationships, your career, who you are and who you'd like to become. It's critical that you really let go and explore your very deepest emotions and thoughts.

- Set a timer and write continuously without worrying about grammar, spelling and punctuation. Don't hold back. The goal is to keep the pen moving and to express yourself as freely as possible. You can write on paper or you can type on a computer.

- The writing is for you and only you. The purpose is to be completely honest with yourself without fear of judgement. You can throw your writing away when you're finished if you like.

- Many people experience feeling a bit sad or depressed after writing. This typically goes away in a couple of hours. If you find that you are getting extremely upset about a topic, simply stop writing or change topics.

There is strength in embracing our vulnerability. When we use writing to lay bare our uncomfortable truths, we reclaim our role as the protagonists in our lives, rather than victims of circumstances beyond our control. While expressive writing is not a panacea – therapy is often necessary for dealing with deeper traumas – it's a powerful, accessible tool for processing the painful events life can throw at us. All it takes is the willingness to pick up a pen and start writing. Through this simple act, we can begin to understand and process our experiences and find a path to healing.

Expressive writing allows us to confront the pain of the past, but moving forward often requires us to step into the unknown. By embracing uncertainty, we can unlock the potential for new possibilities and growth.

Dealing with Uncertainty

The news hit hard. It was mid-December 2021, and the Dutch government had just announced new restrictions: shops and restaurants had to close, and Christmas and New Year gatherings were limited to six people. Borders remained open, but anyone catching Covid had to isolate for ten days. With a tight schedule to return to the UK after New Year's, I worried about getting stuck. On top of that, the mandatory Covid tests added significant extra costs.

That evening, I made the difficult decision to cancel my trip. The risks and expenses seemed too high. For the second year in a row, I wouldn't be home for Christmas, and it broke my heart. I could hear the disappointment in my mother's voice, mirroring my own.

Over the next few days, doubts crept in. Was cancelling really necessary? Was the risk of catching Covid really so high? We would take precautions and everyone was vaccinated. Did it matter that everything was closed? To help make sense of it, I remembered a strategy from a book: using an expected value decision tree. The idea is simple – map out your options, weigh the outcomes by their likelihood and impact, and let the numbers

LETTING GO

guide you. It helps to see a decision from multiple angles, making it easier to balance emotions with logic.

I started with the two main choices: go or stay. For each, I considered the outcomes. If I went and caught Covid, I'd face quarantine, extra costs and miss my UK return (-100). If I didn't catch it, I'd have a memorable Christmas with family (+100). Staying would avoid the risks but mean another holiday without family. If I got Covid at home, it wouldn't be as bad as catching it while in the Netherlands (-40); if I didn't, the UK holiday would be pleasant but less meaningful (+50).

Next, I assigned probabilities. I estimated a 10 per cent chance of getting Covid if I stayed in the UK, and 20 per cent if I went to Amsterdam. I calculated the expected values: going scored a 60, while staying scored a 41. The numbers were clear – I should go. So I did, and I had a wonderful time with no issues getting back.

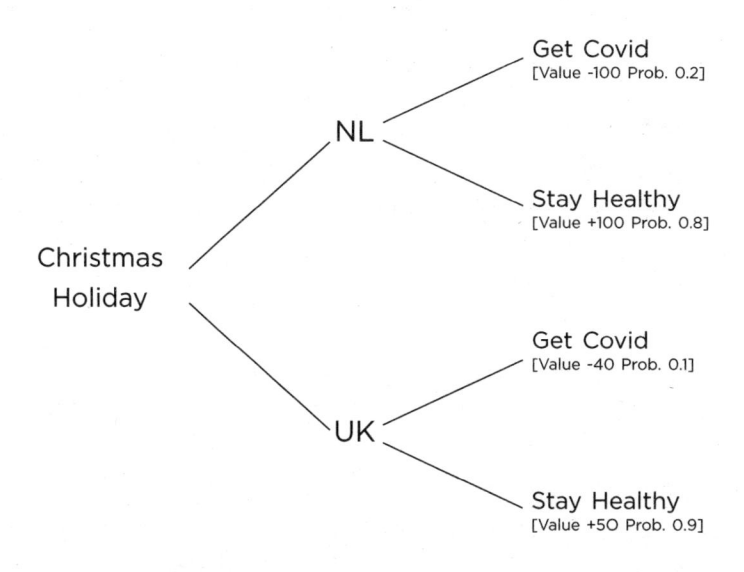

```
Christmas Holiday
├── NL
│   ├── Get Covid [Value -100 Prob. 0.2]
│   └── Stay Healthy [Value +100 Prob. 0.8]
└── UK
    ├── Get Covid [Value -40 Prob. 0.1]
    └── Stay Healthy [Value +50 Prob. 0.9]
```

Expected Value - Go to NL = (-100 x 0.2) + (100x0.8) = 60
Expected Value - Stay in UK = (-40 x 0.1) + (50x0.9) = 41

As we saw in Chapter 8, our brain dislikes uncertainty and it's not particularly keen on losses either. Therefore, it tends to fixate on the worst-case scenario, assigning a higher probability than it might actually deserve. It's a protective mechanism designed to help us avoid uncertainty and potential losses, but it often leads to an exaggerated sense of risk. When we overestimate the likelihood of negative outcomes, it distorts our perception of reality, making us more anxious and less willing to take calculated risks.

This not only affects decisions like travelling during a pandemic, but can also act like a formidable barrier when we're trying to make changes in our lives. When we open ourselves to questioning our engrained behaviours and beliefs, we step into unfamiliar territory where the security of our established views is disrupted. We put ourselves in a position of both uncertainty and potential loss – a prospect that can be frightening and we therefore often resist.

Decision trees help us counter our brain's natural biases by providing an objective framework for weighing potential outcomes. Instead of letting irrational fears of loss and uncertainty dominate, we can use this tool to make decisions based on more realistic probabilities. By breaking down complex choices, we gain a clearer view of the values we assign to outcomes and the likelihood of each possibility. Even when we don't know the exact values or probabilities, decision trees help us think more rationally, allowing us to step outside the emotional fog and see our options – and their impacts – more clearly. This structured process often reveals that what seems very risky is often far more manageable.

Let's give it a try for a hypothetical decision Alex has to make. Alex is often invited to weekend gatherings by his friends. Despite feeling drained and needing time to relax, he always agrees to attend because he doesn't want to disappoint them or miss out on potential fun. Alex could explore his situation by focusing on a specific instance: an invitation to a friend's birthday party. His decision tree might look as follows:

LETTING GO

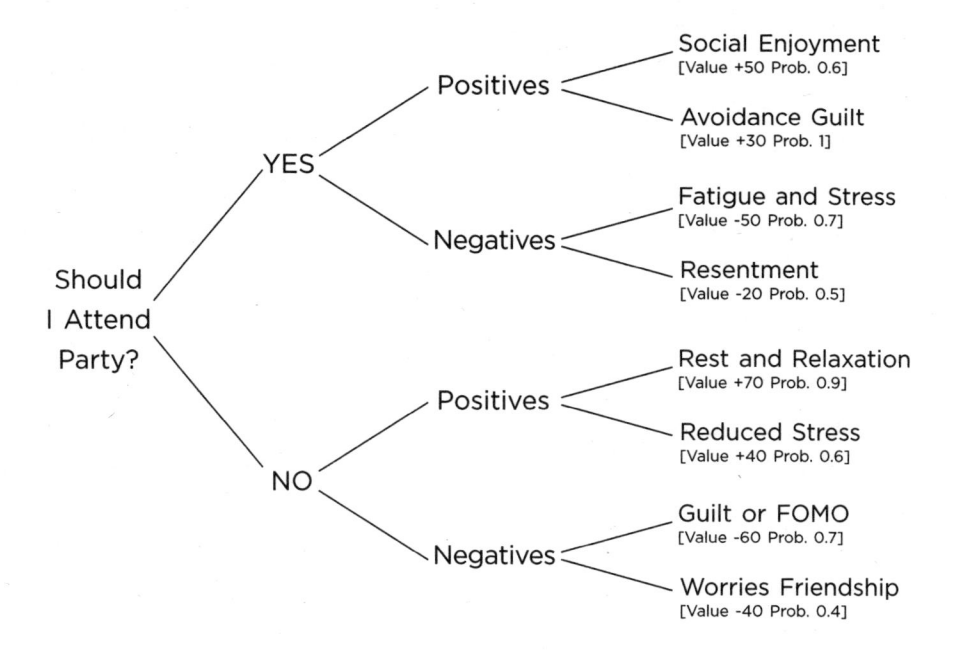

```
                                    ┌─ Social Enjoyment
                                    │  [Value +50 Prob. 0.6]
                        ┌─ Positives ─┤
                        │           └─ Avoidance Guilt
                  YES   │              [Value +30 Prob. 1]
                   ┌────┤
                   │    │           ┌─ Fatigue and Stress
                   │    │           │  [Value -50 Prob. 0.7]
                   │    └─ Negatives ─┤
  Should           │                └─ Resentment
  I Attend ────────┤                   [Value -20 Prob. 0.5]
  Party?           │
                   │                ┌─ Rest and Relaxation
                   │                │  [Value +70 Prob. 0.9]
                   │    ┌─ Positives ─┤
                   │    │           └─ Reduced Stress
                   └────┤              [Value +40 Prob. 0.6]
                  NO    │
                        │           ┌─ Guilt or FOMO
                        │           │  [Value -60 Prob. 0.7]
                        └─ Negatives ─┤
                                    └─ Worries Friendship
                                       [Value -40 Prob. 0.4]
```

Expected Value - Attend Party = (50 x 0.6) + (30 x 1) + (-50 x 0.7) + (-20 x 0.5) = 15
Expected Value - Stay Home = (70 x 0.9) + (40 x 0.6) + (-60 x 0.7) + (-40 x 0.4) = 29

By mapping out these outcomes, Alex can clearly see that while there are benefits to both choices, the cost of attending his friend's party is higher than the reward. His decision tree helps him recognise that, in this case, choosing to stay home will give him more value, even if it feels somewhat uncomfortable in the short-term.

Seeing both costs and benefits of a particular behaviour is important because it makes the trade-offs involved much clearer. While it's not always easy to pinpoint exact values and probabilities, approaching the decision with a rational mindset helps us see things more clearly and make a more informed choice.

Furthermore, it allows us to frame the choice as a loss instead of a gain. This matters as the way a choice is presented can significantly influence our decisions. We tend to be more willing to take a risk to avoid a certain loss than to secure an equivalent gain. By framing something as a gain or a loss, our risk preferences tend to shift accordingly – a phenomenon known as the *framing effect*.

Psychologists Daniel Kahneman and Amos Tversky illustrated this effect in a famous experiment where participants were asked to choose between two medical programmes to combat a hypothetical disease outbreak expected to kill 600 people. When framed as a gain, people preferred a programme that guaranteed saving 200 lives over a riskier one with a 33 per cent chance of saving all 600 and a 67 per cent chance of saving none. But, when framed in terms of lives lost (a loss frame), participants preferred the risky option – the 33 per cent chance that no one would die and 67 per cent chance that all 600 would die – over a programme that guaranteed 400 deaths.[15]

We can leverage this insight to challenge unhelpful beliefs and behaviours. By emphasising what we stand to lose when maintaining a certain behaviour, we may become more open to taking the necessary risks to change. For example, Alex could reframe his decision about attending his friend's birthday party by focusing on the time he would lose for rest and relaxation, which is essential for reducing his stress. This shift in perspective might make it easier for him to embrace the, for him, riskier choice of staying home.

Over time, creating decision trees can shed light on the underlying reasons behind our choices. It allows us to recognise patterns, which in turn may uncover some of our core beliefs. For instance, as Alex analyses his decisions, he might discover that his struggle to decline social invitations stems from a deep-seated belief that he is unworthy of friendship. However, by noticing that his friendships remain intact even when he says no, he can gradually begin to challenge and reshape this belief.

Creating decision trees should boost your confidence in making choices, particularly when they seem risky. There are many ways to create a decision tree, so find a method that resonates with you. If you're looking to integrate decision trees into your life, I can recommend *Bulletproof Problem Solving* by Charles Conn and Robert McLean.[16]

Aversion to uncertainty and loss is just one part of what makes change feel daunting. Social pressure can weigh heavily on us; the fear of judgment, criticism or rejection from family and friends often holds us back. Past failures may lead to scepticism about our ability to succeed, while the effort required to break old habits can feel overwhelming, especially when life is already demanding. Furthermore, the perceived complexity of the change process can be discouraging, particularly if we feel we lack the necessary skills or knowledge. Given these challenges, it's important to start small, focusing on one decision at a time. This approach allows us to gradually build confidence in the process.

Reassessing our approach to measuring success can also help. By choosing the right metrics, we ensure that we're not only making decisions more confidently but also align them with what truly matters to us.

Zero In on What Matters

For the longest time, I avoided Twitter (now X) and LinkedIn. It wasn't just about preserving my focus, though that was a nice side effect; it was because every time I scrolled through those platforms, I was overwhelmed by a sinking feeling that I wasn't accomplishing enough. On the rare occasions when I did log in, I was met with a relentless parade of my colleagues' achievements. There it was: another publication, another conference presentation, another accolade, which made me feel like I was drowning in a sea of academic successes. Every notification, every congratulatory comment on a peer's post, felt like a glaring reminder of how far behind I was. And, as we all know, no one was sharing their struggles, rejections or failures.

In the hyper-competitive world of academia, I pushed myself to constantly churn out papers, meet every deadline, while working hard to be a 'good academic citizen', reviewing others work and participating in committees. Yet, no matter how much I accomplished, it never felt like enough. I couldn't shake the feeling that my peers were always one step ahead – publishing more often, getting their work into more prestigious journals, being invited to speak at more conferences.

It wasn't until I stumbled upon Mark Manson's *The Subtle Art of Not Giving a F*ck* that I began to question the metrics by which I was measuring my success. Manson's message is straightforward yet revolutionary: much of our dissatisfaction in life stems from caring too much about things that ultimately don't matter. We obsess over the wrong metrics – those that society or our peers deem important – because we believe they define our worth. But what if we've been chasing the wrong goals all along?

In my case, the constant comparison to my peers was like running on a treadmill with no end in sight. I was measuring my success by their achievements, by the recognition they received and by the standards that others had set. But these comparisons were fundamentally flawed. They were based on values that didn't align with my own. The truth was, I hadn't taken the time to define what success meant to me personally.

I began to realise that my obsession with external validation – through publications, conference invitations and the approval of my peers – was not only unhealthy but also unproductive. These were not the metrics that truly mattered to me. I had lost sight of why I had entered academia in the first place: the joy of learning, the thrill of discovering new ideas and the satisfaction of mentoring students.

Manson's book emphasises that we are, for the most part, pretty average at most things we do. And that's okay. In fact, it's more than okay – it's normal. By definition we can't all be exceptional. And even if we are exceptional at one thing, we often fall short in other parts of our lives because our time and energy are finite. Yet, we spend so much effort trying to excel at everything, believing that success implies being exceptional in every area of our lives.

Things get even worse if we fall into the perfectionism trap – the belief that we need to perform flawlessly in all, or at least most, aspects of life. Perfectionism pushes us to avoid mistakes and shortcomings at all costs. While it can sometimes drive us to achieve, it can also trap us in a cycle of never feeling good enough. The pursuit of perfection becomes a race without a finish line, leaving us exhausted and unfulfilled.

This drive to be exceptional – or worse, perfect – is often at the root of our unhappiness. We set impossibly high standards for ourselves, believing that anything less is failure. So what should we be focusing on instead? It comes back to our personal values and passions; our 'why', as we discussed in Chapter 3. We need to identify what genuinely matters to us and let go of the rest. This means caring deeply about a few things that resonate with our true selves, rather than scattering our energy across countless pursuits that don't.

For me, this meant redefining success on my own terms. I decided to focus on what brought me genuine fulfilment. Instead of chasing accolades and constantly trying to keep up with my peers, I chose to invest my finite time differently. I began writing this book, channelling my time and energy into a project that truly resonated with me, even if it meant spending less time on my economics research. I began investing more time in mentoring students and junior faculty, helping them navigate their academic journeys. And, most importantly, I stopped measuring my worth by the achievements of others.

I also embraced the fact that my personal life is just as important as my professional life, and that I need to carve out time for it. So I made a conscious decision not to spend my evenings and weekends working, recognising that balance is crucial to my well-being. Of course, that balance went out the window the summer I was finishing this book's manuscript, but I understand that adapting is part of life.

By focusing on what mattered to me, I found a sense of peace and contentment that had long felt out of reach. I realised that success isn't about ticking off a list of achievements, impressing others or striving to be exceptional or perfect – it's about living a life that's true to my own values and passions.

So the next time you feel overwhelmed by the accomplishments of others or the pressure to be perfect, take a step back and ask yourself: what are the things that truly matter to me? Once you have your answer, focus on that – and let go of the rest. Every moment, whether you realise it or not, you're choosing what to care about. Change begins with deciding to care about something different. It's really as simple as that. Still, putting it into practice can be quite challenging – just as accepting life as it is can be hard.

Stop Pushing Back

Imagine you've planned a romantic evening for your partner and are envisioning a night filled with deep conversation and connection. You've meticulously prepared everything, from cooking her favourite meal to setting the perfect ambiance. But when she arrives home, she's exhausted from a demanding day at work and just wants to relax quietly. She quickly eats the meal you prepared and, as soon as she's finished, she retreats to the couch and turns on the TV. As you clean up the table and kitchen, you can't help but feel disappointed, unappreciated and hurt that your efforts seem to go unnoticed. You might even vow never to put in that much effort again.

The truth is, it's not your partner's actions that cause you distress; it's your resistance to the reality of their behaviour. You had a rigid expectation of how she should act, and when she didn't meet that expectation, frustration set in. We often find ourselves caught in a cycle of stress and frustration, but the root of our turmoil usually boils down to one simple factor: our rigid expectations of how life should unfold and how the people in

LETTING GO

our life should behave, whether it's our partner, friend, co-worker or a random stranger.

It's not the external events themselves that cause us distress, but rather our resistance to them. When we cling to a fixed idea of how things should be, we essentially create a barrier between ourselves and reality. This clash between our expectations and what actually happens is where the true source of our distress resides.

To experience how your expectations cause distress, you can try the following exercise. Think about something that's bothering you. Write down a specific statement that captures your idea about the situation. For example, 'My partner should be on time' or 'My boss should appreciate my work'. Note how you feel and behave because this expectation is not being met. Are you frustrated, angry, disappointed? How do you engage with your partner/boss/someone else?

Now take a step back and reflect on how your unease is tied to your desire for things to be different. Picture yourself accepting the situation as it is, without expecting it to change. How do you feel now? Do you notice how your discomfort arises from your insistence that life and the people in it must conform to your specific desires and plans? When you accept a situation as is, you step into a different emotional domain, one with substantially less frustration and disappointment.

It's important to realise that acceptance of a situation doesn't mean passivity or resignation; it's about acknowledging the way things are without unnecessary resistance and make your choices from that perspective. You don't need to stay with your partner if they consistently fail to appreciate your efforts. But not accepting the way they are and repeatedly pushing against it only adds to your frustration and stress. Instead, recognising and accepting who they are can help you decide if you can be happy within this relationship or if it's time to move on.

For help with letting go of the frustration from trying to control what's outside my influence, I turned to the teachings of Byron

Katie – author of *Loving What Is* and creator of 'The Work', a self-inquiry method that challenges stressful thoughts and beliefs. She emphasises the importance of distinguishing between 'your business', 'their business' and 'God's business'.

Katie explains that we typically stress ourselves out by trying to control or interfere with 'their business' – the realm of other people's actions, thoughts and circumstances. For instance, if a project at work isn't going as planned, you might feel stressed because you're trying to manage others' performance. But that's 'their business' and it's beyond your control.

'God's business', in Katie's terminology, refers to natural events and the larger forces of life beyond human control. It's the unpredictable nature of the universe and the flow of events that cannot be dictated by any one person. Like 'their business', we cannot control 'God's business' and we're better off accepting it as is.

'Your business', on the other hand, is where your focus should lie: your own thoughts, actions and reactions. It's about how you choose to respond to the situation. By concentrating on 'your business', you direct your energy towards making positive changes where you can, rather than wasting it on what you cannot change.

If you've read Stephen Covey's *The 7 Habits of Highly Effective People*, you may recall his concepts of the 'Circle of Concern' and 'Circle of Influence'. Covey's 'Circle of Concern' includes all the things we care about, while the smaller 'Circle of Influence' encompasses areas where we can exert control, such as our own thoughts and behaviours. Katie's idea of 'your business' closely aligns with Covey's 'Circle of Influence', emphasising a focus on what we can control. In contrast, 'their business' and 'God's business' fall within Covey's 'Circle of Concern' but outside the 'Circle of Influence'.

Like Covey and Katie, I believe in focusing on what we can influence and releasing the need to control everything else. This mindset reduces stress, enhances our effectiveness and fosters a more proactive approach to life. While it can be tough to stay out of someone else's business, recognising what's truly within our control is an important first step. By letting go of the belief that life and others must act a certain way, we can cultivate a sense of inner peace and live authentically and harmoniously with the world around us.

Now we've equipped ourselves with some strategies to release what no longer serves us, it's time to embrace beliefs that empower us – let's dive into the growth mindset.

Growth Mindset

Even as a four-year-old girl, I knew I was smart. During my first year of kindergarten, I would enthusiastically glance over the puzzles meant for older kids, convinced I could solve them with ease. My mother had taught me to read early, and my father often praised me for my intelligence. At family gatherings, I was affectionately dubbed 'the smart one', and every test I aced or puzzle I completed was met with enthusiastic affirmations of my cleverness.

My father meant well; his compliments aimed to bolster my confidence. However, unintentionally, it established the foundation for what I would later recognise as a fixed mindset. I started associating my self-worth with my intelligence, viewing it as an immutable characteristic – I was either smart or not. This perspective resulted in a need to constantly prove myself and seek validation of my intelligence. It's probably an important reason why I developed imposter syndrome and felt perpetually unworthy of the 'smart' title.

After reading Carol Dweck's groundbreaking book *Mindset*, my perspective about myself and my intelligence underwent a radical change for the better. In this book, she explores two contrasting mindsets: the 'fixed mindset' and the 'growth mindset'. A fixed mindset is the belief that our abilities, such as intelligence, are static traits that cannot be changed. Conversely, a growth mindset is the understanding that abilities can be developed through effort, learning and persistence.

People with a fixed mindset often view failure as a direct reflection of their innate abilities, interpreting it as proof that they lack intelligence or talent. Failure transforms from an action ('I failed') to an identity ('I am a failure'). On the other hand, those with a growth mindset see failure not as an indictment of their innate abilities but as an essential part of their learning process. Though failure can be a painful experience, it's seen as a problem to be faced, dealt with and learned from.

Openness and willingness to self-improve are crucial factors that enable people with a growth mindset to excel. For instance, after performing poorly on a test, college students were given the opportunity to review the tests of other students. Those with a fixed mindset tended to look at the tests of students who did worse than they did, aiming to recover their self-esteem by comparison. Whereas students with a growth mindset examined the tests of peers who had performed far better. They asked themselves: what strategies were these students using? What could they learn from them? By doing so, these students rebuilt their self-esteem not merely by feeling better, but by actually getting better.[17]

The fixed and growth mindsets also impact our perception of effort. People with a fixed mindset tend to view effort as a sign of inadequacy – if you have to work hard, you're not naturally talented. This belief can lead them to shy away from challenges. Those with a growth mindset see effort as the path to mastery and success, recognising that hard work is necessary for developing skills and achieving goals. For them, effort is a vital ingredient for success.

Adopting one mindset or the other places us in a specific world. In the world where traits are seen as fixed, success revolves around demonstrating intelligence or talent – it's about seeking validation. In the world where qualities are viewed as malleable, success is about pushing our boundaries to discover and learn new things – it's about self-development. This has big implications. As plenty of studies have shown: a growth mindset predicts and promotes an increase in challenge seeking, resilience and positive outcomes.[18]

A growth mindset doesn't imply that anyone can achieve anything with hard work alone. It simply means that change is possible under the right conditions and with the right support. It's a powerful belief, as the opposite is very stressful. As Carol Dweck writes: '[If you believe nothing about you can change], every situation feels like a test of your intelligence, personality, or character. Each experience is evaluated: Will I succeed or fail? Will I look smart or dumb? Will I be accepted or rejected?'[19] It perfectly captures the internal struggle I often faced.

How are these mindsets created, you might wonder. The research of Dweck and others has shown that the way children are praised and labelled during childhood plays an important role. When children are praised for their intelligence, such as being told, 'You're so good at maths', it promotes a fixed mindset. This type of personal praise sends the message that their abilities are innate and beyond their control. In contrast, when children receive praise for their effort, like 'I loved seeing how hard you worked on your maths test', it conveys that success is a result of their effort and strategy – factors they can control and improve over time. Praising effort fosters a growth mindset. It encourages children to believe that they can develop and enhance their abilities through hard work and persistence.[20]

You can find out if you have a fixed or growth mindset by reading the following statements and deciding whether you mostly agree or disagree with them:

1. I believe people have a natural limit to how much they can learn, no matter how hard they try.

2. I give up when something is hard or feels impossible to do right.

3. I find inspiration and lessons in the achievements of others.

4. The success of others threatens my self-esteem and sense of worth.

5. I believe effort and persistence are more important than inherent talent for achieving success.

6. Feedback and constructive criticism are essential for improving my performance and skills.

7. I tend to take constructive feedback as personal criticism.

8. I believe that I can always improve and grow in any area if I set my mind to it.

If you find yourself agreeing most with statements 1, 2, 4 and 7, you likely lean towards a fixed mindset. Conversely, if statements 3, 5, 6 and 8 resonate more with you, then you probably embrace a growth mindset. Note that your mindset can vary across different areas of your life. For example, you might have different beliefs regarding your abilities such as intelligence, musical talent, athletic skills or business skills, than you do when it comes to personality traits like resilience, social skills or empathy.

If you find yourself leaning towards a fixed mindset, there's good news: you have the power to change it. Mindsets are simply beliefs – powerful, yes, but ultimately just learned mental frameworks, shaped and reinforced through experience and repetition. Because they are learned, they can also be unlearned and transformed. As we discussed in Part 2, our brain is malleable and capable of learning and adapting throughout our lives, a process known as neuroplasticity. This enables us to reshape ingrained mental patterns and shift our mindset from fixed to growth.

How can we move towards a growth mindset? First, let's understand what doesn't help: simply telling yourself to try harder. If your natural inclination is to see the need for effort as a sign that you're doing something wrong, it's unlikely that you'll change your mindset through willpower alone. The crux lies in shifting your perception of effort and failure; a change that can happen surprisingly quickly.

A recent study examined the impact of just two short online sessions focused on growth mindset principles. Aimed at ninth graders, the intervention taught the students that intellectual abilities are not fixed but can evolve over time. The results were striking: improved grades among lower-achieving students and a boost in enrolment in advanced math courses in tenth grade. This suggests that these students were able to quickly adopt a growth mindset, leading to a significant boost in their performance.[21]

The structure of the intervention could likely benefit us too, though the shift might take longer since teenage brains are more flexible. First, students learned how the brain can change and adapt – similar to what you have read in this book. Second, they heard stories from older students about overcoming challenges through a growth mindset. Perhaps my story can serve as an example for you. Finally, they reflected on their own struggles and wrote a letter of advice to a struggling peer, a technique called *saying-is-believing*.[22] These writing exercises help reinforce the belief that effort leads to improvement and that challenges are opportunities for growth. You can try them too.

To solidify a growth mindset, it helps to shift focus from the end result to the journey itself. This perspective moves the emphasis to appreciating the process of learning and development rather than simply achieving a goal. Every step becomes an opportunity to gain new insights and skills, fostering deeper engagement with the process.

Additionally, pay attention to your self-talk. Cultivate a supportive inner dialogue by celebrating your progress, acknowledging your problem-solving abilities and offering yourself constructive feedback when things don't go as planned.

Above all, don't be afraid of making mistakes. Embrace them as challenges instead, because failures often provide us with the richest learning opportunities. I still remember the first time I caught myself thinking, 'This is tough, but it's helping me improve my work', after receiving harsh feedback on one of my research papers. That's when I realised my mindset had shifted from fixed to growth. I'd stepped into a better world. One you can enter too.

The growth mindset is extremely powerful, but to fully harness its power there's another mindset we need to embrace: the belief that stress can be enhancing.

Synergising Growth and Stress

Picture the following scenario. You've embraced the growth mindset and have chosen to face new challenges head-on. You've let your manager know that you're ready to present your team's findings to the CEO when the occasion arises. Being a strong advocate for empowerment, your manager believes the time has come, and you're about to pitch a new product strategy your team has developed in the boardroom.

Before you even set foot in the room, your heart starts to race, your palms sweat, your breath quickens and your stomach tightens. You instantly identify these signals: stress! You quickly interpret them to mean that you're out of your depth, that failure is imminent. You feel you're about to choke and your confidence drains with every breath you take. The presentation that you initially approached as a challenging opportunity has morphed into a daunting ordeal.

We often view physiological arousal as an inherently negative experience, which leads us to believe that the sensations are signs of imminent failure and that we're out of our depth. As a result, we become anxious and overwhelmed, which only intensifies the stress response and impairs our ability to cope effectively, creating a vicious cycle. Essentially, we become stressed about being stressed. Psychologist Alia Crum refers to this as the 'stress-is-debilitating' mindset.[23]

The stress-is-debilitating mindset is deeply ingrained in our culture. When we talk about managing stress, we usually focus on eradicating it – taking a stroll, drinking chamomile tea or having a relaxing bubble bath. The implicit message is to distract ourselves and eliminate stress when we feel stressed. But an alternative explanation of what we feel is that in the moment we're about to do something that's very important to us, our body is gearing up to the challenge by boosting performance. This is the 'stress-can-be-enhancing mindset'.[24]

Under this mindset, we would interpret the changes in our body as we're about to step into the boardroom in a radically different way. We'd recognise that our elevated heart rate is pumping extra oxygen to our brain, that the sweat is keeping our body cool and that the release of cortisol and adrenaline is enhancing our focus. Viewed this way, stress becomes an ally, a source of energy that propels us to perform at our best. It can be controlled because we choose to take advantage of the enhanced capacity for performance that it fuels, rather than being worried or distracted by it.

What we often overlook is the difference between the stressor, the stress response our interpretation of that response. A stressor is an external event or situation that places demands on our body or mind, like a looming deadline, a complex project or a difficult conversation. The stress response is our body's reaction to the stressor, involving physiological changes like increased heart rate and adrenaline, as well as emotional and cognitive shifts. Lastly, there's our appraisal of the stress response – how we interpret these physiological changes. We can view them as a problem, signalling that we're overwhelmed, or as a resource that energises us to meet the challenge.

We often conflate the experience of stress with our emotional and physiological reactions to a stressor. When saying, 'I'm feeling really stressed', what we really mean is that we've encountered a stressor, noticed the physiological changes in our body and appraised those changes as harmful or overwhelming. What we need to learn is to differentiate the stressor from how we react to it, as often the stressor isn't inherently a bad thing.

Take public speaking as an example. For many, the mere

thought of addressing an audience triggers anxiety, sweating and a racing heart – typical signs of a stress response. If we interpret this as a threat, we amplify feelings of nervousness, making us less effective. However, if we reframe it as an opportunity to share knowledge and connect with others, our response shifts. In this context, a racing heart signals readiness, and sweating means gearing up for action. The stressor – public speaking – remains the same, but how we appraise and experience it transforms. By reshaping our mindset around stress, we end up in a better place.

Why is this important in relation to the growth mindset? The growth mindset encourages us to view challenges as valuable opportunities for learning and self-improvement rather than hazards to avoid. However, if we believe that stress is harmful and beyond our control, we may hesitate to engage in challenging yet stressful learning experiences. The stress response we feel can discourage us from taking these risks. If, on the other hand, we recognise that our stress response can be harnessed as a resource, we're more likely to embrace and tackle those stressful challenges.

A recent study demonstrates the powerful effects of a 30-minute intervention that combined the growth and stress-can-be-enhancing mindsets, showing that these two concepts amplify each other. Ninth graders were encouraged to see struggles as opportunities for growth and to view the stress that arises from these challenges as the body's natural mechanism for overcoming obstacles.

The results were remarkable. The combined mindset intervention significantly improved the students' thoughts about stress, cardiovascular responses, cortisol levels, psychological well-being, academic success and anxiety symptoms during the 2020 Covid lockdowns. Importantly, these positive effects were much stronger compared to those experienced by students who received the growth mindset or the stress-can-be-enhancing mindset intervention alone, underscoring the importance of addressing both mindsets together.[25] While the study focused on adolescents, there's no reason to believe that adults wouldn't benefit similarly from adopting both mindsets.

Embracing both the growth and stress-can-be-enhancing mindsets can make a world of difference. That said, another powerful shift occurs when we focus on what we can achieve by harnessing our unique strengths.

Superpowers

A while back, one of my friends shared a story about her son, whom we shall call Jack. Jack is a bright, imaginative boy whose curiosity knows no bounds. He loves building intricate structures with his Lego sets and spends hours sketching fantastical creatures. However, Jack struggled with reading and writing. Words seemed to dance and blur on the page and, despite working hard, he was always a step behind his classmates.

By the time Jack reached second grade, his teacher noticed his difficulties and recommended an assessment. The diagnosis of dyslexia brought both a sense of relief and concern. Relief, because the struggles Jack faced in reading and writing finally made sense; concern, because of the worry how he would cope in a world that often misunderstands this learning difference.

Ever resolute, my friend decided to help her son see his dyslexia not as a hindrance but as a unique strength. She began telling Jack stories about famous people who had dyslexia – like Leonardo da Vinci and Walt Disney – explaining how their unique ways of thinking led to incredible achievements.

Every day, she helped Jack with his schoolwork using innovative methods that focused on his strengths. They utilised colourful, hands-on learning tools and transformed spelling lessons into games and maths problems into engaging puzzles. Whenever Jack found a task tough, she would remind him of their heroes, reinforcing the belief that his brain just worked differently, enabling him to see and understand the world in ways that others couldn't. As a result, Jack learned to embrace his dyslexia, recognising it as his own unique superpower.

We all possess unique strengths and weaknesses, and our individual ways of perceiving and interacting with the world are what make us who we are. Just like Jack, many of us face challenges that may feel overwhelming, making it hard to see beyond the immediate struggle. However, these very challenges can often be transformed into remarkable strengths with the right mindset and support.

Teaching a child that dyslexia is a superpower rather than a disability can change their outlook on life immensely. If you weren't fortunate like Jack to be taught to focus on your strengths, rather than your (perceived) weaknesses, you can still learn to do so. You have the power to shift your focus to what you can achieve with your unique capabilities, rather than focusing on what you cannot do.

Personally, I spent a long time feeling self-conscious about my introverted nature, often viewing it as a social weakness. However, after reading Susan Cain's book *Quiet*, I began to see my introversion in a new light. I realised it endowed me with unique strengths, such as exceptional listening skills, a deep capacity for reflection and a comfort with solitude. Embracing these introspective qualities, I discovered that they were precisely the attributes I needed to excel in areas that value thoughtful analysis and creativity, like writing this book.

When you begin to see your unique traits as superpowers, you unlock a world of new possibilities. Let your imagination run wild and see where it takes you. You might be astonished by the remarkable achievements you're capable of. If you fight for your limitations you'll get to keep them, but if you choose to challenge them and embrace new possibilities, you'll likely discover a wealth of potential you never knew you had.

The Key Takeaways

Letting go means embracing the natural flow of life and freeing yourself from rigid beliefs and self-limiting behaviours. It's about stopping the futile resistance to things you can't control and instead turn your focus inward. By confronting and releasing your outdated beliefs and unhelpful behaviours, you make room for new, empowering ones. This way you create space for your authentic self, with all its unique qualities and flaws, to emerge and thrive.

- Three levels of cognition – core beliefs, dysfunctional assumptions and automatic negative thoughts (ANTs) – shape your perceptions and responses. Mindfulness, journaling and mood monitoring can help you identify your ANTs. Once you recognise patterns that cause emotional pain, you can challenge and reframe them, and start exploring the dysfunctional assumptions and core beliefs driving these thoughts.

- Your inner voice is always with you and that's a good thing. But when it becomes overly harsh or persistent, it can be destructive. The antidote to excessively fixating on your worries is to consciously zoom out. Techniques such as distanced self-talk, imagining advising a friend and mental time-travelling can help you gain perspective and see the bigger picture.

- Expressive writing helps with processing difficult emotions. This practice provides a safe outlet for feelings and gives perspective as you view your experiences from different angles. It allows you to reclaim your role as the protagonist in your life, rather than feeling like a victim. Write uninterruptedly for 15-30 minutes, repeatedly if needed.

- Stepping into the unknown, especially when there is something to lose, can be challenging. Using decision trees can help clarify the risks and rewards of different choices. By framing a situation in terms of what you would lose if you continue on the same path, you can shift your perspective and become more willing to take a risk.

- Every moment you're choosing what to care about. By accepting your limitations and caring deeply about a few meaningful things – rather than chasing external validation or striving for perfection in every aspect of your life – you likely find greater fulfilment and a more peaceful life.

- It's not external events that cause distress, but your resistance to them. By focusing on what you can control – your own actions and choices – you empower yourself to take meaningful steps and reduce unnecessary anxiety. Redirecting your energy away from trying to influence others' decisions or outcomes beyond your control frees up time and energy to focus on things you can influence.

- A fixed mindset views abilities as static and unchangeable, while a growth mindset sees them as developable through effort, learning and persistence. You can cultivate a growth mindset by shifting your perspective to see effort as a pathway to mastery and failure as an essential part of learning. By embracing the process, you learn to value growth and development rather than just the end result.

- When you learn to view stress as a tool for development (stress-can-be-enhancing mindset) and pair it with the growth mindset, challenges become opportunities to excel and innovate. These two mindsets amplify each other by harnessing stress as fuel for personal and professional growth.

- Embracing your unique traits as superpowers can transform your perspective and unlock new possibilities. By shifting from a mindset of limitation to one of potential, you can discover and harness strengths you may not have realised you possessed, paving the way for remarkable achievements.

10

Dance to the Music

In a small coastal village, a fisherman was lying on the beach, resting and enjoying the sun. A businessman, who was vacationing in the village, walked by and saw the fisherman. The businessman was intrigued by the fisherman's relaxed demeanour and decided to strike up a conversation.

'Why are you lying here, doing nothing?' the businessman asked.

'I've caught enough fish for today,' the fisherman replied.

'But why don't you go out and catch more fish?' the businessman inquired.

'What would I do with them?' the fisherman asked.

'You could sell them and earn more money,' the businessman explained. 'With that extra money, you could buy a bigger boat, catch even more fish, and make even more money. Eventually, you could buy a whole fleet of boats, open your own company, and become very rich.'

'And then what would I do?' the fisherman asked.

'Well, then you could sit back, relax and enjoy life,' the businessman concluded.

The fisherman smiled and looked at the businessman. 'What do you think I'm doing right now?'

Reflecting on my journey, I can't help but see how similar my old mindset was to that businessman's. For years, I believed that success and self-worth were wrapped up in achievements, caught in a cycle of 'more' – more goals, more accolades, more proof that I was 'enough'. But then things shifted. I learned to focus on what truly mattered, which allowed me to filter out distractions, release doubts and tap into my brain's real potential. Slowly, with each small, consistent step, my brain adapted and expanded, revealing a whole new world of possibility.

Yet, even with this clarity, I felt a pull to go further – to understand what truly brings us happiness. The fisherman in the story is a reminder that sometimes we already possess what we're searching for; we're just too caught up to see it. As I reflected on my journey, I realised that the final step lies in accepting that real fulfilment doesn't come from constant striving, but from appreciating what's already here. By letting go of the chase, we may discover that we are already exactly where we need to be.

The Brighter Side of Life

In the late 1980s, within the serene walls of an American convent, a remarkable story began to unfold. Here, a group of researchers stumbled upon an extraordinary opportunity to explore the links between positive emotions and longevity. The subjects of the study were 180 Catholic nuns, members of the School Sisters of Notre Dame, and their lives would provide new insights into how positivity might correlate with health and longevity.

The story began when David Snowdon, a young epidemiologist with a keen interest in ageing and Alzheimer's disease, was granted access to the convent's archives. Here, he found a treasure trove of autobiographical essays written by the nuns in their early twenties, just before taking their vows. This unique dataset offered a rare chance to investigate whether there was a relationship between happiness early in life and later health outcomes.

Snowdon and his team meticulously analysed the essays, focusing on the emotional content of the nuns' writings. They categorised the expressed emotions into positive and negative themes, noting the frequency and intensity of positive emotions such as joy, love, hope and gratitude. The findings were intriguing:

the nuns who expressed more positivity in their early writings lived nearly a decade longer than their less cheerful peers. By the age of eighty-five, over 90 per cent of the happiest nuns were still alive, compared to only about a third of the least happy ones.[1]

As Snowdon and others delved deeper into the lives of the nuns, they found that a positive outlook also correlated with their quality of life. The happiest nuns tended to remain more physically active, socially engaged and mentally resilient in their later years. They also exhibited lower rates of Alzheimer's disease and other forms of dementia.[2]

This groundbreaking 'nun study' is far from an isolated case. Over the years, research has repeatedly shown a connection between positivity and a long, healthy life.[3] But what's truly at play here? What accounts for the relationship between happiness and healthy aging? The answer is not straightforward and involves a complex interplay of factors.

For one, positive emotions often foster stronger social bonds. People who experience frequent joy and positivity tend to be more open and approachable, which encourages close relationships and creates a valuable support network.[4] These connections serve as a protective buffer against stress, offering both emotional comfort and practical assistance during tough times. Social support can even influence physical health, contributing to better immune function, faster recovery from illness and a heightened sense of resilience.[5]

Moreover, positive emotions are linked to healthier lifestyle choices, including improved sleep quality, balanced diets and increased physical activity.[6] People with an optimistic outlook seem generally more motivated to engage in activities that promote their well-being, like regular exercise and nutritious eating. While these habits don't guarantee good health, they certainly tip the scales in favour of staying healthy as we age.

Another key aspect is that positive emotions are associated with lower stress levels. Chronic stress can lead to inflammation, which is linked to a variety of health issues, such as cardiovascular disease and weakened immune system. Those who regularly experience and express positive emotions tend to be less affected by stress-related health problems.[7]

Finally, it's possible that people with a natural tendency towards positive emotions might also have genetic or environmental advantages that contribute to both emotional well-being and strong physical health. In other words, the connection between happiness and longevity might result partly from underlying factors – like a stable upbringing or genetic resilience – that foster both emotional well-being and physical health.

While genetics play a significant role in shaping our ability to keep a positive outlook, this doesn't leave the rest of us powerless.[8] Just as some people are genetically predisposed to a heavier body type while others to a more athletic build, it doesn't render lifestyle choices irrelevant. Almost everyone has the potential to enhance their happiness, regardless of their starting point. Before diving into strategies to unlock this potential, let's first understand what happiness truly means and the reasons why we're not happier.

A Dual Path to Happiness

For the past six months, every morning, at 8.30 sharp, I close the door to my home office, put on my noise cancelling headphones and settle into my chair to start writing. With a fresh cup of coffee by my side, I plunge head first into the mysteries of the human brain. In these quiet hours, each sip of coffee is a moment of pure joy. But that's not all that gives me enjoyment. When I am able to craft a sentence that can turn on a light in someone's mind, or find the perfect story to illuminate a difficult concept, I feel an immense sense of euphoria.

Of course, writing a book is not without its fair share of hurdles. There are days when the words don't come easily; when the complexity of the subject matter feels overwhelming. Sometimes,

I find myself staring at a blank screen, the silence only broken by my timer reminding me that another hour has passed. And there are weekends when I'd rather relax than have to push myself to write. But in these challenging moments, I can remind myself of my purpose: to help others understand how their brains work so they can lead richer, more fulfilling lives. This gives me the strength to push through the difficulties, making even the hardest days rewarding.

In our pursuit of happiness, we often focus on fleeting pleasure or momentary joy. But true happiness comes from a blend of pleasure and purpose. Pleasure, or *hedonic happiness*, is the spontaneous joy and satisfaction derived from life's simple pleasures – a hearty laugh with friends, your favourite dessert or celebrating a milestone. These delightful moments add vibrancy to our lives, rooting us in the present.

Yet relying solely on pleasure would be an unending pursuit of fleeting highs, leaving a void once the excitement fades. This is where purpose, or *eudaimonic happiness*, comes in – living in accordance with our values and engaging in activities that bring a sense of meaning and fulfilment. It's the deeper, long-lasting satisfaction that comes from contributing to something larger than ourselves, pursuing personal growth, fostering strong bonds and making a positive impact on the world around us.

Seeking too much pleasure at the expense of purpose is like indulging in desserts without having a nutritious meal – initially satisfying but ultimately leaving us yearning for something substantial. On the flip side, a life saturated with purpose, devoid of any joy, can lead to burnout, making even the most meaningful pursuits feel burdensome. This is why striking a balance between the two is critical for a happy life. How do we achieve such balance?

The first step is understanding what brings you joy and gives your life meaning. In his book *Happiness by Design*, behavioural scientist Paul Dolan suggests using the Day Reconstructing Method (DRM) where you break your day into 'episodes', such as going for a walk, eating breakfast and commuting to work, then scoring each episode for pleasure and purpose on a scale of 1 to 10.[9] It would look something like this:

Episode	Begin	End	Activity	Who with	Pleasure (0-10)	Purpose (0-10)
1						
2						
3						

Once you've scored your DRM, you likely notice that your sources of pleasure differ from your sources of purpose. Binge-watching your favourite series might offer ample enjoyment but doesn't offer much in terms of purpose, whereas childcare responsibilities may not be as enjoyable but provide a strong sense of purpose. The DRM allows you to visually map out what fuels your happiness and what drains it away. It unveils if your life is optimally balancing pleasure and purpose or if you need to focus more on either the pleasure or purpose aspect. Recognising this makes it easier to say 'no' to activities that tilt the balance too much to one side.

Though the process might seem a bit arduous, the insights garnered from the DRM can be truly eye-opening. Remember our discussion in Chapter 7 about the autopilot mode of living we often fall into? The DRM disrupts this by making us cognisant of elements that enhance or drain our happiness. This awareness not only helps us experience more moments of happiness but also aids in strategically scheduling our days and weeks to include time for relaxation and enjoyment, as well as for steadily working towards our long-term goals.

Each of us will find the optimal balance of pleasure and purpose in different places, and this equilibrium can shift over time. What feels like the right mix for you now might not be the same a year from now, as your circumstances and priorities evolve. It's not about aiming to be exactly in the middle; rather, it's about discovering what works best for you personally. Some may thrive with more pleasure-oriented activities, while others might feel more fulfilled with a purpose-driven day. The key is to regularly reflect and adapt, ensuring that your life aligns with what makes you feel genuinely happy and content. In the end, balance is not something you find, it's something you create.

Now we know we need both pleasure and purpose for our happiness, the next question becomes: why do we so often struggle to find lasting joy?

Why Aren't We Happier?

The morning session of the conference had just concluded, and I needed a break. Stepping outside into the crisp winter air, I decided to take a walk around the frozen lake just beyond the conference centre. To my delight, I spotted Rob, a colleague and friend, already strolling along the path, his breath forming small clouds in the cold air.

We fell into step and talked about the conference and how demanding they can be. But as the quiet settled around us, our conversation naturally shifted to something more personal, something that had been on my mind for a while.

'I've been thinking a lot about the nature of success lately,' I confessed. 'It feels like I'm on this endless treadmill. No matter how much I achieve, it never seems enough.'

'I know exactly what you mean,' Rob replied, 'I always thought that hitting certain milestones would bring lasting satisfaction. But each time I reach one, there's always another just beyond my reach.'

'Right,' I agreed. 'It's like we're conditioned to believe that happiness is always just around the corner, tied to the next big accomplishment. But the satisfaction is always so fleeting.'

Rob sighed; his gaze fixed over the frozen lake. 'It's the hedonic treadmill, isn't it? We adapt so quickly to our successes that they lose their impact almost immediately.'

'Exactly,' I said. 'And it's exhausting. We keep moving the goalpost, thinking that the next achievement will be the one that finally makes us happy.'

Rob nodded thoughtfully. 'Maybe happiness isn't about reaching the next big thing but finding joy in the journey itself.'

I smiled, 'Like this moment, right now. A peaceful walk around a beautiful lake with a friend. No deadlines, no goals – just being here.'

Rob smiled back. 'Exactly!'

As we continued our walk, the cold air invigorating and the conversation flowing easily, I felt a sense of clarity and relief wash over me. The pressures of the conference, the constant chase for the next accolade, seemed to fade into the background. In their place was a simple appreciation for the present moment, and the understanding that true success might just lie in savouring the here and now.

Without realising it, many of us adopt the 'if-then' model of happiness. We tell ourselves: 'if I get that promotion, then I will be happy', 'once I've found the perfect partner, then I'll be truly content' or 'when my child gets into university, then I'll be satisfied'. The problem? By tying our happiness to future events or achievements, the 'if-then' model is supremely effective in preventing us from experiencing everyday happiness.

The 'if-then' model operates on the premise that happiness is conditional, always tied to achieving a specific goal: if only 'X' would happen, then I would be happy – or happier. This way of thinking implies that our present state is never good enough, keeping us in a constant state of waiting for happiness to arrive. It fosters a sense of scarcity and inadequacy, convincing us that our current situation is lacking and that fulfilment lies elsewhere.

Once we achieve a goal, the elation is often short-lived due to what psychologists call the *hedonic treadmill effect*. Generally, even after major positive or negative events, we eventually return to a baseline level of happiness.[10] Regardless of how significant an achievement might be, its impact on our overall happiness is temporary. This so-called *hedonic adaptation* means the satisfaction we seek through the 'if-then' model tends to evaporate quickly, prompting us to chase the next goal in an endless cycle.

To make matters worse, the 'if-then' model often ties happiness to external factors such as career success, material possessions or social status, rather than intrinsic fulfilment. Consequently, we may find ourselves chasing things that aren't genuinely making us happy. And when our happiness depends greatly on external achievements, we're left vulnerable to situations outside our control.

Instead of bringing happiness, the relentless pursuit of goals can drain our mental and physical resources, making it even harder to achieve genuine happiness. In short, the 'if-then' model is a trap – it prevents us from experiencing lasting happiness. By anchoring happiness to the future and tethering it to external achievements, it keeps us in a perpetual state of striving, never quite reaching a place of true contentment.

To truly understand that attaining goals doesn't necessarily lead to lasting happiness, try this simple exercise: reflect on your life a decade ago. Visualise where you were, what you were doing and who you were with. Think about the goals, dreams and desires you had back then. Now identify which ones you have achieved and evaluate their impact on your happiness. Did they bring lasting joy? Are you happier now because of these achievements? The answers might surprise you.[11]

Is there an escape from the 'if-then' model? Absolutely. It involves embracing the present, focusing on intrinsic goals and personal growth. By concentrating on the process rather than the outcome, we can learn to find joy in the journey itself. Practising gratitude and celebrating minor victories helps shift the focus from future achievements to immediate experiences.

To get started, you can try the following exercise. Write down:

- Three things you are grateful for right now.

- Three activities or practices that bring you joy in your daily life.

- Three achievements this week, no matter how small, that brought you closer to one of your goals.

If you make this a regular practice, you'll likely start to appreciate the small, everyday moments more deeply. It also helps shift your focus from the end goal to the journey itself. Setting goals is important – they provide direction, like a compass – but true happiness lies less in reaching a destination and more in savouring the ride. While outcomes are often beyond our control, our actions are always within our grasp.

And you might be glad to know that there's more. Remarkably, we possess the unique ability to generate happiness from within, even when life takes an unfortunate turn.

Happiness on Demand

When the Covid pandemic suddenly interrupted my eagerly awaited and meticulously planned sabbatical, I felt devastated. Finally, I'd allowed myself to jump off the work hamster wheel and indulge in life's simple pleasures, only to find my plans shattered within three weeks. The walls of my home felt like a prison. I couldn't believe my bad luck. Yes, I wasn't forced to return back to work, but what's the point of a sabbatical when the whole world has come to a standstill? I had saved so hard for this much-needed break, and now it was snatched away from me, with no clue when I could take it again.

As the days turned into weeks and weeks into months, my initial frustration slowly gave way to a more positive mood. Immersing myself in learning about the brain, I realised this wasn't a wasted opportunity. The quiet of that period allowed me to experiment with new approaches. Without my usual daily activities and social events, I found ample time for reading and online courses, thus deepening my knowledge of the brain's intricacies. The absence of social pressures provided a unique space for introspection and personal growth.

Fast forward four years, and I marvel at the unexpected turn of events. The premature end of my sabbatical, brought on by the pandemic, was the catalyst for an incredible journey I never saw coming. Not only did it free me from the paralysing grasp of imposter syndrome but also led me to discover a deep love for writing – something I might never have unearthed otherwise. Now, on the brink of publishing my first book, I can hardly believe my good fortune. What felt like a huge setback has turned into the path to something extraordinarily wonderful.

My story is by no means unique; such stories are actually surprisingly common. Take a moment and reflect on your own life. Can you think of a situation that, while seemingly dire at the time, eventually turned out for the better? Maybe a failed relationship led you to the love of your life, a professional setback pushed you to pursue a more fulfilling career or a health issue brought you closer to your loved ones. This is how most people react to negative events. We find a way to make the best of what happened.

Psychologist Dan Gilbert, author of *Stumbling on Happiness*, calls it our ability to synthesise happiness – creating happiness internally when things don't turn out as expected. Unlike natural happiness, which occurs when we get what we want, *synthetic happiness* is about finding contentment and satisfaction in situations where we don't. It reflects our mind's remarkable ability to adapt and find fulfilment despite setbacks.

For instance, imagine going through a painful breakup. Initially, you may feel lost and heartbroken. But over time, you begin to appreciate the freedom of single life – pursuing your own interests, spending more time with people you enjoy hanging out with. You realise that there were aspects of your ex's personality that irked you and that maybe you're better off without him. Gradually, your mind adjusts and you start to feel content; that's synthetic happiness at work.

Behind this natural ability to manufacture happiness lies what psychologists call our *psychological immune system*. Just as our biological immune system protects us from physical ailments, our psychological immune system shields us from emotional distress. It kicks into gear when we face adverse situations, helping us reframe experiences in a more positive light and find meaning even in difficulties.[12]

We often overestimate how badly we'll fare in the face of adversity as we don't factor in the power of our psychological immune system.[13] Gilbert explains, 'Humans are remarkably resilient. We don't get to be knocked down for long. But we don't seem to know this about ourselves. We overestimate how badly we will fare in the face of adversity.'[14] Due to this misjudgement, we often overestimate the lasting and devastating impact of negative events.

The power of our psychological immune system is well illustrated in a study by Daniel Gilbert and Jane Ebert.[15] They asked photography students to take photographs and then select one to keep. The participants were split into two groups. One group was told that they could change their chosen photograph within a certain period, while the other group was told that their choice was final. The results showed that those who could not change their decision ended up liking their chosen photograph more than those who had the option to switch. Why? Our psychological immune system works harder to help us find contentment when decisions are final.

Understanding that we possess a psychological immune system can help us make bolder choices, knowing that our ability to bounce back is stronger than we might think. By recognising how robust our psychological immune system truly is, we can face life's challenges with greater confidence and less fear of what might go wrong.

The strength of our psychological immune system varies from person to person. Some naturally have a strong system, enabling them to quickly recover from setbacks. Others may need to develop and enhance their psychological resilience. The good news is that resilience is a skill that can be cultivated and there are strategies we can employ to help us do that.

Refrain from using the 'bad' label

We all have a natural tendency to focus more on negative experiences, emotions and information compared to positive ones. Evolutionarily, this negativity bias made sense. Our ancestors who were more attuned to potential dangers – the negative aspects of life – were more likely to survive. Our brains thus evolved to give more weight to negative information as a survival mechanism.[16]

We also have a tendency to make instantaneous judgments about everything, quickly labelling events as 'good' or 'bad'. We do this frequently without even realising it. Observe yourself throughout the day: the milk has gone off – bad thing; my early morning meeting got cancelled – good thing, etc.

However, when we label something as bad or negative, our attention tends to be drawn more strongly to it because of our negativity bias. This amplifies our perception of the negative events and can evoke strong emotional responses such as fear, anger or sadness, which can further reinforce our perception of something as bad or undesirable. When we label something as bad or negative, it almost guarantees that we experience it as such.

If positive self-talk feels challenging or insincere, you can first aim to shift to a neutral zone. This involves reframing your perceptions to take a more balanced and realistic view of events, creating a space for a more measured response. Reframing isn't about ignoring the negative but rather trying to see events more objectively. It allows you to notice patterns in your thinking and challenge negative thoughts. Discussing a situation with a friend or considering whether the incident will matter in a few months or years can interrupt your ruminations and help you reappraise your reality, as explained in Chapter 9.

To cultivate a neutral or even positive mindset, begin by observing how you react to various situations. Pay attention to the automatic judgments you make and how quickly you label something as 'bad'. Notice your immediate reaction and try to refrain from labelling it right away. For instance, if you fall and hurt your knee, instead of instantly labelling it as 'bad', use a descriptive and neutral label like, 'I fell and hurt my knee'. On the other hand, be generous with assigning 'good' labels when the situation warrants it.

Eventually, we can go a step further and stop labelling events altogether. We often don't know how things will turn out in the end. What feels 'bad' today might end up being 'good' tomorrow, or the other way around. For instance, losing a job might seem like a setback but could open the door to unexpected opportunities, leading to a more fulfilling role. On the flip side, a promotion that seems 'good' might bring stress or burnout later. By holding off on labelling events too quickly, we give ourselves room to embrace whatever unfolds.

Events themselves are neutral; it is the meaning we attach to them that shapes our emotional responses. Recognising this can help us break the cycle of negativity and cultivate a mindset that is more resilient and adaptable.

Focus on the present

Another way of bolstering our psychological immune system is by trying to stay present in the moment. This helps us focus on what we can control, rather than getting trapped in ruminations about the future, which we are not good at predicting anyhow. By focusing our attention on the here and now, we are less likely to be overwhelmed by thoughts of what might happen in the future and respond to the current situation more effectively.

One of the best ways to train our ability to stay in the present is through mindfulness practices, which are discussed in detail in Chapter 7. Mindfulness encourages us to acknowledge that whatever is happening might not be all-consuming. This practice is not about dismissing our experiences but rather placing them in context. For instance, when faced with a stressful situation, instead of letting it dominate our thoughts, we can observe it from a distance, recognising that it is just one part of our overall experience.

Incorporating mindfulness into our daily routine can significantly enhance our ability to remain grounded. Simple practices such as deep breathing, meditation or even mindful walking can anchor us in the present. Over time, these exercises help build psychological resilience, allowing us to face challenges with a more calm and balanced perspective.

Practise acceptance
Having been through a traumatic event myself, I know very well that in such circumstances, these tips and strategies can seem trite and sometimes even exacerbate the situation by implying that our agonising turmoil is simply a mental hurdle to overcome. In these circumstances, I believe it's more helpful to recognise that the pain and emotions are not only valid but also necessary for the healing process.

When I had to come to terms with the sudden loss of my father, a book taught me a valuable lesson. After another sleepless night, I went for an early morning walk through the silent streets of Washington, DC, and the only place open was a bookstore. I went in and was drawn to a book titled, *When Everything Falls Apart*, which eloquently summed up exactly how I was feeling. Without a second thought, I bought it.

This book, deeply rooted in Buddhist teachings, became my unexpected ally. It invited me to 'lean into the pain', to accept my reality rather than resist it, as resistance only amplifies the suffering. By allowing myself to fully feel the depth of my sorrow and anger, I was able to better process my loss. Gradually, I began to understand and accept the event, stitching my wound and starting to heal. This ordeal, though unimaginably painful, showed me the depths of my resilience. As Daniel Gilbert suggested, we are stronger than we perceive ourselves to be. When I look back, I can see how this traumatic event brought some beautiful things into my life as well.

So, when life deals you a tough hand, try to trust in your psychological resilience and your ability to synthesise happiness.

You may just be surprised by what beauty emerges from the ashes of a seemingly catastrophic event when you allow it. In moments of hardship it can help to keep reminding yourself that 'this too shall pass'. Practice kindness and patience with yourself until it does.

The Happiness Spotlight

Scarcity lies at the heart of economics, capturing the essence of our constant struggle: our resources are limited, but our desires are virtually limitless. This fundamental imbalance forces us to make choices, sometimes tough ones, about how to allocate what little we have, whether it's money, time or energy. Each decision comes with trade-offs: choosing one thing often means forgoing another. For instance, deciding to get a pet to keep you company might mean cutting back on holiday spending.

Our attention, like time and money, is also a scarce resource and requires careful management. Though we may want to pay attention to many things, we can only truly give our attention to one thing at a time. Where we choose to direct that attention will greatly affect our emotional experience. The key question then becomes: are we focusing on things that enhance our happiness? Unfortunately, many of us are not. Instead, we often find ourselves fixating on aspects of life that detract from our happiness, leaving us emotionally drained.

A common trap is placing too much of our attention on external achievements, expecting them to bring us happiness. But, as we've just discussed, these accomplishments typically offer only a fleeting sense of joy. Once the novelty wears off, we find ourselves chasing the next achievement, hoping it will finally bring us fulfilment.

Similarly, we often direct our attention towards acquiring material possessions, believing they will increase our happiness. Yet, the happiness new possessions bring is usually short-lived, as we will shortly see. We quickly return to our previous emotional state, only to crave more things to maintain that fleeting high. Even future planning – necessary to a degree – can spiral into excessive worry about what lies ahead, even though we're notoriously bad at predicting our future emotional states.

Then there's the emotional energy spent on past grievances. When we fixate on past hurts, anger or resentment, we drain our emotional reserves and erode our inner peace. We relive negative experiences, allowing them to consume our thoughts, all while missing opportunities to enjoy the present. The same goes for comparing ourselves to others. This habit not only breeds envy but also diminishes our sense of self-worth. Instead of fostering contentment, these distractions divert our attention from what truly brings us joy.

To make matters worse, we're often unaware of how the *focusing effect* distorts our judgment. Because of this cognitive bias we often place too much emphasis on one specific element of a situation, inflating its significance while ignoring other relevant factors.[17] It can skew our perception of happiness because we overestimate the impact of one detail and fail to see the bigger picture. For instance, someone who has just bought a new car might fixate on a minor scratch, overshadowing the joy of the new purchase. The focusing effect makes the scratch seem more significant than it is, resulting in unnecessary dissatisfaction.

The key to being happier is thus quite straightforward: focus more on what makes you happy and less on what doesn't. While this advice sounds self-evident, it often requires a conscious effort to implement. The first step is to recognise the difference between what we think will make us happy and what actually does. We need to make our happiness salient. Once we've identified the sources of genuine happiness in our lives, the next step is to actively direct our attention towards them.

Earlier in this chapter, you were encouraged to complete a Day Reconstructing Method (DRM) to gain insight into the sources that bring you pleasure and purpose. If you followed through, you should now have a list of positive sources of happiness. The question is: how much attention are you actually giving these sources? Chances are, you're paying them far less attention than you could.

As discussed earlier, our brain is naturally inclined towards negativity, often causing us to focus more on the painful or pointless aspects of our lives. Additionally, much of our time is spent on autopilot, moving through our days without truly engaging with what we're doing. Add to that the fact that we frequently multitask, dividing our attention across various activities, and it's no wonder our happiness can feel elusive.

When we concentrate on the positive aspects of life, we enhance our sense of happiness. When we focus most of our attention on the negative aspects, we reduce it. The same life events and circumstances can affect our mood very differently depending on how much attention we pay to their positive and negative attributes.

Attention is a scarce resource, so it's worth using it wisely. If you love breakfast, make it a mindful experience – savour each bite instead of rushing through it. When spending time with your kids, give them your full attention and put away your phone. If you get a kick out of painting or another hobby, set aside some uninterrupted time to really dive into it. You get the idea.

Happiness is about paying attention to those things that genuinely brings us joy and fulfilment. By focusing our limited attention on the positive, we instantly boost our happiness. Though we each find joy in different places, research has identified some universal drivers of happiness that apply to us all.

What's Money Got to Do with It?

We've all heard the saying, 'Money can't buy happiness.' Yet the idea that we'll be happier if we have more money is intuitively very appealing. Not surprisingly, the question of how money affects our happiness has intrigued researchers for decades. Typically, studies distinguish between two forms of happiness:

evaluative and experienced. *Evaluative happiness* refers to how satisfied we are with our lives when we step back and think about it. It's often influenced by big-picture factors like achievements, relationships and financial status. *Experienced happiness* is about our day-to-day feelings of joy and contentment and the absence of negative emotions like stress or sadness.

In 2010, psychologist Daniel Kahneman and economist Angus Deaton explored the relationship between money and the two types of happiness. Their groundbreaking study revealed that higher income corresponds to greater evaluative happiness, but the impact on experienced happiness plateaus at an annual income of about $75,000. In essence, beyond this point, more money doesn't necessarily mean a better daily emotional experience.[18]

Fast forward to 2021 and some intriguing new research from psychologist Matthew Killingsworth emerged that challenges this long-standing belief. Using a smartphone app, he asked US citizens over the whole income spectrum to answer, in real time, questions like, 'How do you feel right now?' and 'Overall, how satisfied are you with your life?' Similar to the study of Kahneman and Deaton, he found a positive association between income and life-satisfaction. However, his data also revealed a continued positive association between higher income and experienced happiness, even beyond the previously identified $75,000 threshold. These findings suggest that money can keep buying happiness as income increases.[19]

Why does having more money make us happier? The answer isn't straightforward, as many interconnected factors are at play. However, Killingsworth's research offers some valuable insights. Firstly, having more money helps people avoid pain. For those earning less than $80,000, an increase in income is particularly effective at reducing negative feelings. Additional financial resources can ease daily stresses and help mitigate worry about paying bills.

Across the entire income spectrum, positive feelings tend to rise with increases in income. One key reason for this is that more money often translates to greater control over one's life. Financial stability empowers us to make choices that can significantly enhance our quality of life and, in turn, our overall well-being. This sense of control seems to be a major factor in the connection between income and happiness.

Before rushing to make more money, expecting it to boost your happiness, it's important to pause and consider a few caveats. In his book *Happiness*, economist Richard Layard highlights that how happy our money makes us tends to depend on how it compares to what people around us are getting. If you're making a decent salary but see your peers earning significantly more, you might feel a sense of dissatisfaction, regardless of your own financial situation. Conversely, if your income exceeds what most of your friends and colleagues earn, you may feel quite content. Many of us are more concerned about our relative than our absolute income or wealth, more so when we use income as a benchmark for success.[20]

How much our income affects our happiness also depends on how much value we attach to it. Low earners are happier when they deem money unimportant, while high earners are happier when they think money is important. Interestingly, those who equate money with success tend to experience lower well-being.[21] Perhaps because they're more prone to social comparison or because chasing financial success leaves them with little time for fulfilling activities, like spending time with loved ones.

How we spend money significantly impacts our happiness as well. Investing in experiences like theatre, concerts or vacations generally brings more lasting joy than purchasing material goods. This is largely because we adapt more slowly to experiential purchases. Engaging in an experience creates memories and emotions that linger, offering a lasting source of happiness we can revisit. In contrast, material goods often provide a quick spike in satisfaction that fades as we become accustomed to them. Once the novelty wears off, we may find ourselves chasing new possessions to experience that initial thrill again. Shared experiences can also strengthen bonds with loved ones, which, as we will shortly see, is a key driver of happiness.[22]

However, two caveats need to be kept in mind. First, especially because we adapt more slowly to experiential purchases, only positive experiences surpass material purchases in boosting happiness; negative experiences have no benefit over material purchases and sometimes lead to less happiness.[23] Second, the line between experiential and material purchases isn't always clear-cut. I still recall my uncle taking us for a drive in his new Mercedes, his excitement contagious as he described its features and smooth ride. Although I never asked how he felt driving it later on, I imagine the joy didn't fade quickly. When a material purchase continues to bring happiness with each use, it resembles an experience. Ultimately, you're the best judge of which types of purchases bring you long-term happiness, but it's worthwhile to reflect on how you spend your money.

We can use money to buy experiences or material things, but we can also use it to buy time. Many of us feel we lack time, which affects our happiness. Investing in time-saving services removes unpleasant tasks. Whether it's choosing a direct flight over a cheaper, longer one or outsourcing chores like cleaning and shopping, research shows that prioritising time over money consistently leads to greater happiness. This is likely because it reduces stress and frees up time to do things we enjoy.[24] Consider buying time as an investment in your happiness. With the gig economy, outsourcing time-consuming tasks is easier than ever.

Finally, spending money to help others also tends to boost our happiness.[25] Imagine you're at a grocery store, and you see someone in front of you who has to put some items back because they can't afford them. You offer to help by covering the cost of those items. That simple act of kindness can quickly lift your spirits. It is an example of *prosocial spending* – using your money to benefit others.

To feel happy when spending on others, three conditions need to be met: we must feel in control, feel connected to the person or cause we're giving to and believe that our giving is effective.[26] By fulfilling these conditions, we can turn our money into a source of joy for ourselves and others.

It's not just about the act itself but the sense of connection it fosters. When we help others, we create positive social interactions and build stronger relationships, which are key components of our overall well-being. Whether it's donating to a charity, buying a gift for a friend or supporting a local business, pro-social spending can turn money into meaningful moments that enrich both your life and the lives of those around you.[27]

Rather than focusing solely on earning more money in the pursuit of happiness, money might be better thought of as a tool to be deployed to achieve that goal. The real value of money comes from how it helps us create a life that feels genuinely rich and fulfilling. Yet, the greatest happiness often comes from the connections we form with others.

Fostering Connection

After moving to London, the first months were a whirlwind of new experiences and adjustments, but having left all that was familiar behind, I often felt alone. Then, I stumbled upon a little coffee shop, conveniently located on my way to work. I started making a pit stop every morning to grab my oat flat white; a small ritual that soon became an important part of my day.

Within a week, the lady at the counter recognised me. With a warm smile she greeted me and asked about my day as she took my carry cup and processed my payment without needing to ask for my order. She knew my order, as she knew the orders of all the regulars.

While I waited for my coffee to be brewed and my milk steamed, the baristas would engage in friendly chit-chat. We would swap stories, share titbits about our lives or discuss events happening in London. It wasn't just me who received this treatment – all the regulars were greeted with the same warmth and familiarity. Despite the many coffee shops around, there always was a long line of people waiting in this particular one. I guess we all valued the atmosphere and were content to wait ten minutes for our morning brew before heading to the office.

These simple, daily interactions with the staff at Taylor Street Baristas had a big effect on my day. Every time I left the coffee shop, I felt lighter, happier and ready to tackle the day. In that cosy little shop, amidst the smell of freshly brewed coffee, I discovered not only my favourite flat white but something much more precious – the warmth of human connection and its profound impact on my happiness.

In the pursuit of happiness, countless theories and philosophies have been proposed, but one enduring insight comes from the longest-running study on adult life: the Harvard Study of Adult Development that started in 1938. The study tracked a group of Harvard sophomores and disadvantaged youth living in Boston for over eighty years to understand the keys to a happy and healthy life. The findings are clear and compelling: good relationships, not wealth or fame, keep us happier and healthier.

Robert Waldinger, the current director of the study, pinpoints its three key lessons. First, social connections are really good for us and loneliness kills. Those connected with family, friends and the community tend to live happier, healthier and longer lives. Second, quality trumps quantity in relationships. It isn't about the number of friends or marital status, but the strength of close bonds that count. Third, secure relationships not only protect our bodies but also our brains. When we feel we can count on someone else, our memory tends to stay sharper for longer.[28]

Given our ancestors' dependence on forming social bonds and groups for survival, the strong link between human connection and happiness is hardly surprising. As inherently social creatures, we naturally seek interaction and companionship. Sadly, loneliness is on the rise, particularly among younger generations. In the UK, one in five adults feel lonely some of the time and one in fourteen experience it frequently.[29] Various factors can trigger loneliness, such as life changes like divorce, the loss of a loved one, moving to a new city, mental or physical health challenges, or social anxiety. Certain life stages, such as adolescence and old age, are particularly susceptible to feelings of isolation.

We can distinguish between emotional and social loneliness. *Emotional loneliness* arises from the absence of deep, meaningful connections, leaving someone yearning for intimacy and understanding. In contrast, *social loneliness* is more about experiencing that our social network is deficient – a feeling of not belonging or a lack of social integration. We can feel lonely even while having lots of friends, and in a room full of people.

Everyone's experience with loneliness is unique and it might not be easily alleviated. However, there are things we can do that can help mitigate feelings of loneliness. Focusing on the quality rather than the quantity of social connections can be particularly beneficial. While having a large social network has its merits, a few close friends who understand and support us tends to have a bigger positive impact. While nurturing deep relationships requires effort, the rewards tend to be substantial.

Building meaningful connections takes time, but even simple daily interactions – a friendly chat with a barista, a neighbour or a classmate – can greatly enhance our happiness.[30] We often assume that sitting alone during our commute is preferable to striking up a conversation with a stranger, but research shows the opposite: we tend to feel happier when we engage with others rather than isolating ourselves.[31] These micro-connections can foster a sense of belonging and community, helping us feel more connected to the world around us. Even small acts of kindness, like smiling at others or greeting our neighbours, can create ripples of positivity in our lives. To combat social loneliness, we can expand our social circles by joining clubs or groups that align with our interests or participate in community activities.

Our experiences tend to be richer when we put away our smartphones while socialising. People who keep their phones out of sight during meals enjoy the experience more. Even brief distractions from phone use are enough to hinder full engagement and reduce overall enjoyment. Interestingly, even those who value technology report lower satisfaction when distracted by their phones during a meal.[32] Embracing this insight, I now ensure my phone stays in my bag when spending time with friends and family.

Pets can be wonderful companions for those battling loneliness. I remember when I got Tommy, my first cat. His constant companionship and unconditional love – or should I say his love for the treats I offered – made a world of difference. The sound of his footsteps approaching as soon as I turned the key was incredibly comforting. This isn't just my experience; studies found that pets can reduce stress and improve mental health by providing stability and companionship. Caring for a pet establishes a daily routine and fosters a sense of responsibility. Dogs, in particular, excel at sparking social interactions. Taking your dog for a walk can lead to spontaneous conversations with other dog owners, opening doors to new connections.[33]

It's undeniable that social connections are good for both our mental and physical health. However, it's equally important to cultivate periods of solitude. There is a crucial distinction between loneliness and solitude. Loneliness feels like being adrift in a sea of people, whereas solitude is a peaceful retreat you choose for yourself. It's in these moments that you can connect with your inner thoughts and feelings and recharge. Taking time for yourself, away from the hustle and bustle, allows your mind to rejuvenate and your creativity to bloom. Just like a well-tended garden needs both sunshine and rain, our well-being flourishes with a mix of social interactions and peaceful, solitary moments.

We're now almost at the end of the book, but before we part ways, I'd like to leave you with one more tool that never fails to lift my spirits.

Happiness Routines

Every morning, I kick off my day with my WHAM! routine. No, it's not about playing 'Wake Me Up Before You Go-Go' while I brush my teeth (although that would be a fun start). Instead, it's a simple daily ritual that infuses positivity into my day.

The 'W' stands for *Walk*. An invigorating morning stroll not only boosts my spirits and energy levels but also offers a breath of fresh perspective on the unfolding day. It's truly remarkable how a little bit of movement clears my mind and sets a positive tone for the day.

Next comes 'H' – *Hydrate*. Drinking a glass of water the moment I rise replenishes fluids lost during the night, aids in digestion and kicks my brain into action. Maintaining hydration is an absolute must for sustaining energy levels during the day.

'A' signifies *Appreciation*. Setting aside a quiet moment to acknowledge what I'm grateful for cultivates a positive mindset and sets a hopeful tone. This seemingly small act wields a powerful influence on my ability to tackle challenges and seize opportunities.

Finally, there's 'M' – *Mindfulness*. Whether it's a moment of meditation, a deep, restorative breath or simply honing in on the present moment, practising mindfulness acts like an anchor keeping me balanced and grounded.

My WHAM! routine isn't just a series of tasks; it's a way to embrace the day with energy, clarity and positivity. I can highly recommend it.

Chapter 7 already shed light on the value of movement, hydration and mindfulness, now let's explore the power of gratitude. As we just discovered, we all have a tendency to focus on the negative; amplifying negative situations and experiences. This can lead to an overly pessimistic view of our life. Gratitude redirects our attention to life's blessings, thus counteracting our negativity bias by shifting focus from the negative to the positive aspects in our life.

Gratitude is about recognising and acknowledging the goodness in our life and the part others play in this. By practising gratitude, we can foster positive emotions, build emotional resilience and strengthen our relationships, all of which contribute to a happier life. Moreover, the benefits of gratitude to our mental well-being can positively impact our physical health as well.[34]

Practising gratitude is straightforward. Dedicate a few minutes each day to focus on what you're grateful for. You can also start a gratitude journal and write everything down. I do it immediately when I wake up as it helps me to start my day on a positive note. As emphasised in Chapter 7, consistency is key. Choose a time that fits easily in your routine, whether daily or weekly, so that it can become a habit.

For a more powerful experience, move beyond just listing things you're thankful for. Instead, try to genuinely feel the warm, positive emotions. It also helps to vary what you're grateful for, so consider focusing on things you often take for granted like having a roof over your head, a warm bed, clean water coming out of your kitchen tap or your health.

One popular method to enhance your awareness of life's blessings is the 'Three Good Things' exercise.[35] Each night, note down three positive experiences from your day. They could be anything – doing ten instead of eight deadweight lifts in the gym, meeting a work deadline or seeing your child riding a bike unaided for the first time. It helps to also note down why these experiences were meaningful to you. Through this exercise, you also gain valuable insights into what genuinely brings you happiness.

Expressing gratitude to others is also immensely powerful. The find-remind-and-bind theory, developed by positive psychologist Sara Algoe, suggests that gratitude helps us 'find' new social connections, 'remind' ourselves of the value of existing ones and 'bind' us closer to the people who support and nurture us.[36] Think of it as a social glue: when we express gratitude, we not only acknowledge the kindness of others but also reinforce our bonds with them, promoting stronger, more meaningful relationships. This, as we just saw, has a big impact on our happiness.

In long-term relationships, we sometimes end up taking things for granted. As the initial excitement and novelty fade, we might forget to express our appreciation for the small, everyday acts of kindness that our partners show us. By thanking them for the positive impact they have on our life or for doing something that benefits us (even simple things like taking out the trash), we reinforce our emotional bond and foster a positive atmosphere where everyone feels valued. It increases the chance that our relationship remains strong and fulfilling over time.

Let me end with one final suggestion: start looking for glitters throughout your day. 'Glitters' are those small, often overlooked moments of joy and beauty – like the warmth of the morning sun on your face, a kind smile from a stranger, your cat greeting you when you come home or the delightful taste of a glass of wine. By consciously noticing and appreciating those moments, you train your mind to focus on the positive aspects of your life. Even on the most ordinary or challenging days, there are always some glitters to be found.

The Key Takeaways

True happiness emerges from a balance between savouring life's pleasures and engaging in activities that bring a sense of meaning and fulfilment. When you let go of the 'if-then' model of happiness and focus more on the present, intrinsic goals and enjoying the ride, you unlock a deeper, more sustainable form of contentment that isn't dependent on future outcomes. Building meaningful connections and pursuing activities aligned with your core values form the bedrock of enduring happiness and well-being.

- Happy people often enjoy longer, healthier lives, a connection shaped by various factors. Positive emotions can strengthen social ties, promote healthier habits and lower stress – all of which support better health. Additionally, genetics and environmental influences also likely play a significant role.

- True and lasting happiness is found in a harmonious blend of pleasure and purpose. The Day Reconstruction Method (DRM) can serve as a valuable tool to identify the activities and experiences that provide joy and/or meaning in your life, and help you discover the right balance that works for you.

- Without realising it, we often adopt the 'if-then' model, where happiness is conditional on achieving specific goals. It's supremely effective in preventing us from experiencing everyday happiness, as it keeps us in a perpetual state of striving, never quite reaching a place of true contentment. You can escape this model by concentrating on the journey itself, rather than the outcome.

- We are remarkably resilient, often creating synthetic happiness when things don't go as planned. This form of happiness, bolstered by our psychological immune system, helps us find contentment in unexpected, even negative outcomes. You can enhance your resilience by avoiding using the 'bad' label, staying present and practising acceptance.

- Attention is a finite resource, and it matters a great deal how you allocate it. By consciously directing your focus away from life's negative aspects and towards the positive, you can greatly enhance your well-being. By understanding what truly brings you pleasure and purpose, you can begin to redirect your attention there.

- While more money can lead to greater happiness, its effectiveness lies in how you choose to spend it. Prioritising investments in experiences, personal growth, nurturing relationships, buying time and helping others can significantly enhance the joy and fulfilment your money provides.

- Strong social connections are fundamental to your happiness and well-being. Feeling connected to family, friends and your community not only makes you happier but also contributes to a healthier and longer life. The quality of your relationships is more important than the quantity; that being said, even simple daily interactions can significantly boost your happiness.

- The WHAM! routine can help kickstart the day with energy, clarity and positivity. Gratitude, in particular, shifts your focus from what's lacking to what you already have, fostering a more positive mindset throughout the day. By intentionally looking for 'glitters' – small moments of joy and appreciation – you train yourself to notice and cherish the positive, no matter how subtle.

Epilogue

As I watched the final lap of the 4x400m mixed relay at the Paris Olympics, my eyes were glued to the screen. Femke Bol, the Dutch runner, was in full flight, propelling herself forward with every stride. She moved from fourth place, passing the Belgian and then the British runner, until only the American gold favourite remained ahead. With an incredible final push, she closed the gap and crossed the finish line first. The stadium erupted and the Dutch team radiated joy as they celebrated their hard-earned Olympic gold.

Witnessing that incredible victory filled me with admiration for the countless hours of training and commitment distilled into that single, electrifying moment. Those gold medals symbolised more than just a triumph; they represented a lifetime of discipline and perseverance, culminating in a few thrilling seconds.

As I took in their success, I found myself looking back at my own journey. My own 'gold medal' wasn't won in a single, defining moment. Rather, it's the product of a gradual transformation – a shift that unfolded slowly, almost unnoticed. Through consistent efforts to manage myself better, sharpen my thinking and replace my limiting beliefs with more empowering ones, I have crafted a different kind of victory: a life that feels balanced, aligned and sustainable. Instead of a finish line, I have discovered a new way of moving forward.

My journey from insecurity and stress to self-assurance and happiness speaks to the effectiveness of the tools and techniques

I shared in this book. Before I began writing, I already had a range of strategies at my disposal. However, during the writing process, I uncovered even more about the incredible potential of our brain and how to harness that power. This newfound understanding allowed me to further refine my personal strategy. It's an ongoing process that unfolds with each new insight and experience.

Now that I've shared everything I've discovered in these pages, I hope that the tools and techniques that transformed my life will serve as a source of inspiration and guidance for you. What I offer isn't a rigid formula, a one-size-fits-all approach, but a rich array of options. Choose the strategies that resonate with you and align with your unique needs. You don't need to tackle everything at once; progress often comes from taking small, manageable steps. Start with one technique that feels right for you and build from there. Allow yourself the flexibility to adapt and refine these strategies as you move forward, navigating your journey at your own pace.

Each of us possesses the potential to grow, reinvent ourselves and achieve the lives we aspire to lead. So, take the first step on your journey. Explore, learn and evolve; and most importantly, enjoy the process. Your brain's untapped potential awaits. Now, it's your turn to unlock it.

Acknowledgements

This being my first book, I really had no idea what to expect. What has deeply moved me is the generosity of so many people along the way. Their support, encouragement and insights have been invaluable, shaping not only this book but also my experience of writing it.

My heartfelt thanks to Camilla Dubini, who guided me through my first steps in the world of authorship and has remained a trusted confidante ever since. I am incredibly grateful to my agent, Toby Mundy at Aevitas, for believing in me and my book when it was still merely an idea. With his wealth of expertise he helped transform my initial seven pages into a clear and compelling proposal, gently steering the book in the direction where it could have the most impact. Thanks also to Elena Steiert, for her sharp eye and thoughtful feedback that helped refine the proposal. And to the entire Aevitas team, who worked behind the scenes to bring Ignite into the world.

Another special thanks to my publisher, Jamie Hodder-Williams at Bedford Square Publishers. His enthusiasm for the book, trust in me and steady guidance helped me uncover and shape my voice as an author and breathe life into my ideas. To James Nightingale, for polishing the manuscript with care and attention. And to the rest of the BSP team who helped make this book a reality. Thanks also to my Dutch publisher Marjolein Schurink at Cargo/De Bezige Bij, whose excitement about this book, right from the start, and encouragement along the way have been incredibly motivating.

This book benefited immensely from the expertise of many people. As an economist stepping into the world of neuroscience and psychology, there was a lot to learn, and I am deeply grateful to the experts who so generously shared their knowledge and time. Harold Bekkering, Olympia Colizoli, Roshan Cools, Floris De Lange, Hanneke Den Ouden, Martin Dresler, Jan Engelmann, Lisa Genzel, Corina Greven, Erno Hermans, Judith Homberg, Boris Konrad, Uta Noppeney, Sasha Ondobaka, Catalina Ratala, Eelke Spaak and Joel van der Weele your insights have been invaluable in helping me understand the intricacies of the brain. A special thanks to Alan Sanfey for welcoming me to the Donders Institute in Nijmegen and hosting me there. Being part of the DCCN family, and tapping into all the knowledge, has been incredibly helpful. I hope I've done justice to everything I've learned from all of you; any remaining errors are, of course, my own.

I was also fortunate to have a group of friends, colleagues and experts who read early drafts and offered feedback. Kristina Bluwstein, Diana Bonfim, Wandi Bruine de Bruin, Stefanie Bult, Wendy Janssens, Mark Mink, Stefanie Otto, Jolanda Peeters, Arthur Turrell, Arzu Uluc, Femke Van Horen, Laura Van Nierop and Eryk Walczak your thoughtful comments and insights have left their mark on these pages in countless ways.

A heartfelt thanks to Philip Bond, for his invaluable guidance in pushing the boundaries of my thinking and letting me experience the untapped potential of my brain. And to Guido Imbens and Tim Walker for inviting me into their worlds of (intellectual) creativity and offering a glimpse of how they harness their brains to achieve extraordinary things. I am also grateful to David Giles, Andy Haldane, Richard Layard and Huw Pill for their help on this book journey.

This book also benefitted from many conversations I've had with friends, colleagues and even random strangers. These exchanges sparked new ideas and helped refine my thinking. Some of you feature in the stories throughout the book. To respect privacy, I've changed names and, in some cases, adapted the details to craft a more engaging narrative, while staying true to the essence and spirit of the original events.

Writing this book would have been a lot harder without the support of my friends and family. Your encouragement has meant the world to me. A few deserve a special mention: my mother and sister, to whom I've dedicated this book, always there when I need them; my father, whose lessons echo through these pages; Harris, for infusing my life with unbridled joy; Yoshi and Yumi, my constant companions; and Graeme, my partner extraordinaire: master chef, cheerleader, creative collaborator, sounding board, stress-reliever, glitter-bringer and much more. Thank you so much for standing by my side every step of the way.

Endnotes

1. The Art of Prioritising What Matters

1 Newport, Cal. *Deep Work: Rules for focused success in a distracted world.* Piatkus, 2016, p. 186.
2 Harford, Tim. 'The power of saying no.' *Financial Times*, 20 January 2015.
3 Doran, George T. 'There's a SMART way to write management's goals and objectives.' *Management Review* 70.11 (1981): 35–36.
4 Locke, Edwin A. and Gary P. Latham. 'Building a practically useful theory of goal setting and task motivation: A 35-year odyssey.' *American Psychologist* 57.9 (2002): 705–717. Locke and Latham proposed the Goal Setting Theory in the late 1960s and it was further developed over subsequent years. This theory posits that setting specific and challenging goals can lead to higher performance and motivation compared to vague or easy-to-achieve goals. SMART goals are often seen as a practical application of the principles outlined in the theory.
5 Kahneman, Daniel and Amos Tversky. 'Intuitive prediction: Biases and corrective procedures.' *Decision Research*, Perceptronics, 1977.
6 Pareto, Vilfredo. *Cours d'Économie Politique* (in two volumes). F. Rouge & F. Pichon, 1896–1897.
7 Koch, Richard. *The 80/20 Principle: The secret of achieving more with less.* Doubleday, 1998.
8 'Obama's Way', *Vanity Fair*, October 2012.
9 Larcom, Shaun, Ferdinand Rauch and Tim Willems. 'The benefits of forced experimentation: Striking evidence from the London underground network.' *The Quarterly Journal of Economics* 132.4 (2017): 2019–2055.

2. From Distracted to Disciplined

1. Kurzban, Robert. 'Does the brain consume additional glucose during self-control tasks?' *Evolutionary Psychology* 8.2 (2010): 244–259.
2. Hockey, Robert. *The Psychology of Fatigue: Work, effort and control.* Cambridge University Press, 2013.
3. Wiehler, Antonius, Francesca Branzoli, Isaac Adanyeguh, Fanny Mochel and Mathias Pessiglione. 'A neuro–metabolic account of why daylong cognitive work alters the control of economic decisions. *Current Biology* 32.16 (2022): 3564–3575.
4. Ophir, Eyal, Clifford Nass and Anthony D. Wagner. 'Cognitive control in media multitaskers.' *Proceedings of the National Academy of Sciences* 106.37 (2009): 15583–15587; Meyer, David E. and David E. Kieras. 'A computational theory of executive cognitive processes and multiple-task performance: Part I. Basic mechanisms.' *Psychological Review* 104.1 (1997): 3–65.
5. This switch cost effect was first described by psychologist Arthur T. Jersild in *Mental Set and Shift* (no. 89). Columbia University, 1927.
6. Rubenstein, Joshua S, David E. Meyer and Jeffrey E. Evans. 'Executive control of cognitive processes in task switching.' *Journal of Experimental Psychology* 27.4 (2001): 763–797.
7. American Psychological Association, 'Multitasking: Switching costs', 20 March 2006.
8. Bellur, Saraswathi, Kristine L. Nowak and Kyle S. Hull. 'Make it our time: In class multitaskers have lower academic performance.' *Computers in Human Behavior* 53 (2015): 63–70.
9. Muhmenthaler, Michèle C. and Beat Meier. 'Different impact of task switching and response-category conflict on subsequent memory.' *Psychological Research* 85.2 (2021): 679–696.
10. Foerde, K., Knowlton, B. J. and Poldrack, R. A. 'Modulation of competing memory systems by distraction.' *Proceedings of the National Academy of Sciences.* 103.31 (2006): 11778–11783.
11. Watson, Jason M. and David L. Strayer. 'Supertaskers: Profiles in extraordinary multitasking ability.' *Psychonomic Bulletin & Review* 17 (2010): 479–485; Sanbonmatsu, David M, David. L. Strayer, Nathan Medeiros-Ward and Jason M. Watson. 'Who multi-tasks and why? Multi-tasking ability, perceived multi-tasking ability, impulsivity, and sensation seeking.' *PloS One* 8.1 (2013): 1–8.
12. Levitin, Daniel. *The Organized Mind.* Penguin, 2014, p. 170.
13. Cirillo, Francesco. *The Pomodoro Technique.* www.Francescocirillo.com.

14 Csikszentmihalyi, Mihaly. *Beyond Boredom and Anxiety.* Jossey-bass, 2000.
15 Dietrich, Arne. 'Neurocognitive mechanisms underlying the experience of flow.' *Consciousness and Cognition* 13.4 (2004): 746–761.
16 Weber, Rene, Ron Tamborini, Amber Westcott-Baker and Benjamin Kantor 'Theorizing flow and media enjoyment as cognitive synchronization of attentional and reward networks.' *Communication Theory* 19.4 (2009): 397–422.
17 Gold, Joshua, and Joseph Ciorciari. 'A review on the role of the neuroscience of flow states in the modern world.' *Behavioral Sciences* 10.9 (2020): 137.
18 Kalmbach, David A., Logan D. Schneider, Joseph Cheung, Sarah J. Bertrand, Thiruchelvam Kariharan, Allan I. Pack, and Philip R. Gehrman 'Genetic basis of chronotype in humans: Insights from three landmark GWAS.' *Sleep* 40.2 (2017): 1–10.
19 Duffy, Jeanne F., Derk-Jan Dijk, Edward F. Hall and Charles A. Czeisler. 'Relationship of endogenous circadian melatonin and temperature rhythms to self-reported preference for morning or evening activity in young and older people.' *Journal of Investigative Medicine: The Official Publication of the American Federation for Clinical Research* 47.3 (1999): 141–150; Roenneberg, Till, Anna Wirz-Justice and Martha Merrow. 'Life between clocks: Daily temporal patterns of human chronotypes.' *Journal of Biological Rhythms* 18.1 (2003): 80–90.
20 Raichle, Marcus E., Ann Mary MacLeod, Abraham Z. Snyder, William J. Powers, Debra A. Gusnard and Gordon L. Shulman. 'A default mode of brain function.' *Proceedings of the National Academy of Sciences* 98. 2 (2001): 676–682; Gusnard, Debra A., and Marcus E. Raichle. 'Searching for a baseline: functional imaging and the resting human brain.' *Nature Reviews Neuroscience* 2.10 (2001): 685–694.
21 Zeigarnik, Bluma. 'On finished and unfinished tasks.' In Ellis, Willes D., ed. *A Source Book of Gestalt Psychology.* Kegan Paul, Trench, Trubner & Company, 1938, pp. 300–314.
22 Bellezza, Silvia, Neeru Paharia and Anat Keinan. 'Conspicuous consumption of time: When busyness and lack of leisure time become a status symbol.' *Journal of Consumer Research* 44.1 (2017): 118–138.

3. Igniting Your Inner Drive

1 Grant, Adam. M. 'Does intrinsic motivation fuel the prosocial fire? Motivational synergy in predicting persistence, performance, and

productivity.' *Journal of Applied Psychology*, 93.1 (2008): 48–58; Grant, Adam M. and James W. Berry. 'The necessity of others is the mother of invention: Intrinsic and prosocial motivations, perspective taking, and creativity.' *Academy of Management Journal* 54.1 (2011): 73–96.
2. Edward Deci and Richard Ryan first introduced these ideas in their book *Self-Determination and Intrinsic Motivation in Human Behavior.* Springer, 1985.
3. Ryan, Richard M. and Edward L. Deci. 'Intrinsic and extrinsic motivations: Classic definitions and new directions.' *Contemporary Educational Psychology* 25.1 (2000): 54–67.
4. Lepper, Mark R., David Greene and Richard E. Nisbett. 'Undermining children's intrinsic interest with extrinsic reward: A test of the "overjustification" hypothesis.' *Journal of Personality and Social Psychology* 28.1 (1973): 129–137.
5. Stephen Covey popularised this exercise in his book *The 7 Habits of Highly Effective People.* Simon & Schuster, 2013.
6. Šrámek, Petr, M. Šimečková, Ladislav Janský, J. Šavlíková and Stanislav Vybíra. 'Human physiological responses to immersion into water of different temperatures.' *European Journal of Applied Physiology* 81 (2000): 436–442.
7. Berridge, Kent C. and Terry E. Robinson. 'Parsing reward.' *Trends in Neurosciences* 26.9 (2003): 507–513.
8. Schultz, Wolfram, Peter Dayan and P. Read Montague. 'A neural substrate of prediction and reward.' *Science* 275.5306 (1997): 1593–1599.
9. Wise, Roy A. 'Dopamine and reward: the anhedonia hypothesis 30 years on.' *Neurotoxicity Research* 14 (2008): 169–183; Schultz, Wolfram. 'Neuronal reward and decision signals: From theories to data.' *Physiological Reviews* 95.3 (2015): 853–951.
10. Schultz, Wolfram. 'Neuronal reward and decision signals: From theories to data.' *Physiological Reviews* 95.3 (2015): 853–951.
11. See Robert Sapolsky's Pritzker Lecture, 'Dopamine Jackpot', at the California Academy of Sciences on 15 February 2011. Robert Sapolsky trained monkeys to press a bar ten times to receive a good treat on the tenth press. He discovered that dopamine is released not when the reward is received, but in anticipation of it. In a second experiment, when the monkeys received food treats only 50 per cent of the time, dopamine levels doubled, showing that intermitted rewards create stronger anticipation and motivation.
12. https://www.hubermanlab.com/newsletter/tools-to-manage-dopamine-and-improve-motivation-and-drive.

13 Steel, Piers. 'The nature of procrastination: A meta-analytic and theoretical review of quintessential self-regulatory failure.' *Psychological Bulletin* 133.1 (2007): 65–94.
14 Tice, Dianne M. and Roy F. Baumeister. 'Longitudinal study of procrastination, performance, stress, and health: The costs and benefits of dawdling.' *Psychological Science* 8.6 (1997): 454–458.
15 Bisin, Alberto and Kyle Hyndman. 'Present-bias, procrastination and deadlines in a field experiment.' *Games and Economic Behavior* 119 (2020): 339–357.
16 Steel, Piers. *The Procrastination Equation: How to stop putting things off and start getting stuff done.* FT Press, 2012.
17 Hull, Clark L. 'The goal gradient hypothesis.' *Psychological Review*, 39.1 (1932): 25–43.
18 Inzlicht, Michael and Brent W. Roberts. 'The fable of state self-control.' *Current Opinion in Psychology* (2024): 101848.
19 Inzlicht, Michael, Brandon J. Schmeichel and C. Neil Macrae. 'Why self-control seems (but may not be) limited.' *Trends in Cognitive Sciences* 18.3 (2014): 127–133.
20 Hofmann, Wilhelm, Roy F. Baumeister, Georg Förster and Kathleen D. Vohs. 'Everyday temptations: an experience sampling study of desire, conflict, and self-control.' *Journal of Personality and Social Psychology* 102.6 (2012): 1318.
21 Converse, Benjamin A., Lindsay Juarez and Marie Hennecke. 'Self-control and the reasons behind our goals.' *Journal of Personality and Social Psychology* 116.5 (2019): 860; Milyavskaya, Marina, Blair Saunders and Michael Inzlicht. 'Self-control in daily life: Prevalence and effectiveness of diverse self-control strategies.' *Journal of Personality* 89.4 (2021): 634–651.
22 Mischel, Walter, Ebbe B. Ebbesen and Antonette Raskoff Zeiss. 'Cognitive and attentional mechanisms in delay of gratification.' *Journal of Personality and Social Psychology* 21.2 (1972): 204–218.
23 Gollwitzer, Peter M. 'Implementation intentions: Strong effects of simple plans.' *American Psychologist*, 54 (1999): 493–503.
24 Hennecke, Marie and Sebastian Bürgler. 'Many roads lead to Rome: Self-regulatory strategies and their effects on self-control.' *Social and Personality Psychology Compass* 14.6 (2020): e12530.
25 Roemer, Lena, Clemens M. Lechner, Beatrice Rammstedt and Brent W. Roberts. 'The base-rate and longer-term relevance of year-to-year change in personality traits.' *European Journal of Personality* (2024): online.

26 Touroutoglou, Alexandra, Joseph Andreano, Bradford C. Dickerson and Lisa Feldman Barrett. 'The tenacious brain: How the anterior mid-cingulate contributes to achieving goals.' *Cortex* 123 (2020): 12–29.
27 Ibid.
28 Colcombe, Stanley J., Kirk I. Erickson, Paige E. Scalf, Jenny S. Kim, Ruchika Prakash, Edward McAuley, Steriani Elavsky, David X. Marquez, Liang Hu and Arthur F. Kramer. 'Aerobic exercise training increases brain volume in aging humans.' *The Journals of Gerontology Series A: Biological sciences and medical sciences* 61.11 (2006): 1166–1170.
29 Zsadanyi, Sara E., Florian Kurth and Eileen Luders. 'The effects of mindfulness and meditation on the cingulate cortex in the healthy human brain: A review.' *Mindfulness* 12.10 (2021): 2371–2387.
30 Muraven, Mark. 'Building self-control strength: Practicing self-control leads to improved self-control performance.' *Journal of Experimental Social Psychology* 46.2 (2010): 465–468.

4. Memory Magic

1 Joshua Foer uses this analogue in his book *Moonwalking with Einstein: The art and science of remembering everything*. Penguin, 2012, p. 209.
2 Sparrow, Betsy, Jenny Liu and Daniel M. Wegner. 'Google effects on memory: Cognitive consequences of having information at our fingertips.' *Science* 333.6043 (2011): 776–778.
3 Not all sense data reach your brain. Information is lost when it's processed by your retina, cochlea and other sensory organs. Scientists still debate how much is lost. Feldman Barrett, Lisa. *Seven and a Half Lessons About the Brain*. Picador, 2020, p. 153.
4 There is some debate about the relationship between short-term and working memory. Some define working memory as the attention-related aspect of short-term memory. Others argue that working memory includes short-term memory and other process mechanisms that help make use of short-term memory. In practice, the terms are often used interchangeably. See Cowan, Nelson. 'What are the differences between long-term, short-term, and working memory?' *Progress in Brain Research* 169 (2008): 323–338.
5 Miller, George A. 'The magic number seven plus or minus two: Some limits on our capacity for processing information.' *Psychological Review* 63 (1956): 91–97.
6 Cowan, Nelson. 'The magical number 4 in short-term memory: A

reconsideration of mental storage capacity.' *Behavioral and Brain Sciences* 24.1 (2001): 87–114.
7 Feldman Barrett, Lisa. *Seven and a Half Lessons About the Brain.* Picador, 2020, p. 31. Another commonly cited number is 85 billion. The difference is because neurons can be counted by different methods.
8 Not all memories are stored in the cortex. Procedural memories, which involve skills and habits, are primarily stored in the basal ganglia and the cerebellum, rather than the cortex.
9 Rasch, Björn and Jan Born. 'About sleep's role in memory.' *Physiological Reviews* (2013).
10 Diekelmann, Susanne and Jan Born. 'The memory function of sleep.' *Nature Reviews Neuroscience* 11.2 (2013): 114–126.
11 Stickgold, Robert, Laurie Scott, Cynthia Rittenhouse and J. Allan Hobson. 'Sleep-induced changes in associative memory.' *Journal of Cognitive Neuroscience 11.*2 (1999): 182–193.
12 Tempesta, Daniela, Valentina Socci, Luigi De Gennaro and Michele Ferrara. 'Sleep and emotional processing. *Sleep Medicine Reviews* 40 (2018): 183–195.
13 Diekelmann, Susanne and Jan Born. 'The memory function of sleep.' *Nature Reviews Neuroscience* 11.2 (2013): 114–126.
14 Leong, Ruth L. F., June C. Lo and Michael W. L. Chee. 'Systematic review and meta-analyses on the effects of afternoon napping on cognition.' *Sleep Medicine Reviews* 65 (2022): 101666.
15 Talarico, Jennifer M. and David C. Rubin. 'Confidence, not consistency, characterizes flashbulb memories.' *Psychological Science* 14.5 (2003): 455–461; Hirst, William, Elizabeth A. Phelps, Randy L. Buckner, Andrew E. Budson, Alexandru Cuc, John D. E. Gabrieli, Marcia K. Johnson et al. 'Long-term memory for the terrorist attack of September 11: Flashbulb memories, event memories, and the factors that influence their retention.' *Journal of Experimental Psychology: General* 138.2 (2009): 161–176.
16 Loftus, Elizabeth F. and Jacqueline E. Pickrell. 'The formation of false memories.' *Psychiatric Annals* 25.12 (1995): 720–725.
17 The same brain networks light up when we remember past experiences and when we imagine future events. Addis, Donna Rose, Alana T. Wong, and Daniel L. Schacter. 'Remembering the past and imagining the future: Common and distinct neural substrates during event construction and elaboration.' *Neuropsychologia* 45.7 (2007): 1363–1377.
18 Ebbinghaus, Hermann, *Memory: A contribution to experimental*

psychology, 1885. The experiment was recently replicated with very similar results. Murre, Jaap M. J. and Joeri Dros. 'Replication and analysis of Ebbinghaus' forgetting curve.' *PloS One 10.7* (2015).

19 One of the problems with this theory is that it's difficult to demonstrate that time alone is responsible for declines in recall.

20 De Quervain, Dominique J-F. and Andreas Papassotiropoulos. 'Identification of a genetic cluster influencing memory performance and hippocampal activity in humans.' *Proceedings of the National Academy of Sciences* 103.11 (2006): 4270–4274; De Quervain, Dominique J–F., Iris-Tatjana Kolassa, Sandra Ackermann, Amanda Aerni, Peter Boesiger, Philippe Demougin, Thomas Elbert et al. 'PKCα is genetically linked to memory capacity in healthy subjects and to risk for posttraumatic stress disorder in genocide survivors.' *Proceedings of the National Academy of Sciences* 109.22 (2012): 8746–8751.

21 Standing, Lionel. 'Learning 10000 pictures.' *Quarterly Journal of Experimental Psychology* 25.2 (1973): 207–222.

22 Brady, Timothy F., Talia Konkle, George A. Alvarez and Aude Oliva. 'Visual long-term memory has a massive storage capacity for object details.' *Proceedings of the National Academy of Sciences* 105.38 (2008): 14325–14329.

23 The VVIQ was developed by British psychologist David Marks in 1973. It has since been widely used and validated across different populations and contexts, making it a standard tool for measuring visual imagery vividness.

24 Chase, William G. and K. Anders Ericsson. 'Skill and working memory.' *Psychology of Learning and Motivation* (vol. 16). Academic Press, 1982, 1–58.

25 Thalmann, Mirko, Alessandra S. Souza and Klaus Oberauer. 'How does chunking help working memory?' *Journal of Experimental Psychology: Learning, memory, and cognition* 45.1 (2019): 37–55.

26 Foer, Joshua. *Moonwalking with Einstein: The art and science of remembering everything*. Penguin, 2012.

27 Graeber, Thomas, Christopher Roth and Florian Zimmermann. 'Stories, statistics, and memory.' *The Quarterly Journal of Economics* 139.4 (2024): 2181–2225.

28 Maguire, Eleanor A., Elizabeth R. Valentine, John M. Wilding and Narinder Kapur. 'Routes to remembering: The brains behind superior memory.' *Nature Neuroscience* 6. 1 (2003): 90–95.

29 Yates, Frances A. *The Art of Memory*. Routledge & Kegan, 1966.

30 Konrad, Boris. *De Geheimen van Ons Geheugen.* Ambo/Anthos, 2018, p. 210.
31 Wagner, Isabella C., Boris N. Konrad, Philipp Schuster, Sarah Weisig, Dimitris Repantis, Kathrin Ohla, Simone Kühn et al. 'Durable memories and efficient neural coding through mnemonic training using the method of loci.' *Science Advances* 7.10 (2021).
32 Horsley, Kevin. *Unlimited memory: How to use advanced learning strategies to learn faster, remember more and be more productive.* TCKpublishing.com, 2016, pp. 66–72.

5. Learning How to Learn

1 Woollett, Katherine and Eleanor A. Maguire. 'Acquiring 'the Knowledge' of London's layout drives structural brain changes.' *Current Biology* 21.24 (2011): 2109–2114.
2 Feldman Barrett, Lisa. *Seven and a Half Lessons About the Brain*, Picador, 2020, p. 50.
3 The phenomenon is more formally known as Hebb's principle. Hebb, Donald O. *The Organization of Behavior: A neuropsychological theory.* Psychology Press, 2002.
4 Gilmore, John H., Rebecca C. Knickmeyer and Wei Gao. 'Imaging structural and functional brain development in early childhood.' *Nature Reviews Neuroscience* 19.3 (2018): 123–137.
5 Swiss psychologist Jean Piaget is credited with the early development of the concept of schemas, which he used to explain a stage theory of cognitive development, particularly in children. The concept of schemas was later popularised in 1932 by British psychologist Frederic Bartlett, who conducted experimental research on how schemas influence memory.
6 Van Kesteren, Marlieke T. R., Dirk J. Ruiter, Guillén Fernández and Richard N. Henson. 'How schema and novelty augment memory formation.' *Trends in Neurosciences* 35.4 (2012): 211–219. This study also found that when the rubber duck was placed in a bakery, participants remembered it vividly. The stark difference between expectations (a bakery filled with bread and pastries) and reality (a rubber duck in the midst of it) made the scenario so unusual that it stood out in their memories. This illustrates how both fitting within a familiar schema and standing out against it can enhance our ability to remember information.
7 Tajfel, Henri and Alan L. Wilkes. 'Classification and quantitative judgement.' *British Journal of Psychology* 54.2 (1963): 101–114.

8 Ross, Lee. 'The intuitive psychologist and his shortcomings: Distortions in the attribution process.' *Advances in Experimental Social Psychology* (vol. 10). Academic Press, 1977, 173–220.
9 de Groot, Adriaan, D. *Thought and Choice in Chess*. The Hague, Mouton Publishers, 1965.
10 Chase, William G. and Herbert A. Simon. 'Perception in chess.' *Cognitive Psychology* 4.1 (1973): 55–81.
11 Klein, Gary A., Roberta Calderwood and Anne Clinton-Cirocco. 'Rapid decision making on the fire ground.' *Proceedings of the Human Factors Society Annual Meeting* 30.6 (1986): 576–580.
12 The idea that 10,000 hours of practice is required to become an expert was popularised by Malcolm Gladwell in his book *Outliers*. He based this number on research by Anders Ericsson, however the '10,000-hour rule' has been widely misunderstood. Gladwell simplified Ericsson's research, which actually emphasised the quality and type of practice rather than just the number of hours. Furthermore, subsequent studies show that the path to expertise varies across fields and individuals and there is no magic number for mastering a skill. Malcolm Gladwell, *Outliers: The story of success*. Penguin, 2009.
13 Gobet, Fernand and Guillermo Campitelli. 'The role of domain-specific practice, handedness, and starting age in chess.' *Developmental Psychology* 43.1 (2007): 159–172. This study found a large amount of variability in total amount of deliberate practice even among master-level chess players – from slightly more than 3,000 to more than 23,000 hours.
14 Ericsson, K. Anders, Ralf T. Krampe and Clemens Tesch–Römer. 'The role of deliberate practice in the acquisition of expert performance.' *Psychological Review* 100.3 (1993): 363–406; Deakin, Janice M. and Stephen Cobley. 'A search for deliberate practice.' *Expert Performance in Sports* (2003): 115–36.
15 Ericsson, K. Anders, Ralf T. Krampe and Clemens Tesch–Römer. 'The role of deliberate practice in the acquisition of expert performance.' *Psychological Review* 100.3 (1993): 363–406.
16 Ericsson, K. Anders, Robert R. Hoffman, Aaron Kozbelt and A. Mark Williams, eds. *The Cambridge Handbook of Expertise and Expert Performance*. Cambridge University Press, 2018; McNamara, Brooke N., David Z. Hambrick and Frederick L. Oswald. 'Deliberate practice and performance in music, games, sports, education, and professions: A meta-analysis.' *Psychological Science* 25.8 (2014): 1608–1618; Hambrick, David Z., Frederick L. Oswald, Erik M. Altmann, Elizabeth

J. Meinz, Fernand Gobet and Guillermo Campitelli. 'Deliberate practice: Is that all it takes to become an expert?' *Intelligence* 45 (2014): 34–45.
17 Oakley, Barbara. *A Mind for Numbers*, TarcherPerigee, 2014, pp. 61–63. The 'illusion of competence' as discussed here is related to the *Dunning-Kruger effect*, but it is not the same. The Dunning-Kruger effect is a cognitive bias in which individuals with low ability or knowledge in a particular domain tend to overestimate their competence, while those with high ability or expertise may underestimate their competence. Kruger, Justin and David Dunning. 'Unskilled and unaware of it: How difficulties in recognizing one's own incompetence lead to inflated self-assessments.' *Journal of Personality and Social Psychology* 77.6 (1999): 1121–1134.
18 Karpicke, Jeffrey D. and Henry L. Roediger III. 'The critical importance of retrieval for learning.' *Science* 319.5865 (2008): 966–968.
19 Dunlosky, John, Katherine A. Rawson, Elizabeth J. Marsh, Mitchell J. Nathan and Daniel T. Willingham. 'Improving students' learning with effective learning techniques: Promising directions from cognitive and educational psychology.' *Psychological Science in the Public Interest* 14.1 (2013): 4–58.
20 Baddeley, Alan, Michael W. Eysenck and Michael C. Anderson. *Memory*. Psychology Press, 2009, pp. 71–73; Carpenter, Shana K., Nicholas J. Cepeda, Doug Rohrer, Sean H.K. Kang, and Harold Pashler. 'Using spacing to enhance diverse forms of learning: Review of recent research and implications for instruction.' *Educational Psychology Review* 24 (2012): 369–378.
21 Karpicke, Jeffrey D. and Henry L. Roediger III. 'The critical importance of retrieval for learning.' *Science* 319.5865 (2008): 966–968.
22 Deslauriers, Louis, Logan S. McCarty, Kelly Miller, Kristina Callaghan and Greg Kestin. 'Measuring actual learning versus feeling of learning in response to being actively engaged in the classroom.' *Proceedings of the National Academy of Sciences* 116.39 (2019): 19251–19257.
23 Bradshaw, Gary L. and John R. Anderson. 'Elaborative encoding as an explanation of levels of processing.' *Journal of Verbal Learning and Verbal Behavior* 21.2 (1982): 165–174.
24 Cherry, E. Colin. 'Some experiments on the recognition of speech, with one and with two ears.' *The Journal of the Acoustical Society of America* 25.5 (1953): 975–979.
25 Hallam, Susan and Raymond MacDonald. 'The effects of music in community and educational settings.' *The Oxford Handbook of Music Psychology* (2009): 471–480.

26 Smith, Steven M., Arthur Glenberg and Robert A. Bjork. 'Environmental context and human memory.' *Memory & Cognition* 6.4 (1978): 342–353; Smith, Steven M. 'Background music and context-dependent memory.' *The American Journal of Psychology* (1985): 591–603; Herz, Rachel S. 'The effects of cue distinctiveness on odor-based context-dependent memory.' *Memory & Cognition* 25 (1997): 375–380.

27 Godden, Duncan R. and Alan D. Baddeley. 'Context-dependent memory in two natural environments: On land and underwater.' *British Journal of Psychology* 66.3 (1975): 325–331. A replication study was unable to replicate the findings of the experiment. There are, however, noticeable differences between the original and replication study, in particular the period over which recall took place. It is therefore hard to conclude that the original study cannot be replicated. Murre, Jaap M. J. 'The Godden and Baddeley (1975) experiment on context-dependent memory on land and underwater: A replication.' *Royal Society Open Science* 8.11 (2021): 200724.

28 Schneiderman, Neil, Gail Ironson and Scott D. Siegel. 'Stress and health: Psychological, behavioral, and biological determinants.' *Annual Review of Clinical Psychology* 1.1 (2005): 607–628.

29 Roozendaal, Benno, Bruce S. McEwen and Sumantra Chattarji. 'Stress, memory and the amygdala.' *Nature Reviews Neuroscience* 10.6 (2009): 423–433.

30 This inverted U-shape is also known as the Yerkes-Dodson Law, a psychological principle that describes the relationship between arousal (stress) and performance formulated by psychologists Robert Yerkes and John Dodson in 1908.

31 Hermans, Erno J., Marloes J. A. G. Henckens, Marian Joëls and Guillén Fernández. 'Dynamic adaptation of large-scale brain networks in response to acute stressors.' *Trends in Neurosciences* 37.6 (2014): 304–314.

32 Krause, Florian, Nikos Kogias, Martin Krentz, Michael Lührs, Rainer Goebel and Erno J. Hermans. 'Self-regulation of stress-related large-scale brain network balance using real-time fMRI neurofeedback.' *Neuroimage* 243 (2021): 118527. Participants in the study were trained to down regulate the salience network but, for ease of exposition, I refer to the amygdala which is an important part of the salience network.

33 Hopper, Susan I., Sherrie L. Murray, Lucille R. Ferrara and Joanne K. Singleton. 'Effectiveness of diaphragmatic breathing for reducing physiological and psychological stress in adults: A quantitative systematic

review.' *JBI Evidence Synthesis* 17.9 (2019): 1855–1876; Perciavalle, Valentina, Marta Blandini, Paola Fecarotta, Andrea Buscemi, Donatella Di Corrado, Luana Bertolo, Fulvia Fichera and Marinella Coco. 'The role of deep breathing on stress.' *Neurological Sciences* 38.3 (2017): 451–458.

34 Crum, Alia J., Peter Salovey and Shawn Achor. 'Rethinking stress: The role of mindsets in determining the stress response.' *Journal of Personality and Social Psychology* 104.4 (2013): 716.

35 Mueller, Pam A. and Daniel M. Oppenheimer. 'The pen is mightier than the keyboard: Advantages of longhand over laptop note taking.' *Psychological Science* 25.6 (2014): 1159–1168.

36 Kiewra, Kenneth A. 'Investigating notetaking and review: A depth of processing alternative.' *Educational Psychologist* 20.1 (1985): 23–32.

37 Homa, Donald. 'An assessment of two extraordinary speed-readers.' *Bulletin of the Psychonomic Society* 21.2 (1983): 123–126.

38 Rayner, Keith, Elizabeth R. Schotter, Michael E. J. Masson, Mary C. Potter and Rebecca Treiman. 'So much to read, so little time: How do we read, and can speed reading help?' *Psychological Science in the Public Interest* 17.1 (2016): 4–34.

39 Rayner, Keith and Robert E. Morrison. 'Eye movements and identifying words in parafoveal vision.' *Bulletin of the Psychonomic Society* 17.3 (1981): 135–138; Bouma, Herman. 'Visual search and reading: Eye movements and functional visual field: A tutorial review.' *Attention and Performance VII* (2022): 115–147.

40 Rayner, Keith, Elizabeth R. Schotter, Michael E. J. Masson, Mary C. Potter and Rebecca Treiman. 'So much to read, so little time: How do we read, and can speed reading help?' *Psychological Science in the Public Interest* 17.1 (2016): 4–34.

41 Reichle, Erik D., Simon P. Liversedge, Denis Drieghe, Hazel I. Blythe, Holly S. S. L. Joseph, Sarah J. White and Keith Rayner. 'Using EZ Reader to examine the concurrent development of eye-movement control and reading skill.' *Developmental Review* 33.2 (2013): 110–149.

42 Rayner, Keith, Elizabeth R. Schotter, Michael E. J. Masson, Mary C. Potter, and Rebecca Treiman. 'So much to read, so little time: How do we read, and can speed reading help?' *Psychological Science in the Public Interest* 17.1 (2016): 4–34.

43 The Cattell-Horn-Carroll theory is an integration of two previously established theoretical models of intelligence: The theory of fluid and crystallised intelligence (Gf-Gc) of Raymond Cattell and John Horn, and John Carroll's three-stratum theory, a hierarchical, three-stratum

model of intelligence. Horn, John L. and Raymond B. Cattell. 'Refinement and test of the theory of fluid and crystallized general intelligences.' *Journal of Educational Psychology* 57.5 (1966): 253–270; Carroll, John B. *Human Cognitive Abilities: A survey of factor-analytic studies*. Cambridge University Press, 1993.

6. When Creativity Strikes

1. The idea that memory and creativity are two sides of the same coin is even embedded in the English language. The Latin root 'inventio' is the basis for two words in modern English: inventory and invention. To invent, you first need a well-stocked inventory – a bank of existing ideas to draw from.
2. Gilhooly, Kenneth J. and Mary L. M. Gilhooly. *Aging and Creativity*. Academic Press, 2021.
3. Ellamil, Melissa, Charles Dobson, Mark Beeman and Kalina Christoff. 'Evaluative and generative modes of thought during the creative process.' *Neuroimage* 59.2 (2012): 1783–1794; Beaty, Roger E., Mathias Benedek, Paul J. Silvia and Daniel L. Schacter. 'Creative cognition and brain network dynamics.' *Trends in Cognitive Sciences* 20.2 (2016): 87–95.
4. Beaty, Roger E., Yoed N. Kenett, Alexander P. Christensen, Monica D. Rosenberg, Mathias Benedek, Qunlin Chen, Andreas Fink et al. 'Robust prediction of individual creative ability from brain functional connectivity.' *Proceedings of the National Academy of Sciences* 115.5 (2018): 1087–1092. In addition to stronger functional connections between the default and control networks, connectivity of the salience network (the network involved in switching between the default and control networks) matters too.
5. Mind-wandering can positively affect the generation of novel ideas when it occurs at the right time and in the right context. Zedelius, Claire M. and Jonathan W. Schooler. 'The richness of inner experience: Relating styles of daydreaming to creative processes.' *Frontiers in Psychology* 6 (2016): 1–7; Beaty, Roger E. 'The creative brain.' *Cerebrum: The Dana forum on brain science*. (vol. 2020). Dana Foundation, 2020.
6. Kaplan, Fred. *Dickens: A biography*. Harper & Row, 1988.
7. Baird, Benjamin, Jonathan Smallwood, Michael D. Mrazek, Julia W. Y. Kam, Michael S. Franklin and Jonathan W. Schooler. 'Inspired by distraction: Mind wandering facilitates creative incubation.' *Psychological Science* 23.10 (2012): 1117–1122.

8   Gable, Shelly L., Elizabeth A. Hopper and Jonathan W. Schooler. 'When the muses strike: Creative ideas of physicists and writers routinely occur during mind wandering.' *Psychological Science* 30.3 (2019): 396–404.
9   This so-called Alternative Uses Task was developed by Joy P. Guilford in the 1960s. Guilford, Joy P. *The Nature of Human Intelligence.* McGraw-Hill, 1967.
10 Duncker, Karl and Lynne S. Lees. 'On problem-solving.' *Psychological Monographs* 58.5 (1945): i–113.
11 Divergent thinking is often equated with lateral thinking. However, British psychologist Edward de Bono, who coined the term, explains that divergent thinking is just one aspect of lateral thinking. De Bono, Edward. *Serious Creativity.* Vermilion, 1992, p. 90.
12 The theoretical foundation of divergent and convergent thinking is rooted in the work of Guilford who postulated that both modes of thought are necessary for problem solving. Guilford, Joy P. *The Nature of Human Intelligence.* McGraw-Hill, 1967.
13 Hoogman, Martine, Marije Stolte, Matthijs Baas and Evelyn Kroesbergen. 'Creativity and ADHD: A review of behavioral studies, the effect of psychostimulants and neural underpinnings.' *Neuroscience & Biobehavioral Reviews* 119 (2020): 66–85.
14 Torrance, E. Paul. *The Torrance Tests of Creative Thinking.* Prentice Hall, 1968.
15 Guilford, Joy P. *The Nature of Human Intelligence.* McGraw-Hill, 1967.
16 Mednick, Sarnoff. 'The associative basis of the creative process.' *Psychological Review* 69.3 (1962): 220–232.
17 De Bono, Edward. *Serious Creativity.* Vermilion, 1992, pp. 258–267.
18 Ibid., pp. 121–127.
19 Eberle, Bob. *Scamper: Games for imagination development.* Prentice Hall, 1971. The technique builds upon the earlier work of Alex Osborn who initially referred to the creative technique as a 'think up', which he introduced in 1938 and formalised in his book *Applied Imagination.* Osborn, Alex F. *Applied Imagination: Principles and procedures of creative problem solving.* Scribner, 1953.
20 Salvador Dali learned this technique from the Capuchin monks of Toledo. Dali, Salvador. *50 Secrets of Magic Craftsmanship.* Dover Publications Inc, 1992, p. 36.
21 Lacaux, Célia, Thomas Andrillon, Céleste Bastoul, Yannis Idir, Alexandrine Fonteix-Galet, Isabelle Arnulf and Delphine Oudiette. 'Sleep onset is a creative sweet spot.' *Science Advances,* 7.50 (2021):

1–9; Horowitz, Adam Haar, Kathleen Esfahany, Tomás Vega Gálvez, Pattie Maes and Robert Stickgold. 'Targeted dream incubation at sleep onset increases post-sleep creative performance.' *Scientific Reports*, 13.1 (2023): 7319.
22 Horowitz, Adam Haar, Kathleen Esfahany, Tomás Vega Gálvez, Pattie Maes and Robert Stickgold. 'Targeted dream incubation at sleep onset increases post-sleep creative performance.' *Scientific Reports*, 13.1 (2023): 7319.
23 Rubin, Rick. *The Creative Art*. Canongate Books, 2023, p. 77.

7. The Brain Gym

1 Philip Bond runs a consultancy specialising in solving challenging problems in fields ranging from F1 and Olympic sports through to aerospace and medical AI. He also works as a success coach enabling individuals and companies to achieve exceptional levels of performance. He is professor of creativity and innovation at the University of Manchester and formerly held a visiting fellowship in the Department of Mathematics at Oxford and visiting professorships in engineering mathematics and computer science at the University of Bristol. He has twice held the Guinness world record for the 'Everest test of memory', the so-called matrix memorisation of the number pi.
2 Wood, Wendy, Jeffrey M. Quinn and Deborah A. Kashy. 'Habits in everyday life: Thought, emotion, and action.' *Journal of Personality and Social Psychology* 83.6 (2002): 1281–1297.
3 Wood, Wendy. *Good Habits, Bad Habits*. Macmillan, 2019, p. 13.
4 Although much is still unknown about neuronal timing, dopamine seems to promote habit learning for less than a minute. Shindou, Tomomi, Mayumi Shindou, Sakurako Watanabe and Jeffery Wickens. 'A silent eligibility trace enables dopamine-dependent synaptic plasticity for reinforcement learning in the mouse striatum.' *European Journal of Neuroscience* 49.5 (2019): 726–736.
5 Armitage, Christopher J. 'Can the theory of planned behaviour predict the maintenance of physical activity?' *Health Psychology* 24.3 (2005): 235–245.
6 Wood, Wendy. *Good Habits, Bad Habits*. Macmillan, 2019, p. 126.
7 www.humanbenchmark.com.
8 www.raiseyouriq.com.
9 This is just one version of image streaming and there are various, more advanced practices available. The technique has been popularized

in by Win Wegner. His claims that image streaming increases IQ have not been scientifically proven. Wenger, Win and Richard Poe. *The Einstein Factor: A proven new method for increasing your intelligence.* Penguin Random House, 1995.

10 Katz, Benjamin, Priti Shah and David E. Meyer. 'How to play 20 questions with nature and lose: Reflections on 100 years of brain-training research.' *Proceedings of the National Academy of Sciences* 115.40 (2018): 9897–9904.

11 Foroughi, Cyrus K., Samuel S. Monfort, Martin Paczynski, Patrick E. McKnight and P. M. Greenwood. 'Placebo effects in cognitive training.' *Proceedings of the National Academy of Sciences* 113.27 (2016): 7470–7474.

12 Katz, Benjamin, Priti Shah, and David E. Meyer. 'How to play 20 questions with nature and lose: Reflections on 100 years of brain-training research.' *Proceedings of the National Academy of Sciences* 115.40 (2018): 9897–9904.

13 Dunning, Darren L. and Joni Holmes. 'Does working memory training promote the use of strategies on untrained working memory tasks?' *Memory & Cognition* 42 (2014): 854–862.

14 Katz, Benjamin, Priti Shah, and David E. Meyer. 'How to play 20 questions with nature and lose: Reflections on 100 years of brain-training research.' *Proceedings of the National Academy of Sciences* 115.40 (2018): 9897–9904.

15 Dresler, Martin, William R. Shirer, Boris N. Konrad, Nils C. J. Müller, Isabella C. Wagner, Guillén Fernández, Michael Czisch and Michael D. Greicius. 'Mnemonic training reshapes brain networks to support superior memory.' *Neuron* 93.5 (2017): 1227–1235.

16 Konrad, Boris. *De Geheimen van Ons Geheugen.* Ambo Anthos, 2016, p. 192.

17 Erickson, Kirk I., Charles Hillman, Chelsea M. Stillman, Rachel M. Ballard, Bonny Bloodgood, David E. Conroy, Richard Macko, David X. Marquez, Steven J. Petruzzello and Kenneth E. Powell. 'Physical activity, cognition, and brain outcomes: A review of the 2018 physical activity guidelines.' *Medicine and Science in Sports and Exercise* 51.6 (2019): 1242–1251.

18 Zhu, Jianwei, Fenfen Ge, Yu Zeng, Yuanyuan Qu, Wenwen Chen, Huazhen Yang, Lei Yang, Fang Fang and Huan Song. 'Physical and mental activity, disease susceptibility, and risk of dementia: A prospective cohort study based on UK biobank.' *Neurology* 99.8 (2022) e799-e813. See also James et al (2023) who tracked more than 1,400

British people for thirty years, showing that more physical activity was associated with better cognitive performance at age 69. James, Sarah-Naomi, Yu-Jie Chiou, Nasri Fatih, Louisa P. Needham, Jonathan M. Schott and Marcus Richards. 'Timing of physical activity across adulthood on later-life cognition: 30 years follow-up in the 1946 British birth cohort.' *Journal of Neurology, Neurosurgery & Psychiatry* 94.5 (2023): 349–356.

19 Ciria, Luis F., Rafael Román-Caballero, Miguel A. Vadillo, Darias Holgado, Antonio Luque-Casado, Pandelis Perakakis and Daniel Sanabria. 'An umbrella review of randomised control trials on the effects of physical exercise on cognition.' *Nature Human Behaviour* 7.6 (2023): 928–941.

20 Cheval, Boris, Liza Darrous, Karmel W. Choi, Yann C. Klimentidis, David A. Raichlen, Gene E. Alexander, Stéphane Cullati, Zoltán Kutalik and Matthieu P. Boisgontier. 'Genetic insights into the causal relationship between physical activity and cognitive functioning.' *Scientific Reports* 13.1 (2023): 5310.

21 Erickson, Kirk I., Charles Hillman, Chelsea M. Stillman, Rachel M. Ballard, Bonny Bloodgood, David E. Conroy, Richard Macko, David X. Marquez, Steven J. Petruzzello and Kenneth E. Powell. 'Physical activity, cognition, and brain outcomes: A review of the 2018 physical activity guidelines.' *Medicine and Science in Sports and Exercise* 51.6 (2019): 1242–1251.

22 Gibbons et al (2023) found that just six minutes of intense cycling has a big impact on the production of BDNF in young healthy adults. Intensity of the workout mattered – just six minutes of high-intensity cycling increased BDNF by four to five times more than a leisurely ninety-minute ride. Gibbons, Travis D., James D. Cotter, Philip N. Ainslie, Wickliffe C. Abraham, Bruce G. Mockett, Holly A. Campbell, Emma M. W. Jones, Elliott J. Jenkins and Kate N. Thomas. 'Fasting for 20 h does not affect exercise-induced increases in circulating BDNF in humans.' *The Journal of Physiology* 601.11 (2023): 2121–2137.

23 Firth, Joseph, Brendon Stubbs, Davy Vancampfort, Felipe Schuch, Jim Lagopoulos, Simon Rosenbaum and Philip B. Ward. 'Effect of aerobic exercise on hippocampal volume in humans: A systematic review and meta-analysis.' *Neuroimage* 166 (2018): 230–238. Van Praag, Henriette. 'Neurogenesis and exercise: Past and future directions.' *Neuromolecular Medicine* 10 (2008): 128–140.

24 Dolezal, Brett A., Eric V. Neufeld, David M. Boland, Jennifer L. Martin and Christopher B. Cooper. 'Interrelationship between sleep and

exercise: A systematic review.' *Advances in Preventive Medicine* 2017.1 (2017): 1364387.

25 Stults-Kolehmainen, Matthew A. and Rajita Sinha. 'The effects of stress on physical activity and exercise.' *Sports Medicine* 44 (2014): 81–121.

26 https://www.who.int/news-room/fact-sheets/detail/physical-activity

27 Tabata, Izumi, Kouji Nishimura, Motoki Kouzaki, Yuusuke Hirai, Futoshi Ogita, Motohiko Miyachi and Kaoru Yamamoto. 'Effects of moderate-intensity endurance and high-intensity intermittent training on anaerobic capacity and VO2 max.' *Medicine and Science in Sports and Exercise* 28 (1996): 1327–1330.

28 Killingsworth, Matthew A. and Daniel T. Gilbert. 'A wandering mind is an unhappy mind.' *Science* 330.6006 (2010): 932–932.

29 Tang, Yi-Yuan, Britta K. Hölzel and Michael I. Posner. 'The neuroscience of mindfulness meditation.' *Nature Reviews Neuroscience* 16.4 (2015): 213–225; Basso, Julia C., Alexandra McHale, Victoria Ende, Douglas J. Oberlin and Wendy A. Suzuki. 'Brief, daily meditation enhances attention, memory, mood, and emotional regulation in non-experienced meditators.' *Behavioural Brain Research* 356 (2019): 208–220.

30 Basso, Julia C., Alexandra McHale, Victoria Ende, Douglas J. Oberlin and Wendy A. Suzuki. 'Brief, daily meditation enhances attention, memory, mood, and emotional regulation in non-experienced meditators.' *Behavioural Brain Research* 356 (2019): 208–220.

31 Tang, Yi-Yuan, Britta K. Hölzel and Michael I. Posner. 'The neuroscience of mindfulness meditation.' *Nature Reviews Neuroscience* 16.4 (2015): 213–225; Young, Katherine S., Anne Maj van der Velden, Michelle G. Craske, Karen Johanne Pallesen, Lone Fjorback, Andreas Roepstorff and Christine E. Parsons. 'The impact of mindfulness-based interventions on brain activity: A systematic review of functional magnetic resonance imaging studies.' *Neuroscience & Biobehavioral Reviews* 84 (2018): 424–433.

32 Kabat-Zinn, Jon. *Wherever You Go, There You Are: Mindfulness meditation in everyday life.* Hyperion, 1994.

33 Lange, Tanja, Stoyan Dimitrov, Thomas Bollinger, Susanne Diekelmann and Jan Born. 'Sleep after vaccination boosts immunological memory.' *The Journal of Immunology*, 187.1 (2011): 283–290.

34 Rosenblum, Yevgenia, Frederik D. Weber, Michael Rak, Zsófia Zavecz, Nicolas Kunath, Barbara Breitenstein, Björn Rasch et al. 'Sustained polyphasic sleep restriction abolishes human growth hormone release.' *Sleep* 47. 2 (2024): 1–12.

35 Watson, Nathaniel F., M. Safwan Badr, Gregory Belenky, Donald L. Bliwise, Orfeu M. Buxton, Daniel Buysse et al. 'Recommended amount of sleep for a healthy adult: a joint consensus statement of the American Academy of Sleep Medicine and Sleep Research Society.' *Journal of Clinical Sleep Medicine* 11.6 (2015): 591–592.
36 https://www.sleepfoundation.org/sleep-hygiene/healthy-sleep-tips; https://aasm.org/resources/pdf/products/howtosleepbetter_web.pdf
37 Blume, Christine, Christian Cajochen, Isabel Schöllhorn, Helen C. Slawik and Manuel Spitschan. 'Effects of calibrated blue–yellow changes in light on the human circadian clock.' *Nature Human Behaviour* 8. 3 (2024): 590–605. This study finds that our body clock doesn't respond much to shifts in light colour towards warmer tones, like yellow, if the overall brightness stays the same.
38 Blanchard, James and S. J. A. Sawers. 'The absolute bioavailability of caffeine in man.' *European Journal of Clinical Pharmacology* 24 (1983): 93–98.
39 https://www.sleepfoundation.org/nutrition/alcohol-and-sleep.
40 Walker, Matthew. *Why We Sleep*. Penguin Random House, 2018, p. 291.
41 Ficca, Gianluca, John Axelsson, Daniel J. Mollicone, Vincenzo Muto and Michael V. Vitiello. 'Naps, cognition and performance.' *Sleep Medicine Reviews* 14.4 (2010): 249–258.
42 Yamada, Yosuke, Xueying Zhang, Mary E. T. Henderson, Hiroyuki Sagayama, Herman Pontzer, Daiki Watanabe, Tsukasa Yoshida et al. 'Variation in human water turnover associated with environmental and lifestyle factors.' *Science* 378. 6622 (2022): 909–915.
43 Dresler, Martin, Anders Sandberg, Kathrin Ohla, Christoph Bublitz, Carlos Trenado, Aleksandra Mroczko-Wąsowicz, Simone Kühn and Dimitris Repantis 'Non-pharmacological cognitive enhancement.' *Neuropharmacology* 64 (2013): 529–543.
44 Dyall, Simon C. 'Long-chain omega-3 fatty acids and the brain: A review of the independent and shared effects of EPA, DPA and DHA.' *Frontiers in Aging Neuroscience* 7 (2015): 52; Luchtman, Dirk W. and Cai Song. 'Cognitive enhancement by omega-3 fatty acids from childhood to old age: Findings from animal and clinical studies' *Neuropharmacology* 64 (2013): 550–565.
45 For a review of the literature on effects of coffee see Dresler, Martin, Anders Sandberg, Kathrin Ohla, Christoph Bublitz, Carlos Trenado, Aleksandra Mroczko-Wąsowicz, Simone Kühn and Dimitris Repantis 'Non-pharmacological cognitive enhancement.' *Neuropharmacology*

64 (2013): 529–543; Scholey, Andrew and Lauren Owen. 'Effects of chocolate on cognitive function and mood: A systematic review.' *Nutrition Reviews* 71.10 (2013): 665–681.

8. Inner Truths

1 Jang, Kerry L., Robert R. McCrae, Alois Angleitner, Rainer Riemann and W. John Livesley. 'Heritability of facet-level traits in a cross-cultural twin sample: Support for a hierarchical model of personality.' *Journal of Personality and Social Psychology* 74.6 (1998): 1556–1565; Lubinski, David. 'Scientific and social significance of assessing individual differences: "Sinking shafts at a few critical points".' *Annual Review of Psychology* 51.1 (2000): 405–444.
2 Bowlby, John. *Attachment and Loss: Separation, anxiety and anger* (vol. 2). Hogarth Press, 1973.
3 Heritability refers to how much genetic differences account for variations in a trait (like height or intelligence) among people. It doesn't indicate how much of a trait in one person comes from their genes. Heritability isn't constant; it can change if the variability of a trait changes in a group. While heritability helps us understand how much variation exists within a group, it doesn't explain why one group may be different from another. However, it does indicate how environmental changes might influence the average level of a trait in a population. See Nolen-Hoeksema, Susan, Barbara Fredrickson, Geoffrey R. Loftus and Christel Lutz. *Atkinson and Hilgard's Introduction to Psychology* (16th edition). Cengage Learning, 2014, p. 424.
4 McAdams, Dan P. 'The psychology of life stories.' *Review of General Psychology* 5.2 (2001): 100–122.
5 Ashton, Michael C. and Kibeom Lee. 'A theoretical basis for the major dimensions of personality.' *European Journal of Personality* 15.5 (2001): 327–353.
6 Schwartz, Shalom H. 'Universals in the content and structure of values: Theoretical advances and empirical tests in 20 countries.' *Advances in Experimental Social Psychology* (vol. 25). Academic Press, 1992, 1–65.
7 Dobewall, Henrik, Raül Tormos and Christin-Melanie Vauclair. 'Normative value change across the human life cycle: Similarities and differences across Europe.' *Journal of Adult Development* 24 (2017): 263–276; Bardi, Anat, Kathryn E. Buchanan, Robin Goodwin, Letitia Slabu and Mark Robinson. 'Value stability and change during self-chosen

life transitions: Self-selection versus socialization effects.' *Journal of Personality and Social Psychology* 106.1 (2014): 131–147.
8 Inglehart, Ronald and Wayne E. Baker. 'Modernization, cultural change, and the persistence of traditional values.' *American Sociological Review* 65.1 (2000): 19–51.
9 Schwartz, Shalom H. 'Universals in the content and structure of values: Theoretical advances and empirical tests in 20 countries.' *Advances in Experimental Social Psychology* (vol. 25). Academic Press, 1992, 1–65; Schwartz, Shalom H., Gila Melech, Arielle Lehmann, Steven Burgess, Mari Harris and Vicki Owens. 'Extending the cross-cultural validity of the theory of basic human values with a different method of measurement.' *Journal of Cross-cultural Psychology* 32.5 (2001): 519–542.
10 Festinger, Leon. *A Theory of Cognitive Dissonance*. Stanford University Press, 1957.
11 Beck, Aaron. T. *Cognitive Therapy and the Emotional Disorders*. International Universities Press, 1976.
12 Clark, Andy. 'Whatever next? Predictive brains, situated agents, and the future of cognitive science.' *Behavioral and Brain Sciences* 36.3 (2013): 181–204.
13 Simons, Daniel J. and Christopher F. Chabris. 'Gorillas in our midst: Sustained inattentional blindness for dynamic events.' *Perception* 28.9 (1999): 1059–1074. Other tests have confirmed that we can also be 'blind' to auditory information as well as touch and smell information. https://www.bps.org.uk/research-digest/beyond-invisible-gorilla
14 Seth, Anil. *Being You: A new science of consciousness*. Penguin, 2021.
15 Friston, Karl. 'The free-energy principle: A unified brain theory?' *Nature Reviews Neuroscience* 11.2 (2010): 127–138.
16 Barrett, Lisa Feldman, *Seven and a Half Lessons About the Brain*, 2020, Picador, p. 66.
17 De Berker, Archy O., Robb B. Rutledge, Christoph Mathys, Louise Marshall, Gemma F. Cross, Raymond J. Dolan and Sven Bestmann. 'Computations of uncertainty mediate acute stress responses in humans.' *Nature Communications* 7.1 (2016): 10996.
18 Kahneman, Daniel and Amos Tversky. 'Prospect theory: An analysis of decision under risk.' *Econometrica* 47.2 (1979): 363–391.
19 Morriss, Jayne, Martin Gell and Carien M. van Reekum. 'The uncertain brain: A co-ordinate based meta-analysis of the neural signatures supporting uncertainty during different contexts.' *Neuroscience & Biobehavioral Reviews* 96 (2019): 241–249.

20 Kahneman, Daniel and Amos Tversky. 'Prospect theory: An analysis of decision under risk.' *Econometrica* 47.2 (1979): 363–391.
21 Vallone, Robert P., Lee Ross and Mark R. Lepper. 'The hostile media phenomenon: Biased perception and perceptions of media bias in coverage of the Beirut massacre.' *Journal of Personality and Social Psychology* 49.3 (1985): 577–585.

9. Letting Go

1 Klarreich, E. 'Huygens's clocks revisited.' *American Scientist* 90, July–August 2002.
2 This principle applies to all tuning forks (and resonant systems) that share the same natural frequency.
3 Kross, Ethan and Ozlem Ayduk. 'Self-distancing: Theory, research, and current directions.' *Advances in Experimental Social Psychology* (vol. 55). Academic Press, 2017. 81–136; Nejad, Ayna Baladi, Philippe Fossati and Cédric Lemogne. 'Self-referential processing, rumination, and cortical midline structures in major depression.' *Frontiers in Human Neuroscience* 7 (2013): 666.
4 Lyubomirsky, Sonja, Kari L. Tucker, Nicole D. Caldwell and Kimberly Berg. 'Why ruminators are poor problem solvers: clues from the phenomenology of dysphoric rumination.' *Journal of Personality and Social Psychology* 77.5 (1999): 1041–1060.
5 Nolen-Hoeksema, Susan, Blair E. Wisco and Sonja Lyubomirsky. 'Rethinking rumination.' *Perspectives on Psychological Science* 3.5 (2008): 400–424.
6 Ibid.
7 Kross, Ethan. *Chatter: The voice in our head (and how to harness it)*. Vermillion, 2022, p. 48.
8 Moser, Jason S., Adrienne Dougherty, Whitney I. Mattson, Benjamin Katz, Tim P. Moran, Darwin Guevarra, Holly Shablack et al. 'Third-person self-talk facilitates emotion regulation without engaging cognitive control: Converging evidence from ERP and fMRI.' *Scientific Reports* 7.1 (2017): 4519.
9 Neubauer, Andreas B., Joshua M. Smyth and Martin J. Sliwinski. 'Age differences in proactive coping with minor hassles in daily life.' *The Journals of Gerontology: Series B.* 74.1 (2019): 7–16.
10 Frankl, Viktor E. *Man's Search for Meaning*. Beacon Press, 2006. (Originally published in 1946.)
11 Pennebaker, James W. and Sandra K. Beall. 'Confronting a traumatic

12. Frattaroli, Joanne. 'Experimental disclosure and its moderators: a meta-analysis.' *Psychological Bulletin* 132.6 (2006): 823–865; Baikie, Karen A. and Kay Wilhelm. 'Emotional and physical health benefits of expressive writing.' *Advances in Psychiatric Treatment* 11.5 (2005): 338–346; Reinhold, Maren, Paul-Christian Bürkner and Heinz Holling. 'Effects of expressive writing on depressive symptoms – A meta-analysis.' *Clinical Psychology: Science and practice* 25.1 (2018): 80; DiMenichi, Brynne C. and Lauren L. Richmond. 'Reflecting on past failures leads to increased perseverance and sustained attention.' *Journal of Cognitive Psychology* 27.2 (2015): 180–193.
13. Smyth, Joshua M., Jill R. Hockemeyer and Heather Tulloch. 'Expressive writing and post-traumatic stress disorder: Effects on trauma symptoms, mood states, and cortisol reactivity.' *British Journal of Health Psychology* 13.1 (2008): 85–93; Lieberman, Matthew D., Naomi I. Eisenberger, Molly J. Crockett, Sabrina M. Tom, Jennifer H. Pfeifer and Baldwin M. Way. 'Putting feelings into words.' *Psychological Science* 18.5 (2007): 421–428.
14. https://liberalarts.utexas.edu/psychology/faculty/pennebak. See also Smyth, Joshua and Rebecca Helm. 'Focused expressive writing as self-help for stress and trauma.' *Journal of Clinical Psychology* 59.2 (2003): 227–235.
15. Kahneman, Daniel and Amos Tversky. 'Prospect theory: An analysis of decision under risk.' *Econometrica* 47.2 (1979): 363–391.
16. Conn, Charles and Robert McLean. *Bulletproof Problem Solving: The one skill that changes everything.* Wiley, 2018.
17. Nussbaum, A. David and Carol S. Dweck. 'Defensiveness versus remediation: Self-theories and modes of self-esteem maintenance.' *Personality and Social Psychology Bulletin* 34.5 (2008): 599–612. See also Moser et al (2011) who show at the neural level an enhanced focus on learning after errors for students with a growth mindset about their intelligence. Moser, Jason S., Hans S. Schroder, Carrie Heeter, Tim P. Moran and Yu-Hao Lee. 'Mind your errors: Evidence for a neural mechanism linking growth mind-set to adaptive posterror adjustments.' *Psychological Science* 22.12 (2011): 1484–1489.
18. Dweck, Carol S. and David S. Yeager. 'Mindsets: A view from two eras.' *Perspectives on Psychological Science* 14.3 (2019): 481–496.
19. Dweck, Carol S. *Mindset: How you can fulfill your potential.* Constable & Robinson, 2012, p.6.

20 Mueller, Claudia M. and Carol S. Dweck. 'Praise for intelligence can undermine children's motivation and performance.' *Journal of Personality and Social Psychology* 75.1 (1998): 33–52; Kamins, Melissa L. and Carol S. Dweck. 'Person versus process praise and criticism: implications for contingent self-worth and coping.' *Developmental Psychology* 35.3 (1999): 835–847.

21 Yeager, David S., Paul Hanselman, Gregory M. Walton, Jared S. Murray, Robert Crosnoe, Chandra Muller, Elizabeth Tipton, et al. 'A national experiment reveals where a growth mindset improves achievement.' *Nature* 573.7774 (2019): 364–369.

22 Aronson, Elliot. 'The power of self-persuasion.' *American Psychologist* 54.11 (1999): 875.

23 Crum, Alia J., Peter Salovey and Shawn Achor. 'Rethinking stress: The role of mindsets in determining the stress response.' *Journal of Personality and Social Psychology* 104.4 (2013): 716–733.

24 Ibid.

25 Yeager, David S., Christopher J. Bryan, James J. Gross, Jared S. Murray, Danielle Krettek Cobb, Pedro H. F. Santos, Hannah Gravelding, Meghann Johnson and Jeremy P. Jamieson. 'A synergistic mindsets intervention protects adolescents from stress.' *Nature* 607.7919 (2022): 512–520.

10. Dance to the Music

1 Danner, Deborah D., David A. Snowdon and Wallace V. Friesen. 'Positive emotions in early life and longevity: Findings from the nun study.' *Journal of Personality and Social Psychology* 80.5 (2001): 804–813.

2 Snowdon, David. *Aging with Grace: What the nun study teaches us about leading longer, healthier, and more meaningful lives.* Bantam, 2002.

3 Diener, Ed and Micaela Y. Chan. 'Happy people live longer: Subjective well-being contributes to health and longevity.' *Applied Psychology: Health and Well-being* 3.1 (2011): 1–43; Zhang, Yujing and Buxin Han. 'Positive affect and mortality risk in older adults: A meta-analysis.' *PsyCh Journal* 5.2 (2016): 125–138.

4 Pressman, Sarah D., Brooke N. Jenkins and Judith T. Moskowitz. 'Positive affect and health: What do we know and where next should we go?' *Annual Review of Psychology* 70.1 (2019): 627–650.

5 Kiecolt-Glaser, Janice K., Jean-Philippe Gouin and Liisa Hantsoo. 'Close

relationships, inflammation, and health.' *Neuroscience & Biobehavioral Reviews* 35.1 (2010): 33–38.
6. Pressman, Sarah D., Brooke N. Jenkins and Judith T. Moskowitz. 'Positive affect and health: What do we know and where next should we go?' *Annual Review of Psychology* 70.1 (2019): 627–650.
7. Ibid.
8. Lykken, David and Auke Tellegen. 'Happiness is a stochastic phenomenon.' *Psychological Science* 7.3 (1996): 186–189.
9. Dolan, Paul. *Happiness by Design*. Penguin Random House, 2014, pp. 110–111. The day reconstructing method was originally designed by Daniel Kahneman and colleagues. Kahneman, Daniel, Alan B. Krueger, David A. Schkade, Norbert Schwarz and Arthur A. Stone. 'A survey method for characterizing daily life experience: The day reconstruction method.' *Science* 306.5702 (2004): 1776–1780.
10. Conditions like post-traumatic stress disorder (PTSD) can significantly disrupt this process. PTSD can lead to long-lasting changes in well-being, making it more difficult for individuals to return to their pre-trauma baseline happiness.
11. This exercise is adapted from Rao, Srikumar. *Happiness at Work*, McGraw Hill, 2010, p. 74.
12. Gilbert, Daniel T., Elizabeth C. Pinel, Timothy D. Wilson, Stephen J. Blumberg and Thalia P. Wheatley. 'Immune neglect: A source of durability bias in affective forecasting.' *Journal of Personality and Social Psychology* 75.3 (1998): 617–638.
13. This phenomenon, known as *affective forecasting*, reveals that people often overestimate the impact of future events on their happiness. We think winning the lottery will make us blissful forever or that a breakup will leave us devastated indefinitely. However, studies consistently show that our emotional reactions to these events are less intense and more fleeting than we anticipate. Wilson, Timothy D. and Daniel T. Gilbert. 'Affective forecasting: Knowing what to want.' *Current Directions in Psychological Science* 14.3 (2005): 131–134.
14. Gilbert, Daniel T. 'On the surprising science of happiness.' The TED Interview, October 2019.
15. Gilbert, Daniel T., and Jane E.J. Ebert. 'Decisions and revisions: the affective forecasting of changeable outcomes.' *Journal of Personality and Social Psychology* 82.4 (2002): 503–514.
16. Rozin, Paul and Edward B. Royzman. 'Negativity bias, negativity dominance, and contagion.' *Personality and Social Psychology Review* 5.4 (2001): 296–320; Baumeister, Roy F., Ellen Bratslavsky, Catrin

Finkenauer and Kathleen D. Vohs. 'Bad is stronger than good.' *Review of General Psychology* 5.4 (2001): 323–370.

17 Schkade, David A. and Daniel Kahneman. 'Does living in California make people happy? A focusing illusion in judgments of life satisfaction.' *Psychological Science* 9.5 (1998): 340–346.

18 Kahneman, Daniel and Angus Deaton. 'High income improves evaluation of life but not emotional well-being.' *Proceedings of the National Academy of Sciences* 107.38 (2010): 16489–16493. A similar conclusion was reached in a more recent global analysis of the same dataset. Jebb, Andrew T., Louis Tay, Ed Diener and Shigehiro Oishi. 'Happiness, income satiation and turning points around the world.' *Nature Human Behaviour* 2.1 (2018): 33–38.

19 Killingsworth, Matthew A. 'Experienced well-being rises with income, even above $75,000 per year.' *Proceedings of the National Academy of Sciences* 118.4 (2021). Killingsworth highlights several factors that might explain the differences in findings. Notably, Kahneman and Deaton's study uses a binary measure of experienced well-being (yes/no), which limits the ability to register improvements once the higher level is achieved. In contrast, Killingsworth measures experienced well-being on a continuous response scale ranging from 'very bad' to 'very good', allowing for more nuanced data. Additionally, Killingsworth's study collects real-time reports of experienced well-being, whereas Kahneman and Deaton relied on surveys asking people to recall their feelings during a specific past period. This retrospective approach may not accurately reflect actual emotional experiences.

20 Layard, Richard. *Happiness: Lessons from a new science.* Penguin, 2011, pp. 43–47.

21 Killingsworth, Matthew A. 'Experienced well-being rises with income, even above $75,000 per year.' *Proceedings of the National Academy of Sciences* 118.4 (2021).

22 Gilovich, Thomas and Amit Kumar. 'We'll always have Paris: The hedonic payoff from experiential and material investments.' *Advances in Experimental Social Psychology.* 51 (2015): 147–187.

23 Nicolao, Leonardo, Julie R. Irwin and Joseph K. Goodman. 'Happiness for sale: Do experiential purchases make consumers happier than material purchases?' *Journal of Consumer Research* 36.2 (2009): 188–198.

24 Whillans, Ashley V., Elizabeth W. Dunn, Paul Smeets, Rene Bekkers and Michael I. Norton. 'Buying time promotes happiness.' *Proceedings of the National Academy of Sciences* 114.32 (2017): 8523–8527;

Whillans, Ashley V. and Elizabeth W. Dunn. 'Valuing time over money is associated with greater social connection.' *Journal of Social and Personal Relationships* 36.8 (2019): 2549–2565.

25 Dunn, Elizabeth W., Ashley V. Whillans, Michael I. Norton and Lara B. Aknin. 'Prosocial spending and buying time: Money as a tool for increasing subjective well-being.' *Advances in Experimental Social Psychology*. 61 (2020): 67–126.

26 Lok, Iris and Elizabeth W. Dunn. 'Under what conditions does prosocial spending promote happiness?' *Collabra: Psychology* 6.1 (2020): 5.

27 Aknin, Lara B., Elizabeth W. Dunn, Jason Proulx, Iris Lok and Michael I. Norton. 'Does spending money on others promote happiness? A registered replication report.' *Journal of Personality and Social Psychology* 119.2 (2020). An earlier study showing that prosocial spending leads to happiness is Dunn, Elizabeth W., Lara B. Aknin and Michael I. Norton. 'Spending money on others promotes happiness.' *Science* 319.5870 (2008): 1687–1688.

28 Waldinger, Robert. 'What makes a good life? Lessons from the longest study on happiness.' TED Talk, January 2016.

29 https://www.ons.gov.uk/peoplepopulationandcommunity/wellbeing/bulletins/publicopinionsandsocialtrendsgreatbritain/13december2023to1january2024.

30 Sandstrom, Gillian M. and Elizabeth W. Dunn. 'Social interactions and well-being: The surprising power of weak ties.' *Personality and Social Psychology Bulletin* 40.7 (2014): 910–922.

31 Epley, Nicholas and Juliana Schroeder. 'Mistakenly seeking solitude.' *Journal of Experimental Psychology: General* 143.5 (2014): 1980–1999.

32 Dwyer, Ryan J., Kostadin Kushlev and Elizabeth W. Dunn. 'Smartphone use undermines enjoyment of face-to-face social interactions.' *Journal of Experimental Social Psychology* 78 (2018): 233–239.

33 McConnell, Allen R., Christina M. Brown, Tonya M. Shoda, Laura E. Stayton and Colleen E. Martin. 'Friends with benefits: On the positive consequences of pet ownership.' *Journal of Personality and Social Psychology* 101.6 (2011): 1239–1252; Wood, Lisa, Karen Martin, Hayley Christian, Andrea Nathan, Claire Lauritsen, Steve Houghton, Ichiro Kawachi and Sandra McCune. 'The pet factor – companion animals as a conduit for getting to know people, friendship formation and social support.' *PloS One* 10.4 (2015).

34 Emmons, Robert A. and Michael E. McCullough. 'Counting blessings versus burdens: An experimental investigation of gratitude and subjective well-being in daily life.' *Journal of Personality and Social Psychology*

84.2 (2003): 377–389; Wood, Alex M., Jeffrey J. Froh and Adam W. A. Geraghty. 'Gratitude and well-being: A review and theoretical integration.' *Clinical Psychology Review* 30.7 (2010): 890–905; Jans-Beken, Lilian, Nele Jacobs, Mayke Janssens, Sanne Peeters, Jennifer Reijnders, Lilian Lechner and Johan Lataster. 'Gratitude and health: An updated review.' *The Journal of Positive Psychology* 15.6 (2020): 743–782.

35 Seligman, Martin E. P., Tracy A. Steen, Nansook Park and Christopher Peterson. 'Positive psychology progress: Empirical validation of interventions.' *American Psychologist* 60.5 (2005): 410–421.

36 Algoe, Sara B. 'Find, remind, and bind: The functions of gratitude in everyday relationships.' *Social and Personality Psychology Compass* 6.6 (2012): 455–469.

Index

80/20 rule *see* Pareto principle
9/11 attacks 89
active learning 122, 124, 142, 143
active recall 122–123, 124
AI (Artificial Intelligence) 83, 98, 148
Algoe, Sara 293
Allen, David 44
Alles Mag Dag (Anything Goes Day) 20–23
Alzheimer's 181–182, 189, 268, 269
amygdala 37, 128–130, 185, 216–217, 240
Angrist, Joshua 146
anterior mid cingulate cortex (aMCC) 75–76, 78
Ashton, Michael 205
automatic negative thoughts (ANTs) 230–231, 234–235, 237

Babcock, Linda 6
Baddeley, Alan 128
Baker/baker paradox 99
Beck, Aaron 208, 229–230
biological clock 39

body method 81, 103–104, 106, 112
Bond, Philip xv, 157, 171–172, 177–178, 300
Bowlby, John 202
brain training *see* cognitive workouts
brain, nutrition for 193–196
brain-derived neurotrophic factor (BDNF) 182
brainstorming 158
brainwaves 36
breathing exercises 130–131
Burkeman, Oliver 21
busyness 45–47, 49
Buzan, Tony 162

caffeine 62, 191, 192, 193, 194,
Cain, Susan 262
Cattell-Horn-Carroll (CHC) theory 141–142
chess 32, 119–120
childhood 115–116, 202, 208, 255
chronotype 39–40, 190,
chunking 100–102, 119, 180
circadian rhythm 39

Cirillo, Francesco 33
Clear, James 69–70
cocktail party effect 126
cognitive behavioural theory
 (CBT) 208, 230
cognitive workouts 177–181
collaboration 164–166
compound interest
 (analogy) 82–83
confirmation bias 119, 208–209, 215
Conn, Charles 247
constrained optimisation xvii
context-dependent
 memory 127–128
convergent thinking 154–157
core beliefs 207–209, 213–214, 217–218, 224, 229–232
cortex 27, 30, 36–37, 75–76, 86–88, 118, 128–129, 180, 185, 240
cortisol 128, 185, 234, 240, 259, 260
Covey, Stephen 10, 252
Covid 46, 242–243, 260, 276
creativity xv, 21–22, 36, 145–169
Crum, Alia 258
Csikszentmihalyi, Mihaly 35

Day Reconstructing method
 (DRM) 271–272
daydreaming 22, 151
de Bono, Edward 159
de Groot, Adriaan 119
Deaton, Angus 285
Deci, Edward 53
decision fatigue 18–19
decision trees 242–247
deliberate practice 120–121, 143
dementia 181–182, 269

diminishing marginal returns
 25, 28
divergent thinking 154–157, 169
Dolan, Paul 271
dopamine 30, 37, 58–63, 71, 77, 174, 183,
Doran, George 8
dream journal 162–163
Duncker's radiation problem 154
Dweck, Carol 253, 255
dysfunctional
 assumptions 230–31, 263
dyslexia 261–262

Ebbinghaus, Hermann 93–94
Eberle, Bob 160
Ebert, Jane 278
Einstein, Albert 148
Eisenhower Matrix 10–13
Ericsson, Anders 100–101
executive function 182, 196
exercise, physical 181–183
expressive writing 238–242

fatigue, mental 26–28, 48
Ferrante, Elena 96
flashbulb memories 89
flow 32, 34–38, 47–48
focused work 32, 35–36, 38, 42, 48
Foer, Joshua 102–103
FOMO (fear of missing out) 46
forgetting curve 93–94, 123–124
framing effect 245–246
Frankl, Victor 238
functional fixedness 154

Gilbert, Daniel 183–184, 277–278, 281
glitters (small moments of
 joy) 294, 296

INDEX

glucose 26–27, 189, 193–194
glutamate 27
glycaemic index (GI) 194, 196
Godden, Duncan 128
golden hours 38–39, 41, 47, 48
gratitude 292–294
Great British Bake-Off, The (TV show) 125–126
Greene, David 55
growth mindset 253–258, 260–261

habits 18–19, 23, 69–70, 75–76, 78, 122, 172–177, 187, 195
happiness 183–185, 268–278, 282–296,
Harford, Tim 5
hedonic treadmill 273–275
HEXACO framework 204–205
hippocampus 30, 86–88, 114–115, 118, 128–129, 180, 182
Homa, Donald 135
hormones 39, 128, 185, 189–190, 234
Horsley, Kevin 108
hydration, importance of for brain 193–194, 196, 209, 211, 292
hyperbolic discounting 4

identity 201–206, 217, 223–224
if-then model 274–275
illusion of competence 121, 123
Imbens, Guido 31–32, 145–146
imposter syndrome xiii, xv, 140, 171–172, 221, 229, 253, 277
ISEEOU (mnemonic) 97, 104, 111

Jordan, Michael 70
journaling 231, 263

Kahneman, Daniel 246, 285
Kaizen (Japanese philosophy) 149
Katie, Byron 251–252
Killingsworth, Matthew 183–184, 285
Knowledge, the (of London taxi drivers) 114–115
Konrad, Boris 107, 181
Kross, Ethan 235
Kwik, Jim xiv, 81

Lanting, Frans 39
Layard, Richard 286, 300
Lee, Kibeom 205
Lepper, Mark 55
Loftus, Elizabeth 90
loneliness 289–291
long-term memory 85–86, 93–94, 100, 101, 103, 111, 117, 123–124

Manson, Mark 248–249
McAdams, Dan 203
McLean, Robert 247
Mecking, Olga 21
meditation 36, 184–188, 196
memorisation contests 102–103
memory *see* long-term- and short-term memory
memory athletes 107
memory traces 86, 99, 103, 105, 123–124
mental chatter 232–237
Mestral, George de *see* Velcro, invention of
method of loci 103, 106–107, 112
mind mapping 162
mind wandering 42, 150–152, 168–169, 184

mindfulness 76, 184–185, 187, 196, 230–231, 280–281, 292
mnemonics 96–98, 104, 108, 111
money, effect on happiness of 284–288
mood monitoring 231, 263
motivation 27, 37–38, 52–67, 73–78, 116, 165
Mueller, Pam 132
multitasking 28–31, 48

narrative identity 202–203
neural hooks 138, 143
neurons 36, 86–87, 93, 115, 116–117
neuroplasticity 142–143
Newport, Cal 4
Niksen (Dutch: doing nothing) 21, 23
Nisbett, Richard 55
non-REM sleep 87, 162
Noppeney, Uta 140
norepinephrine 183
note taking 132–134, 144

Oakley, Barbara 121
Obama, Barack 18
Oppenheimer, Daniel 132
opportunity cost 5, 16, 18, 22

pain, mental 237–242
Pareto principle 14–16, 23, 47
Pastoor, Rick 13
Pavlov, Ivan 38, 127
Pennebaker, James 239–241
perfectionism 16, 205, 249
personality traits 155, 202–206, 223, 234, 256
Peyser, Brenda 6
planning fallacy 14

Pomodoro technique 33–34, 38, 48
procrastination 63–67
productivity 15, 21, 25, 33, 39–42, 46–49, 63–64
psychological immune system 277–278, 280, 295

Raichle, Marcus 42
random input technique 159
Rao, Srikumar xvi
RAT (Remote Associates Test) 155
Rayner, Keith 136
REM sleep 88, 191
Remains of the Day (film) 199–200
Rubin, Rick 166–167
Ryan, Richard 53

SCAMPER technique 160–161, 169
schemas 116–119, 207
Schwartz theory of values 205–206
self-control 73–76, 78
self-determination theory (SDT) 53–54
self-doubt xiii, xiv, 166–169
self-quizzing 124, 143
Seneca 58
serotonin 183
short-term memory 85–86, 110, 141
Simonides of Ceos 106
Sinek, Simon 56
Six Thinking Hats (problem solving technique) 159–160
sleep 39–40, 87–89, 162–163, 188–193

INDEX

SMART framework 7–8, 22–23, 64–67, 69, 78
Snowdon, David 268–269
social media 4, 247
spaced repetition 123–124, 142, 143
speed reading 135–139
Standing, Lionel 96–97
stress 62–63, 128–132, 182–183, 184–185, 234, 240, 252, 258–261, 269–270
stressors 237, 259–260
sunk cost fallacy 17
superpowers 262, 265
synapses 86, 116–117

Tabata, Izumi 183
task switching 29
time management xix, 15, 19, 20, 98
Torrance Test of Creative Thinking (TTCT) 155
Tuitert, Mark 51–52

Tversky, Amos 246
tyrosine (amino acid) 62

utility maximisation 68–69

VAC (Visualise, Associate and Chunk) 95–96, 102
Velcro, invention of 146–147
Vesterlund, Lise 6
Visual Vividness Imagery Questionnaire (VVIQ) 98

Waldinger, Robert 289
Wechsler Adult Intelligence Scale 142
Weingart, Lauri 6
WHAM! Routine 292
willpower 73–76
Woodcock-Johnson IV (cognitive test) 142

Zeigarnik effect 42–43

About the Author

Photo credit © Graeme Bulcraig

Neeltje van Horen is professor of financial economics at the University of Amsterdam and has worked for various policy institutions, including the World Bank, the Dutch Central Bank and the Bank of England.

She is a sought-after speaker and regularly publishes in leading academic journals. She divides her time between London and Amsterdam.

Bedford Square Publishers

Bedford Square Publishers is an independent publisher of fiction and non-fiction, founded in 2022 in the historic streets of Bedford Square London and the sea mist shrouded green of Bedford Square Brighton.

Our goal is to discover irresistible stories and voices that illuminate our world.

We are passionate about connecting our authors to readers across the globe and our independence allows us to do this in original and nimble ways.

The team at Bedford Square Publishers has years of experience and we aim to use that knowledge and creative insight, alongside evolving technology, to reach the right readers for our books. From the ones who read a lot, to the ones who don't consider themselves readers, we aim to find those who will love our books and talk about them as much as we do.

We are hunting for vital new voices from all backgrounds – with books that take the reader to new places and transform perceptions of the world we live in.

Follow us on social media for the latest Bedford Square Publishers news.

@bedsqpublishers
facebook.com/bedfordsq.publishers/
@bedfordsq.publishers

https://bedfordsquarepublishers.co.uk/